Global Democracy

This book presents the key debates about globalization and links them with the growing, related discussion of the possible development of global democracy.

Global Democracy covers the relevant literatures and explores some of the major debates. The first part of the book brings together three major theorists and three critiques of their work – David Held on the potential advantages of globalization for the furtherance of democracy; Paul Hirst and Grahame Thompson questioning the idea of globalization, and Danilo Zolo questioning the need for some kind of international governance. The second part of the book looks at possible structures and processes of global democratization, such as the UN, global civil society, diminished state sovereignty and the EU. There are contributions from major thinkers such as Boutros Boutros-Ghali.

This book provides exposition and critical examination of the latest thinking of leading authorities in the newly important fields of globalization and global democracy. It will be a valuable textbook and resource for students of International Relations, Politics, Political Theory, and those taking courses in democratization and globalization.

Barry Holden is Senior Lecturer in Politics at the University of Reading. He is the author of *The Nature of Democracy* and *Understanding Liberal Democracy* and he edited *The Ethical Dimensions of Global Change*.

Global Democracy

Key debates

Edited by Barry Holden

London and New York

First published 2000 by Routledge
11 New Fetter Lane, London EC4P 4EE

Simultaneously published in the USA and Canada
by Routledge
29 West 35th Street, New York, NY 10001

Routledge is an imprint of the Taylor & Francis Group

Transferred to Digital Printing 2003

Typeset in Sabon by Taylor & Francis Books Ltd
Printed and bound in Great Britain by Biddles Ltd,
Guildford and King's Lynn

British Library Cataloguing in Publication Data
A catalogue record for this book is available from the British Library

Library of Congress Cataloging-in-Publication Data
Global democracy : key debates / edited by Barry Holden.
p.   cm.
Includes bibliographical references and index.
alk. paper
1. Democracy. 2. Democratization. 3. Post-communism.
I. Holden, Barry.
JC421.G56   1999   99-41428
320.9′049–dc21   CIP

ISBN 0–415–19878–X (pbk)
ISBN 0–415–19879–8 (hbk)

Contents

List of illustrations   vii
Notes on contributors   ix
Preface   xii

Introduction   1
BARRY HOLDEN

PART I
Theoretical issues   **15**

1 The changing contours of political community: rethinking
   democracy in the context of globalization   17
   DAVID HELD

2 A critique of Held   32
   MICHAEL SAWARD

3 Global myths and national policies   47
   PAUL HIRST AND GRAHAME THOMPSON

4 Hirst and Thompson's 'Global myths and national
   policies': a reply   60
   JONATHAN PERRATON

5 The lords of peace: from the Holy Alliance to the new
   international criminal tribunals   73
   DANILO ZOLO

6 Neither cosmopolitanism nor realism: a response to
Danilo Zolo   87
TONY COATES

PART II
Structures and processes   **103**

7 An agenda for democratization: democratization at the
international level   105
BOUTROS BOUTROS-GHALI

8 The United Nations as an agency of global democracy   125
DANIELE ARCHIBUGI, SVEVA BALDUINI AND MARCO DONATI

9 Alternative models for global democracy   143
JOHAN GALTUNG

10 Global civil society and the democratic prospect   162
RICHARD FALK

11 Globalization, sovereignty and policy-making: insights
from European integration   179
JONATHAN GOLUB

Globalization and democracy – an afterword   202
RICHARD BELLAMY AND R. J. BARRY JONES

Index   217

Illustrations

Figures

2.1 Characterizing democratic mechanisms   39
A1   Types of governance   205

Tables

3.1 Ratio of merchandise trade to GDP at current prices
     (exports and imports combined) 1913–93   50
3.2 Percentage distribution of MNC sales to home
     region/country, 1987 and 1992–93   52
3.3 Percentage distribution of MNC assets to home
     region/country, 1987 and 1992–93   52
4.1 Trade–GDP ratios for developed countries in constant prices
     (percentages)   62
9.1 A typology of world citizens   150
11.1 Welfare state and social policy indicators in the EU   192

Contributors

Daniele Archibugi is a director at the Italian National Research Council in Rome. He has worked on the history of peace ideas and the reform of the United Nations and he is one of the promoters of the model of cosmopolitical democracy. Amongst his recent publications are (as co-editor and contributor) *Cosmopolitan Democracy: An Agenda for a New World Order, Re-imagining Political Community: Studies in Cosmopolitan Democracy* and a special issue of *Peace Review* on Global Democracy.

Sveva Balduini graduated from the University of Rome. He is a consultant at ISFOL, an institute for the development of vocational training, in Rome.

R. J. Barry Jones is Professor of International Relations in the Department of Politics at the University of Reading and co-director of the Centre for the Study of Global Change and Governance. His latest book is *The World Turned Upside Down?: Globalization and the Future of the State* (forthcoming). He is also preparing an edited volume (with Yale Ferguson of Rutgers University) on *Political Space: The New Frontier of International Relations*. A number of his recent papers and chapters address the issues of globalization and its effects on the state and upon general well-being and prosperity.

Richard Bellamy is Professor of Politics and International Relations at the University of Reading. His many publications include *Liberalism and Modern Society, Liberalism and Pluralism: Towards a Politics of Compromise, Rethinking Liberalism* and, as co-editor, *Constitutionalism in Transformation* and *Pluralism and Liberal Neutrality*. He is currently co-ordinating a TSER and Leverhulme project on European Citizenship.

Boutros Boutros-Ghali is the former Secretary-General of the United Nations (1992–1996) and he is chairperson of the UNESCO International Panel on Democracy and Development. He has also been the Egyptian Deputy Prime Minister for Foreign Affairs and Professor in International Law and International Relations at Cairo University. He has published many books and articles in English, French and Arabic.

Tony Coates is a lecturer in politics at the University of Reading. In addition to several chapters dealing with international ethics he is author of *The Ethics of War* and editor of and contributor to *International Justice* (forthcoming).

Marco Donati graduated from the University of Rome and was a postgraduate at the University of Sussex. He is currently responsible for a humanitarian camp in Kosova.

Richard Falk has been a member of the Princeton faculty since 1961 where he is Albert G. Milbank Professor of International Law and Practice. He is the author of several books including *Law in an Emerging Global Village: a Post-Westphalian Perspective* and *Predatory Globalization: a Critique*.

Johan Galtung is Professor of Peace Studies at a number of universities around the world and director of TRANSCEND, a peace and development network. He has published more than eighty books, including *Peace by Peaceful Means* and *Human Rights in Another Key*.

Jonathan Golub is a lecturer in politics at the University of Reading. He has published on environmental policy, judicial politics and European integration theory. His most recent work is 'In the shadow of the vote? Decision making in the European Community' in *International Organisation*, Autumn 1999.

David Held is Professor of Politics and Sociology at the Open University. Among his recent publications are (as co-author) *Global Transformations: Politics, Economics and Culture, Models of Democracy, Democracy and the Global Order: From the Modern State to Cosmopolitan Governance* and (as co-editor) *Re-imagining Political Community: Studies in Cosmopolitan Democracy*.

Paul Hirst is Professor of Social Theory at Birkbeck College, University of London and Academic Director of the London Consortium Graduate Programme in Humanities and Cultural Studies. His recent books include *Globalisation in Question* (second edition), with Grahame Thompson, and *From Statism to Pluralism*.

Barry Holden is a senior lecturer in politics at the University of Reading and co-director of the Centre for the Study of Global Change and Governance. He is the author of *The Nature of Democracy* and *Understanding Liberal Democracy*, and the editor of and contributor to *The Ethical Dimension of Global Change*. His most recent work is 'International social justice, global warming and global democracy' in

Tony Coates (ed.) *International Justice* (forthcoming).

Jonathan Perraton is a lecturer in economics and Deputy Director of the Political Economy Research Centre at the University of Sheffield. He is author (with David Held, Anthony McGrew and David Goldblatt) of *Global Transformations: Politics, Economics and Culture* and several articles on international economics and globalization.

Michael Saward is a senior lecturer in politics at Royal Holloway, University of London. He is the author of *The Terms of Democracy* and chapters and articles on democracy and green political theory.

Grahame Thompson is Professor of Political Economy at the Open University. His main area of interest is in international political economy, particularly the issue of globalization. He is also publishing in the area of the discourse of economics and critiques of traditional economics. He is the co-author (with Paul Hirst) of *Globalisation in Question* and he is beginning a book on the nature and significance of network forms of organization.

Danilo Zolo is Professor of Reflexive Epistemology Philosophy and Sociology of Law at the University of Florence. His publications include *Democracy and Complexity* and *Cosmopolis: Prospects for World Government*.

Preface

This book is the outcome of a conference on 'Global Democracy', hosted by the Centre for the Study of Global Change and Governance in the Department of Politics at the University of Reading. Papers at that conference formed the basis for five of the chapters in this volume (Chapters One, Two, Three, Five and Six). Other authors were invited to contribute subsequently. Most contributors had the opportunity to read and reflect on others' chapters. Different versions of some chapters (Chapters One, Three and Ten) have appeared elsewhere, and Chapter Seven is a reproduction (with the author's permission) of a section of Boutros Boutros-Ghali's *An Agenda for Democracy* published by the United Nations in 1996.

I should like to acknowledge the roles of Tony Coates, in organizing the original conference, and Richard Bellamy, in generating this book – the ideas for both the conference and for the book itself came from him. I should also like to thank Pat Hicks and Melanie Richardson for their invaluable help in preparing the manuscript when they were already under great pressure from their normal departmental work. Finally, I should like to thank my wife, Barbara, for enduring once again the disruption of family life during the preparation of a book.

Barry Holden

Introduction

Barry Holden

It is now commonplace to maintain that, with the end of the cold war and the downfall of communism, there has been a 'triumph' of democracy. This view has been criticized, and the extent of the spread of democracy can be disputed. None the less the idea of democracy – the idea that it is the best form of government – is very widely accepted. Even if one does not accept that 'the principles of democratic government [are] triumphing' (Hadenius 1997: 1), one can at least agree that '[n]ever before has the idea of democratic government been more popular' (Archibugi, Held and Köhler 1998a: 2). Indeed, it can be said that '[a]mong the twentieth century's most important legacies to the new millennium [is] ... the assertion of democracy as the legitimate system of government' (Archibugi, Held and Köhler 1998a: 1).

What is primarily at issue here, of course, is the traditional idea of democracy within states. However, the international pre-eminence of intra-state democracy is now beginning to flow over into the international order, so that the 'triumph' of democratic notions 'may well prove to be ... the fulcrum on which the future development of global society will turn' (Franck 1992). For this and other reasons (indicated overleaf) there has recently been a growing interest in the idea of 'global democracy', as the subject matter of a number of recent books testifies (for example, Archibugi and Held 1995; Held 1995; McGrew 1997; Archibugi, Held and Köhler 1998b). But what global democracy is, and to what extent its existence is likely or desirable, are matters about which there is considerable controversy. There is in fact quite a debate going on, the nature of which is illustrated in the contributions that follow. These questions about global democracy raise closely related issues concerning globalization; and these, too, are debated in the pages that follow. In fact, as Richard Bellamy and Barry Jones say in their 'Afterword':

> Three key questions animate the contributions to this volume: does globalization challenge established patterns of territorially-based governance (democratic or otherwise); do global issues and dynamics

require effective governance at a supranational or transnational level; and is it either feasible or desirable for global governance to be based upon democratic principles and practices?

Let us turn to an outline of the matters involved in the treatment of these questions by considering first what is meant by the term 'global democracy'. The meaning is somewhat fluid, and this, of course, is one of the matters at issue. And nor is this the only term used; others, such as 'cosmopolitan', 'transnational' and 'supranational democracy', are commonly employed to convey similar types of idea. However, as an initial characterization, we might say that the central notion in the idea of global democracy is that of democracy at a level above or beyond the nation-state. This can simply mean democracy that transcends states, without specifying geographical reach or how many states, but it can also mean democracy that covers the globe, the world as one big democracy (the epithets 'transnational' and 'supranational' may refer more readily to the former and 'cosmopolitan' and 'global' to the latter); both perspectives feature in the chapters that follow. This kind of idea involves some fundamental rethinking of the nature of democracy. Its various features, and the reasons for its genesis, are discussed in the chapters that follow, but a preliminary indication can be given. As I have said elsewhere:

> ...there is developing a theory of 'cosmopolitan democracy'. To sum this up, one could say that the core idea of democracy, rule by the people, needs – and is starting – to be rethought because of changes in the world that may be rendering obsolete received notions of 'rule' and 'the people'. The traditional idea of democracy centres on the state. The state gives content to 'rule by the people'. It does this by specifying 'rule' as 'that which is done by the state', 'the people' as 'those who are citizens of the state', and accordingly 'rule by the people' as 'control of the state by its citizens'. Now changes are afoot that are undermining this account.
>
> (Holden 1996: 138–9)

We can see suggested here some reasons for the growing interest in, and the nature of other questions involved in the debate about, global democracy. In particular there are questions about the changes which are said to be 'undermining this account'. There is great interest in such changes; and there is also considerable controversy – controversy concerning their nature, extent and significance.

The term 'globalization' is commonly used to refer to, or sum up, the kinds of changes referred to here. 'Globalization', then, refers to global processes that are said to be changing the nature of the international realm, modifying states' autonomy, interconnecting them more closely together, and having the potential to bring about an integrated world society rather than a system of separate autonomous states. There is a particular focus on economic processes and the idea that an integrated world economy has developed: in the words of Hirst and Thompson (Chapter Three), '[i]t is widely believed that distinct national economies with their own dynamics have dissolved into the world system'.

As is shown in the chapters that follow – particularly Chapters Three and Four – there is considerable controversy about the nature, extent and significance of globalization. We shall be glancing at the issues covered in a moment, when we indicate the content of the various chapters, but here we should highlight the connection between globalization and global democracy. The nub of this connection has already been indicated: the changes undermining the traditional account of democracy are pre-eminently those covered by the term 'globalization'. More specifically, to the extent that the autonomy of states is reduced – by the globalization processes – the ability of the people in a state to control what happens to them, through controlling the state, is diminished. In other words, the ability of the people to rule is diminished. A postulated remedy for this is to develop means other than the state by which people can control what happens to them. And, given that the processes requiring control transcend states, so, then, must these alternative means of popular control also transcend states: hence transnational or global democracy.

Notice, too, an important corollary of this: if the means of popular control transcend state boundaries, so, then, must the assemblages of people using these means – 'the people', and 'rule by the people' become redefined. There may be a variation in extent from assemblages which cross the borders of some (perhaps very few) states to an assemblage of the whole world: the world might be conceived as a unit and an integrated global society may be seen as requiring global popular control. (It is worth remarking here that environmental problems – above all that of combating global warming – may also involve the whole world as a unit.)

An associated matter here is the extent to which such 'assemblages' can, or need to, be communities (see especially Chapters One and Two). And when the focus is on the whole world then the matter becomes one of the extent to which one can validly speak of a global community or a 'community of mankind'.

There might well be some mutual reinforcement here: global democracy may depend to a degree on the existence of a global community, but globalization processes and moves towards global democracy may themselves help to create such a community. Be that as it may, there is in fact a long tradition of thought about the world as one political community (for a recent discussion see Heater 1996). This can be called the cosmopolitan tradition, and it involves assumptions about the universal validity of moral (and indeed other) ideas; assumptions which are necessarily involved in theorizing about global democracy (indeed, as indicated above, a synonym for 'global democracy' is 'cosmopolitan democracy'). But these assumptions are controversial and come up against an alternative communitarian and (arguably) relativist perspective, according to which moral – and other – ideas are appropriate only to their own particular cultures and communities. Here, then, is another important theme in the global democracy debate, and one which is particularly the focus of Chapters Five and Six.

Let us now turn to the structure of the book and to an indication of what is covered in the individual chapters. The book is divided into two main parts. Part One focuses on key theoretical issues. The chapters by Held, Hirst and Thompson, and Zolo give contrasting accounts of global democracy, globalization and cosmopolitanism; and each is followed by a critical assessment. Part Two is concerned with possible institutions, structures and processes for realizing global democracy. Here various ideas concerning the United Nations, 'global civil society' and the lessons of the European Union are examined. Finally there is an 'Afterword' in which Bellamy and Jones reflect on the main themes discussed in the body of the book and offer some conclusions of their own.

In Chapter One, David Held, perhaps the key figure in the emerging field of studies concerned with global democracy (see, in particular, Held 1993; 1995; 1998), focuses on the implications of globalization for political communities and democracy. 'Political communities', he points out, 'are in the process of being transformed', and the type of transformation with which he is particularly concerned is 'the progressive enmeshment of human communities with each other' flowing from 'the growing interconnectedness of states and societies'. Historically, the theory and practice of liberal democracy has been integrally connected with nation-states and based on the presupposition that such communities control their own destinies. The theory of democracy has taken 'for granted the link between the demos, citizenship, electoral mechanisms, the nature of consent, and the boundaries of the nation-state'. Held then considers globalization – which he argues is best thought of as a multi-dimensional phenomenon – and the way in which it has undermined the distinctiveness and efficacy of the nation-state and state-centric democratic politics. Salient features include global environmental problems, the weakening of the territorial basis of the nature of political community and identity, and the increasing constraint on 'the autonomy of democratically elected governments...by sources of unelected and unrepresentative economic power'. Clearly there are profound challenges to democracy here, but Held discerns new developments and opportunities too. These centre on the potentialities for the development of a global rule of law and for transnational processes of governance being brought under some kind of democratic control. In short, Held argues that, although there are clearly dangers, globalization also presents opportunities for a more effective form of democracy – transnational, global or cosmopolitan democracy.

In Chapter Two, Michael Saward expresses some doubts about the globalization thesis and, indeed, whether it has implications for global democracy. He none the less holds the view that 'the rethinking of demo-cratic structures and processes within and beyond national boundaries – and entertaining the idea of cosmopolitan democracy – is a worthy goal and object of debate in its own right'. He is, in fact, generally sympathetic with the spirit of Held's contribution. However, Saward does question important aspects of the latter's argument by focusing on 'a key issue of democracy today – how and where should democratic decisions now be made?' This is central to his concern with the question of how we might identify and generate the structures and mechanisms of transnational democracy. He starts from Held's contentions that the normally assumed congruence 'between a given population and the decisions and powers of a particular government is being undermined by the contemporary range, importance and intensity of cross-border issues'; that, therefore, units of democratic decision-making should, where necessary, cross national borders and be shaped around the principle that those who participate in, or consent to, a governmental decision should be all those who are affected by it; and that this use of the 'all-affected principle' should down-grade national–territorial conceptions of political community.

Saward has two, interrelated, concerns. First, he questions Held's idea that shifting the focus from national–territorial communities should primarily involve instituting new permanent (sub-national and suprana-tional) *territorial* layers of government. Saward instead wants to pay 'more attention to a number of intermediate and more fine-grained possibilities' – and he explores 'four possible democratic responses to cross-border demands and issues'. He wishes to give somewhat greater prominence to the all-affected principle: while he concedes the principle has fatal flaws as 'the primary means of delineating political communities', he does maintain it 'has great attractions as an important supplementary guide to mecha-nisms and institutions'. His second concern is that there is a need for a fuller discussion of democratic mechanisms than Held provides. And Saward focuses on the mechanisms of democratic decision-making that might be used in the 'communities of fate' thrown together by cross-border issues. He discusses five such mechanisms in particular: the cross-border referendum, the deliberative forum, reciprocal representation, functional representation and intensive accountability.

Saward, then, endorses the spirit of Held's thinking but suggests we 'may be missing something important if we insist on territorial arrange-ments above the level of the nation-state which, in essence, mirror the territorial rationale and indirect democratic basis of conventional national political organisation in the contemporary world'.

In the next two chapters, the focus moves to the issue of globalization itself. Hirst and Thompson, in Chapter Three, question the evidence for the existence of a process of globalization and maintain that an erroneous acceptance of its existence and importance subverts belief in the feasibility of the project of the social democratic left. The 'new conventional wisdom', they argue, is that the process of globalization means that states 'cannot singly or collectively govern world markets'. Social solidarity and the possibilities of national schemes for welfare and economic redistribution and regulation are thereby undermined, while the whole world becomes 'like a quasi-colony for the business class'. However, 'the evidence does not sustain the extreme globalist thesis', and 'the scope for national and bloc policy (and therefore for active reform) is far greater than the pessimists who believe in the dominance of world market forces allow'. National autonomy is limited, but not markedly more so today than in earlier periods. There are governance problems in the international economy, but these 'stem from conflicting national interests much more than they do from "global" market forces'; and the constraints on social welfare policies are domestic rather than the product of globalization.

Perraton, in his critique of Hirst and Thompson in Chapter Four, maintains that the evidence does show the existence of significant processes of globalization. He accepts that there 'is certainly plenty to challenge in the extreme or "hyperglobalization" arguments'. And he contends that this is indeed the kind of challenge mounted by Hirst and Thompson. However, this 'does not simply support their contention that nothing substantive has changed'. They are misled, he maintains, by erroneously supposing that the existence of globalization processes entails a unique end-point to which they are inexorably moving. Demonstration of the non-existence of such inexorable movement does not, then, amount to a denial of the existence of significant processes of globalization. Perraton goes on to provide evidence for their existence and to argue that national autonomy has thereby been diminished: it is 'not that national governments have lost all power to firms or markets, but that their power has diminished substantially relative to these institutions'. He concludes, in effect, with a call for the replacement of the globalization debate by the task of '[e]xamining how the world economy has changed and what possibilities remain for governments' which 'would help identify areas for effective international co-operation and governance of the world economy'.

In Chapter Five, Zolo mounts a fundamental attack on the whole cosmopolitan viewpoint, which, he would maintain, is shared by many of the other contributors to this volume (Held and Falk being specifically mentioned). Up to this point, contributors have been concerned with assessments of globalization, global democracy and the relationships between them, but Zolo challenges the whole conceptual framework which tends to inform such assessments. More specifically, he rejects the notion that in order to avoid international disorder – and, indeed, planetary disaster – the international anarchy of the 'system of sovereign states which was established by the Peace of Westphalia (1648)' must be replaced by a new political and legal structure of international power, 'a kind of modern Cosmopolis'. He attacks 'legal globalism' which, finding 'its philosophical basis in the Kantian idea of the moral unity of humankind', maintains that 'the globalization of law as one legal system' is necessary for the avoidance of global disorder. Together with an awareness of the processes of globalization, this cosmopolitan legal globalism will 'in the judgement of Falk, Held and their followers...gradually point the way towards planetary social integration and thereby constitute the premise for the construction of a world constitutional state and a transnational democracy'.

For Zolo, however, what his whole cosmopolitan or globalist philosophy really involves is the imposition of parochial Western values on the rest of the world, and, rather than cultural globalization, what we have is an imperialist projection of Western culture, resulting in 'a process of "creolisation"' which produces, instead of 'communitarian integration', 'contamination, resistance and disorder'. Nor is the implicit assumption that 'processes of globalization of the international economy tend to reduce the gap between the economies' of the rich and the poor countries justified. It is, then, erroneous to think that globalization can in any way 'be equated with the socio-economic integration of the planet'; an erroneous idea that is, however, commonly accompanied by another, the pernicious idea that the United Nations has some kind of global authority rather than being a creature of the industrial powers (especially the United States) – which results in 'a restricted number of military powers engag[ing] increasingly in "humanitarian" interventionism'. The combination of moral and cultural imperialism and a propensity for military intervention increases the likelihood of war. Also, 'legal globalism' and the 'global authority view' of the United Nations has given rise to 'a kind of "judicial internationalism"' resulting in the new International War Tribunals, and now, also, an International Criminal Tribunal. But not only do these tribunals, arising from a spurious cosmopolitan base, dispense Western rather than universal 'justice', they also rest on the mistaken notion that judicial sanctions can prevent violent conflict. Zolo concludes that we should aim only at a 'minimal international order' in which the unavoidability of conflict must be acknowledged: indeed, he says, 'the realistic assumption on which my proposal rests is that only in and through conflict can peace be achieved'.

Tony Coates, in his response to Zolo in Chapter Six, picks up on the paradox that a condemnation of cosmopolitanism for its war-like propensities co-exists with a positive evaluation of (what must necessarily be violent) conflict: 'Here...is a writer who dons the mantle of pacifism while upholding the necessity and value of war.' In fact, Coates is in sympathy with a good deal of what Zolo says, and he agrees in rejecting the kind of cosmopolitanism that characterizes the viewpoint of many of the other contributors which, while projecting particular Western values, spuriously claims universality. However, he does take issue with Zolo's underlying moral relativism, resulting as it does in a rejection of universalism as such. Coates's key point here is a denial that '*all* forms of universalism are...antagonistic to particular moral communities or cultures'.

Cosmopolitanism's universalism is linked with that of the natural law tradition, but Coates reminds us of crucial differences within that tradition between the Enlightenment ideas underlying modern cosmopolitanism and the non-Enlightenment tradition of natural law. The latter 'is "universalist" without being "cosmopolitan"' and seeks 'to reconcile the normative unity of mankind with the facts of cultural and moral diversity'. Coates, then, remains sensitive to cultural diversity and the danger of 'moral imperialism' inherent in modern cosmopolitanism, but in recognizing also the moral universalism of the 'normative unity of mankind' he does not, for example, reject (as Zolo does) all possibility of humanitarian intervention.

The contributors in Part Two, concerned with the question – or, in Golub's case, the questioning – of the realization of the global democracy project, work within the kind of cosmopolitan framework criticized by Zolo and Coates. The contribution from Boutros Boutros-Ghali, the former Secretary General of the United Nations (Chapter Seven), consists of a key section from his *Agenda for Democratization*. The latter is an important text which Boutros-Ghali presented to the United Nations in December 1996 (its importance is discussed in Chapter Eight). In this section, Boutros-Ghali argues that '[d]emocratization internationally is necessary on three interrelated fronts': democratization of the United Nations itself, the provision for more participation on the international scene by actors other than states, and the achievement of 'a culture of democracy internationally'. This last 'will not only require a society of States committed to democratic principles and processes; it will also demand an enlarged international civil society deeply involved in democratic institutions, whether State, inter-state or supra-State, private or quasi-private', committed to political pluralism and imbued with the procedures and traditional culture of democracy. International democracy is a valid idea despite the fact that there are 'substantial differences between democratization at the international level and democratization within States'; and in fact '[g]rowing recognition of the practical importance of democracy within States has...contributed to growing recognition of the practical importance of democracy among States, and generated increased demand for democratization internationally'. The growth of globalization, interdependence and environmental pressures also contributes to this demand. 'Today, decisions concerning global matters carry with them far-reaching domestic consequences.' Such decisions require democratizing: 'unrepresentative decisions on global issues can run counter to democratization within a State and undermine a people's commitment to it' (and of course there is the also inherent desirability of democratizing decisions that affect people's daily lives).

There are, in fact, signs that processes of international democratization are already taking place:

...[t]he overall result is that globalization is creating chains of deci-sions and political associations which link different levels of political representation. In other words, what is emerging are de facto linkages extending from individual citizens all the way to international organi-zations, grappling with global problems and prospects. The forces at work in the world today are thus demanding and enabling an unprece-dented democratization of international politics and decision-making.

Boutros-Ghali then goes on to look at some of the structures, processes and actors that are involved. Included here are the integration of new non-state actors – especially the powerful 'transnational entities involved in business and finance' – into existing international structures and mecha-nisms; the role of regional organizations, non-governmental organizations and local authorities; the function of business and industry; and the role of the media. But it is on the importance of democratizing the United Nations itself, and enhancing its role in strengthening international law, that he concentrates most particularly.

It is the importance of the United Nations as an agency of global democracy that is the subject of Chapter Eight, by Archibugi, Balduini and Donati, which includes an assessment of the significance of Boutros-Ghali's text. After an initial consideration of the general importance of democracy in the world today, it is argued that 'in the era of globalization, and with the ending of the cold war, the issue of democracy has to be understood in a much more extensive way than the traditional narrowly state-based idea of it involves'. An understanding of global democracy, similar to Boutros-Ghali's, is developed from this, and attention then turns to how it is to be promoted. The only international actor capable of promoting global democracy is the United Nations. Such a role for the organization was foreseen by Boutros-Ghali, and here we see the impor-tance of *An Agenda for Democratization* (the impact of which was, unfortunately, diminished by Boutros-Ghali's immediate departure from office). Archibugi, Balduini and Donati then examine the *Agenda*'s ideas for the promotion of global democracy by the United Nations. These include assisting states in internal democratization, democratizing its own structure, and seeking to develop a greater world role for institutions and actors other than states; but it is noted that there is 'no mention of the more ambitious project of a People's Assembly' (a project discussed by Johan Galtung in Chapter Nine). Archibugi, Balduini and Donati close with an assessment of the United Nations and democratization after Boutros-Ghali. They conclude that under the new Secretary-General, although the impetus for global democratization may have declined, it has not disappeared; and is now articulated 'in terms of pragmatism rather than of a comprehensive and long-term political project'.

In Chapter Nine, Galtung discusses alternative models for global democracy in a world that is 'yielding to borderless postmodernity with its considerable problems'. He begins with the modern process of democratization within states, but argues that, for various reasons, the 'sum of state democracies is not necessarily global democracy'. World democratization, which is under way (and Galtung points to specific developments), thus needs to go further. But what should this involve? 'If globalization means that decision-making moves to the global level, and democracy is the right to participate in decisions concerning oneself, then only one conclusion is possible: give people the institutionalized right to articulate their concern in such a way that it has a bearing on global decision-making.' But how is this to be achieved? In clarifying this, Galtung considers the role of 'world citizens', various candidates for which have been suggested – states, transnational corporations, civil society and its components – but each, by itself, is deficient as a building block of global democracy. Towns and cities – peace-oriented (unlike states) and cosmopolitan (through being communication centres) – are better candidates. But in fact all of these should be actors in global democracy, which 'is interconnected democracy, at the world level'. The mistake is to gamble only on states and to conclude that 'what has to be democratized under conditions of globalization is a world state organization' – the candidate usually suggested being the United Nations.

The existing United Nations structure should indeed be democratized, but this is not enough. Galtung then details his positive suggestions, which include world referenda and a directly elected United Nations People's Assembly. The latter would be added to the existing United Nations General Assembly – and would eventually be the only UN body with decision-making power – along with three more (consultative) bodies for representing respectively corporations, local authorities and non-governmental organizations. He concludes with an admonition: 'States beware: as other key actors...catch the linkage between globalization and democracy while states fail to do so...these other systems [of representation] may overtake and pass the states-system as carriers of the popular will.' Indeed, '[b]eing expressions of an ethos of non-territoriality and fluidity one of them may' eventually become more important than the United Nations General Assembly.

Richard Falk's concern with global democracy, expressed in Chapter Ten, focuses more on developing global civil society than on institutional structures. After noting that talk of 'global' rather than 'transnational' civil society highlights 'the degree to which the orientation is not one of crossing borders, but of inhabiting and constructing a polity appropriate for a global village', he distinguishes global civil society from global market forces. The former, as 'globalization-from-below', opposes and modifies the negative (there are also positive) features of the latter's 'globalization-from-above'. These negative features essentially involve defects of the market, including its neglect of public goods. Referring to Hirst and Thompson (1996), Falk maintains that with 'those social forces associated with globalization-from-below...it remains possible and essential to promote the social agenda [and global public goods] while retaining the benefits of globalization-from-above'. Elements of global civil society have, among other things, attempted to protect the global commons (the activities of Greenpeace being notable), but such attempts have not been 'based on either a coherent critique or alternative ideology'.

Falk then develops the argument that this defect can be remedied by 'the banner of democracy, but democracy reformulated in relation to the basic aspirations of peoples everywhere to participate in the processes that are shaping their lives'. This idea of 'normative democracy' is both global – following David Held's account, but with a greater emphasis on 'the agency and role of global civil society' – and inclusive of more than the bare procedural requirements of liberal democracy. Falk concludes that normative democracy can orchestrate globalization-from-below to seek 'a politics of reconciliation that maintains much of the openness and dynamism associated with globalization-from-above, while countering its pressures to privatize and marketize the production of public goods'. The role of the state in this remains critical though ambivalent: 'it is not even now a matter of intrinsic opposition between the state as instrument of globalization-from-above and social movements as instrument of globalization-from-below', since there can emerge 'coalitions between states and social movements...as is evident in relation to many questions of environment, development and human rights'.

In Chapter Eleven, Jonathan Golub considers what we might learn about globalization and global democracy from considering aspects of the functioning and development of the European Union. He remarks that alarmists' concern about globalization derives essentially from a fear about states losing their sovereignty over basic policy-making functions. 'For these observers, the "punchline" seems to boil down to this: that democratic states are now unable to maintain the high social and environmental standards which continue to attract public support.' States are constrained to adopt policies that keep producers and investors happy '[r]egardless of what citizens might prefer' in terms of raising environmental and welfare standards. Such observers predict, in fact, a 'race to the bottom', with states being constrained to accept ever-lower standards. Other commentators are more sanguine, and contend that states remain in sufficient control of their own policies or that the development of international institutions will avert the race to the bottom. And then 'there are those who advocate some novel form of global democracy to remedy what they see as the twin problems of obsolete nation-states and inherently inadequate state-centred international institutions'.

In appraising these differing analyses, the experience of Europe can be useful: European integration can be seen as global integration – globalization – in miniature. Golub contends that 'European integration uncovers lessons which are particularly salient to central aspects of the globalization debate...[and] provides almost a laboratory experiment of what changes might occur to national sovereignty, policy choices and effective governance if one could fast forward the globalization process'. After a detailed review of the evidence in the fields of environmental and social policy, he concludes that '[a]larmists will be surprised by the fact that European integration has greatly intensified transnational exchange without unleashing anything like a race to the bottom'; and he also shows that this is not primarily due to supranational institutions. He further concludes that his evidence 'sharply contradicts the presumptions of cosmopolitan democracy and undermines the impetus for its utopian prescriptions'. In the European experience there has not been – and hence globally there is unlikely to be – anything like that collapse of national democratic control the presumption of which is so central to the advocacy of transnational democracy. Democratic reform, according to Golub, should be concerned not with unnecessary and utopian schemes for global democracy but with reform of democracy at the national level.

In their 'Afterword', Richard Bellamy and Barry Jones pick out the critical issues emerging from the preceding chapters by focusing, as we saw earlier, on three key questions as animating the contributions to this volume. After broadly categorizing contributors' positions with respect to these questions, they move on 'to examine an assumption commonly held by global democrats of all shades. Namely, that democracy is self-evidently a basic good that all wish to enjoy, and that the central issue is how it might best be realized in global conditions.' There are, they acknowledge, 'a variety of forces making for the transformation of democracy beyond the nation-state', but they maintain that these require different sorts of responses, not all of them democratic. After distinguishing differing forms of governance and addressing the presumption that democracy is a basic good, Bellamy and Jones argue that whether, where and what type of supranational democracy is desirable depend on circumstances. A crucial complication here is the difficulty in identifying where a people properly exists, a matter in which a commitment to democracy cannot itself provide any guidance. 'The people may be self-determining but cannot themselves determine who they are' and 'which demos can speak and when are not matters they can decide democratically for themselves'.

In their conclusion to these reflections on globalization, global governance and the place of democracy, Bellamy and Jones suggest a mixed picture in which traditional forms of government might be supplemented by the *ad hoc* emergence of new types of global governance and where 'the degree to which government must or can always be democratic' remains an open question. What is likely is the 'evolution of, and collaboration between, established liberal democracies rooted in nation-states. Thus the seeds of global democracy lie in governance *with* governments.' More messy, perhaps, than a system of the kind desired by global democracy theorists, but 'much more likely to satisfy the preconditions for the establishment of democracy and deliver the desired benefits than grander schemes for a cosmopolitan political order'.

In the chapters that follow, then, differing viewpoints are brought to bear on the newly developing subject of global democracy. This involves debate about not only global democracy as such but also such closely connected matters as cosmopolitanism, globalization and the lessons of the European Union. These are all matters which are of central and growing importance in international relations and international political economy, as well as in political theory and political studies generally. It is hoped that the book as a whole will provide a useful guide and contribution to work in this critical field of study.

References

Archibugi, D. and Held, D. (eds) (1995) *Cosmopolitan Democracy*, Cambridge: Polity Press.

Archibugi, D., Held, D. and Köhler, M. (1998a) 'Introduction', in Archibugi, Held and Köhler (1998b).

——(eds) (1998b) *Re-imagining Political Community*, Cambridge: Polity Press.

Franck, T. M. (1992) 'The Emerging Right to Democratic Governance', *American Journal of International Law*, 86: 46–91.

Hadenius, A. (1997) 'Victory and Crisis: Introduction', in A. Hadenius (ed.), *Democracy's Victory and Crisis*, Cambridge: Cambridge University Press.

Heater, D. (1996) *World Citizenship and Government: Cosmopolitan Ideas in the History of Western Political Thought*, Basingstoke: Macmillan.

Held, D. (1993) 'From City States to a Cosmopolitan Order?', in D. Held (ed.), *Prospects for Democracy*, Cambridge: Polity Press.

——(1995) *Democracy and the Global Order*, Cambridge: Polity Press.

——(1998) 'Democracy and Globalization', in Archibugi, Held and Köhler (1998b).

Hirst, P. and Thompson, G. (1966) *Globalization in Question*, Cambridge: Polity Press.

Holden, B. (1996) 'Democratic Theory and Global Warming', in B. Holden (ed.), *The Ethical Dimensions of Global Change*, Basingstoke: Macmillan.

McGrew, A. (ed.) (1997) *The Transformation of Democracy?*, Cambridge and Milton Keynes: Polity Press in association with The Open University Press.

Part I
Theoretical issues

1 The changing contours of political community

Rethinking democracy in the context of globalization

David Held

Political communities are in the process of being transformed. Of course, transformation can take many forms. But one type of transformation is of particular concern in this paper: the progressive enmeshment of human communities with each other. Over the last few centuries, human communities have come into increasing contact with each other; their collective fortunes have become intertwined. I want to dwell on this and its implications.

The focus will be on the changing nature of political community in the context of the growing interconnectedness of states and societies – in short, globalization. The paper has a number of parts.[1] In the first part, I explore some of the key assumptions and presuppositions of liberal democracy; above all, its conception of political community. In the second part, I explore changing forms of globalization. In my view, globalization has been with us for some time, but its extensity, intensity and impact have changed fundamentally. In the third and final part, the implications of changing forms of globalization are explored in relation to the prospects of democratic political community.

The presuppositions of liberal democracy

Until the eighteenth century, democracy was generally associated with the gathering of citizens in assemblies and public meeting places. From the late eighteenth century, it began to be thought of as the right of citizens to participate in the determination of the collective will, but now through the medium of elected representatives (Bobbio 1989). The theory of liberal or representative democracy fundamentally shifted the terms of reference of democratic thought: the practical limits that a sizeable citizenry imposes on democracy – which had been the focus of so much critical (anti-democratic) attention – were thought to be eradicable. Representative democracy could now be celebrated as both accountable and feasible government, potentially stable over great territories and time spans (see Dahl 1989: 28–30). As one of the best-known advocates of the representative system put it, 'by ingrafting representation upon democracy' a system of government is created that is capable of embracing 'all the various interests and every extent of territory and population' (Paine 1987: 281). Representative democracy could even be heralded, as James Mill wrote, 'as the grand discovery of modern times' in which 'the solution of all difficulties, both speculative and practical, would be found' (quoted in Sabine 1963: 695). Accordingly, the theory and practice of democratic government broke away from its traditional association with small states and cities, opening itself to become the legitimating creed of the emerging world of modern nation-states.

Built, as it was, against the background of the formation of the modern nation-state, the development of liberal democracy took place within a particular conceptual space (cf. Walker 1988; Connolly 1991; McGrew 1997b). Modern democratic theory and practice was constructed upon national, territorial foundations. National communities, and theories of national communities, were based on the presupposition that political communities could, in principle, control their destinies and citizens could come to identify sufficiently with each other such that they might think and act together with a view of what was best for all of them; that is, with a view of the common good (Sandel 1996: 202). It was taken for granted that, bar internal difficulties, the demos, the extent of the franchise, the form and scope of representation and the nature and meaning of consent – in fact all the key elements of self-determination – could be specified with respect to geography: systems of representation and democratic accountability could be neatly meshed with the spatial reach of sites of power in a circumscribed territory. Moreover, as a consequence of this, clear-cut distinctions could be elaborated – and national institutions built upon – the difference between 'internal' and 'external' policy, between domestic and foreign affairs.

Of course, the construction of a national democratic community was often deeply contested, as different social, economic and cultural groups fought with each other about the nature of this community and about their own status within it. None the less, the theory of democracy, particularly as it developed in the nineteenth and twentieth centuries, could take for granted the link between the demos, citizenship, electoral mechanisms, the nature of consent, and the boundaries of the nation-state. The fates of different political communities may be intertwined, but the appropriate place for determining the foundation of 'national fate' is the national community itself. Accordingly, modern democratic theory and democratic politics assume a symmetry and congruence between citizen-voters and national decision-makers. Through the ballot box, citizen-voters are, in principle, able to hold decision-makers to account; and, as a result of electoral consent, decision-makers are able to make and pursue law and policy legitimately for their constituents, ultimately the people, in a fixed, territorially-based community.

Changing forms of regional and global order

At the centre of the dominant theoretical approaches to democratic politics is an uncritically appropriated concept of the territorial political community. And the difficulty with this is that political communities have rarely – if ever – existed in isolation as bounded geographical totalities; they are better thought of as overlapping networks of interaction. These networks crystallize around different sites and forms of power – economic, political, military, cultural, among others – producing diverse patterns of activity which do not correspond in any simple and straightforward way to territorial boundaries (see Mann 1986: ch. 1). Modern political communities are, and have always been, locked into a diversity of processes and structures which range in and through them. The theory and practice of the democratic sovereign state has always been in some tension with the actuality of state sovereignty and autonomy. How, then, should one understand these patterns of interconnections, and their changing form over time? And how should one understand their political implications, in particular for sovereignty, autonomy and the democratic political community?

The term 'globalization' captures some of the changes which shape the nature of the political and the prospects of political community; unpacking this term helps create a framework for addressing some of the issues to be explored. Globalization can be understood in relation to a set of processes which shift the spatial form of human organization and activity to transcontinental or inter-regional patterns of activity, interaction and the exercise of power (see Held *et al.* 1999[2]). It involves a stretching and deepening of social relations and institutions across space and time such that, on the one hand, day-to-day activities are increasingly influenced by events happening on the other side of the globe and, on the other, the practices and decisions of local groups or communities can have significant global reverberations (see Giddens 1990). It is possible to distinguish different *historical forms of globalization* in terms of (1) the extensiveness of networks of relations and connections; (2) the intensity of flows and levels of activity within these networks; and (3) the impact of these phenomena on particular bounded communities. It is not a case of saying, as many do, that formerly there was no globalization, and there is now; rather, it is a case of recognizing that forms of globalization have changed over time and that these can be systematically understood by reference to points 1–3 above. Such an historical approach to globalization contrasts with the current fashion to suggest either that globalization is fundamentally new – the 'hyper-globalization school', with its insistence that global markets are now fully established (see Ohmae 1990) – or that there is nothing unprecedented about contemporary levels of international economic and social interaction since they resemble those of the gold standard era, the 'sceptical school' (see Hirst and Thompson 1996 and ch. 3 in this volume).

Globalization is neither a singular condition nor a linear process.

Rather, it is best thought of as a multi-dimensional phenomenon involving domains of activity and interaction that include the economic, political, technological, military, legal, cultural and environmental. Each of these spheres involves different patterns of relations and activities. A general account of globalization cannot simply predict from one domain what will occur in another. It is necessary to keep these distinctive domains separate and to build a theory of globalization and its impact on particular political communities from an understanding of what is happening in each and every one of them.

At least two tasks are necessary in order to pursue this objective, although, of course, not to complete it. First, it is important to illustrate some of the fundamental alterations in the patterns of interconnectedness among political communities. Second, it is important to set out some of the political implications of these changes. In what follows, I start by illustrating some of the transformations which have brought a change in the organization and meaning of political community.

1   Among the significant developments which are changing the nature of political community are global economic processes, especially growth in trade, production and financial transactions, organized in part by rapidly expanding multinational companies. Trade has grown substantially, reaching unprecedented levels, particularly in the period following the Second World War. Not only has there been an increase in intra-regional trade around the world, but there has also been sustained growth among regions as well (see Perraton *et al.* 1997). More countries are involved in global trading arrangements, for instance India and China, and more people and nations are affected by such arrangements. If there is a further lowering of tariff barriers across the world, along with a further reduction of transportation and communication costs, these trends are likely to continue and to further the extension, intensity and impact of trade relations on other domains of life. The expansion of global financial flows has, moreover, been particularly rapid in the last 10–15 years. Foreign exchange turnover has mushroomed and is now around 1.2 trillion US dollars a day. Much of this financial activity is speculative and generates fluctuations in prices (of stocks, shares, futures, etc.) in excess of those which can be accounted for by changes in the fundamentals of asset values. The enormous growth of global financial flows across borders, linked to the liberalization of capital markets from the late 1970s, has created a more integrated financial system than has ever been known.

Underpinning this economic shift has been the growth of multinational corporations, both productive and financial. Approximately 20,000 multinational corporations now account for a quarter to a third of world output, 70 per cent of world trade and 80 per cent of foreign direct investment. They are essential to the diffusion of skills and technology, and they are key players in the international money markets. In addition, multinational corporations can have profound effects on macroeconomic policy. They can respond to variations in interest rates by raising finance in whichever capital market is most favourable. They can shift their demand for employment to countries with much lower employment costs. And in the area of industrial policy, especially technology policy, they can move activities to where the maximum benefits accrue.

It is easy to misrepresent the political significance of the globalization of economic activity. There are those, earlier referred to as the 'hyper-globalizers', who argue that we now live in a world in which social and economic processes operate predominantly at a global level (see Ohmae 1990; Reich 1991). According to these thinkers, national political communities are now immersed in a sea of global economic flows and are inevitably 'decision-takers' in this context. For many neo-liberal thinkers, this is a welcome development; a world market order based on the principles of free trade and minimum regulation is the guarantee of liberty, efficiency and effective government (see Hayek 1960: 405–6). By contrast, however, there are those who are more reserved about the extent and benefits of the globalization of economic activity. They point out, for instance, that for all the expansion in global flows of trade and investment the majority of economic activity still occurs on a more restricted spatial scale – in national economies and in the OECD countries. They also point out that the historical evidence suggests that contemporary forms of international economic interaction are not without precedent – and they refer to the gold standard era for some substantial and interesting comparisons (see Hirst and Thompson 1996; cf. Perraton *et al.* 1997, and ch. 4 in this volume).

But the claims of the hyper-globalizers and their critics mis-state much of what is significant about contemporary economic globalization for politics. Nation-states continue to be immensely powerful, and enjoy access to a formidable range of resources, bureaucratic infrastructural capacity and technologies of coordination and control. The continuing lobbying of states by multinational corporations confirms the enduring importance of states to the mediation and regulation of economic activity. Yet it is wrong to argue that globalization is a mere illusion, an ideological veil, that allows politicians simply to disguise the causes of poor performance and policy failure. Although the rhetoric of hyper-globalization has provided many an elected politician with a conceptual resource for refusing political responsibility, globalization has significant and discernible characteristics which alter the balance of resources, economic and political, within and across borders.

Among the most important of these characteristics is the tangible growth in the enmeshment of national economies in global economic transactions (i.e., a growing proportion of the economy in nearly all nations involves international economic exchanges with an increasing number of countries). This increase in the extent and intensity of economic interconnectedness has altered the relation between economic and political power. One shift has been particularly significant:

> ...the historic expansion of exit options for capital in financial markets relative to national capital controls, national banking regulations and national investment strategies, and the sheer volume of privately held capital relative to national reserves. Exit options for corporations making direct investments have also expanded...the balance of power has shifted in favour of capital *vis-à-vis* both national governments and national labour movements.
>
> (Goldblatt *et al.* 1997: 74)

As a result, the autonomy of democratically elected governments has been, and is increasingly, constrained by sources of unelected and unrepresentative economic power. These have the effect of making adjustment to the international economy (and, above all, to global financial markets) a fixed point of orientation in economic policy, and of encouraging an acceptance of the 'decision signals' of its leading agents and forces as one, if not the, standard of rational decision-making. The options for political communities, and the costs and benefits of them, ineluctably alter.

2   Within the realms of the media and culture there are also grounds for thinking that there is a growing disjuncture between the idea of the democratic state as an independent, accountable centre of power bounded by fixed borders – in this case, a centre of national culture, able to foster and sustain a national identity – and interlinked changes in the spheres of media and cultural exchange. A number of developments in recent times can be highlighted. English has spread as the dominant language of elite cultures throughout the world: it is now the dominant language in business, computing, law, science and politics. The internationalization and globalization of telecommunications have been extraordinarily rapid: international telephone traffic increased more than fourfold between 1983 and 1995; there has been a massive increase in transnational cable links; there has been an explosion in satellite links; and the Internet has provided a remarkable increase in the infrastructure of horizontal and lateral communication capacity within and across borders. Moreover, substantial multimedia conglomerates have developed, such as the Murdoch empire and Time-Warner. In addition, there has been a huge increase in tourism. For example, in 1960 there were 70 million international tourists, while in 1994 there were nearly 500 million. And in television and film there are similar trends.

None of the above examples, or the accumulative impact of parallel cases, should be taken to imply the development of a single global, media-led culture (consider the impact of Star television in India). But certainly, taken together, these developments do imply that many new forms of communication media range in and across borders, linking nations and peoples in new ways. The creation and recreation of new forms of identity – often linked to patterns of consumption and the entertainment industries – are not to be underestimated. In this context, the capacity of national political leaders to sustain a national culture has become more complex and difficult. Even in China, for example, where the authorities sought to restrict access to and use of Western media, films and the Internet, it has found this extremely difficult to do, especially with regard to young people. All independent states may retain a legal claim to 'effective supremacy over what occurs within their territories', but this is significantly compromised by the growing enmeshment of 'the national' with transnational influences (see Keohane 1995). The determination of political community, and the nature of political identity within it, become less a territorial matter and more a matter of transaction, exchange and bargaining across a complex set of transnational networks. At the very least, national political communities by no means simply determine the structure, education and cultural flows in and through which citizens are cultivated. Citizens' values and judgements are now formed in a complex web of national, international and global cultural exchange.

3 Environmental problems and challenges are perhaps the clearest and starkest examples of the global shift in human organization and activity, creating some of the most fundamental pressures on the efficacy of the nation-state and state-centric democratic politics. There are three types of problems at issue:

a The first is shared problems involving the global commons, i.e., fundamental elements of the ecosystem, and among the most significant challenges here are global warming and ozone depletion.
b A second category of global environmental problems involves the interlinked challenges of demographic expansion and resource consumption. Pressing examples under this heading include desertification, questions of bio-diversity and threats to the existence of certain species.
c A third category of problems is transboundary pollution, such as acid rain, river pollutants or the contaminated rain which fell in connection with Chernobyl.

In response to the progressive development of, and publicity surrounding, environmental problems in the last two decades, there has been an interlinked process of cultural and political globalization as illustrated by the emergence of new cultural, scientific and intellectual networks; new environmental movements with transnational organizations and transnational concerns; and new institutions and conventions like those agreed in 1992 at the Earth Summit in Brazil. Not all environmental problems are, of course, global; such an implication would be entirely false. But there has been a striking shift in the physical and environmental conditions – that is, in the extent and intensity of environmental problems – affecting human affairs in general. These processes have moved politics dramatically away from an activity which crystallizes first and foremost around state and interstate concerns. It is clearer than ever that the fortunes of political communities and peoples can no longer be simply understood in exclusively national or territorial terms. As one commentator aptly noted:

> ...in the context of intense global and regional interconnectedness, the very idea of political community as an exclusive territorially delimited unit is at best unconvincing and at worst anachronistic. In a world in which global warming connects the long-term fate of many Pacific islands to the actions of tens of millions of private motorists across the globe, the conventional territorial conception of political community appears profoundly inadequate. Globalization weaves together, in highly complex and abstract systems, the fate of households, communities and peoples in distant regions of the globe.
>
> (McGrew 1997b: 237)

Political communities are locked into a diversity of processes and structures which range across them. It can be no surprise, then, that national communities do not make decisions and policies exclusively for themselves, and that governments today do not simply determine what is right or appropriate for their own citizens alone. While it would be a mistake to conclude that political communities are without distinctive degrees of division or cleavage at their borders, they are clearly shaped by multiple cross-border interaction networks and power systems. Thus, questions are raised both about the fate of the idea of political community and about the appropriate locus for the articulation of the democratic political good. The proper 'home' of politics and democracy becomes a quite puzzling matter.

4   Changes in the development of international law have placed individuals, governments and non-governmental organizations under new systems of legal regulation. International law recognizes powers and constraints, and rights and duties, which have qualified the principle of state sovereignty in a number of important respects; sovereignty *per se* is no longer a straightforward guarantee of international legitimacy. Entrenched in certain legal instruments is the view that a legitimate state must be a democratic state that upholds certain common values (see Crawford 1994). One significant area in this regard covers human rights law and human rights regimes.

Of all the international declarations of rights, the European Convention for the Protection of Human Rights and Fundamental Freedoms (1950) is particularly noteworthy. In marked contrast to the Universal Declaration of Human Rights and the subsequent UN Covenants of Rights, the European Convention was concerned, as its preamble indicates, 'to take the first steps for the collective enforcement of certain of the rights stated in the Universal Declaration'. The European initiative was and remains a most radical legal innovation: an innovation which, against the stream of state history, allows individual citizens to initiate proceedings against their own governments. Within this framework, states are no longer free to treat their own citizens as they think fit (see Capotorti 1983: 977). Human rights regimes have also been promoted in other regions of the world, partly in response to United Nations encouragement that such rights should be entrenched at regional levels (see Evans 1997).

Each of the main UN human rights covenants has now been ratified by over 140 out of 190 states, and more are expected to ratify them. Increasing numbers of states appear willing to accept, in principle, general duties of protection and provision, as well as of restraint, in their own procedures and practices (see Beetham 1998). Clearly these commitments are rarely backed by coercive powers of enforcement. However, the demands of the new international human rights regimes – formal and informal – have created a plethora of transnational groups, movements, agencies and lawyers all engaged in reworking the nature of national politics, national sovereignty and state accountability.

In international law, accordingly, there has been a gradual shift away from the principle that state sovereignty must be safeguarded irrespective of its consequences for individuals, groups and organizations. Respect for the autonomy of the subject, and for an extensive range of human rights, creates a new set of ordering principles in political affairs which can delimit and curtail the principle of effective state power. Along with other international legal changes (see Cassese 1986; Held 1995, ch. 5), these developments are indicative of an alteration in the weight granted, on the one hand, to claims made on behalf of the state system and, on the other hand, to those made on behalf of an alternative organizing principle of world order, in which an unqualified state sovereignty no longer reigns supreme.

5   While all the developments described so far have helped engender a shift away from a purely state-centred international system of 'high politics' to new and novel forms of geo-governance, a further interesting example of this process can be drawn from the very heart of the idea of a sovereign state – national security and defence policy. There has been a notable increase in emphasis upon collective defence and cooperative security. The enormous costs, technological requirements and domestic burdens of defence are contributing to the strengthening of multilateral and collective defence arrangements as well as international military cooperation and coordination (see Held *et al.*, 1999, chs 2 and 3, for an

elaboration and discussion). The rising density of technological connections between states now challenges the very idea of national security and
national arms procurement. Some of the most advanced weapons-systems
in the world today, e.g. fighter aircraft, depend on components which
come from many countries.[3] There has been a globalization of military
technology linked to a transnationalization of defence production. And the
proliferation of weapons of mass destruction makes all states insecure and
problematizes the very notions of 'friends' and 'enemies'.

Even in the sphere of defence and arms production and manufacture,
the notion of a singular, discrete and delimited political community
appears problematic. Indeed, even in this realm, any conception of
sovereignty and autonomy which assumes that they denote an indivisible,
illimitable, exclusive and perpetual form of public power – embodied
within an individual state – is increasingly challenged and eroded.

Democracy and globalization: in sum

At the end of the second millennium, as indicated previously, political
communities and civilizations can no longer be characterized simply as
'discrete worlds'; they are enmeshed and entrenched in complex structures
of overlapping forces, relations and movements (cf. Fernández-Armesto
1995). Four points can be noted to help characterize the changing relationship between globalization and democratic nation-states.

First, the locus of effective political power can no longer be assumed to
be national governments – effective power is shared, bartered and struggled over by diverse forces and agencies at national, regional and
international levels. Second, the idea of a political community of fate – of a
self-determining collectivity – can no longer meaningfully be located
within the boundaries of a single nation-state alone. Some of the most
fundamental forces and processes which determine the nature of life-
chances within and across political communities are now beyond the reach
of nation-states. The system of national political communities persists, of
course; but it is articulated and re-articulated today with complex
economic, organizational, administrative, legal and cultural processes and
structures which limit and check its efficacy. If these processes and structures are not acknowledged and brought into the political process
themselves, they will tend to bypass or circumvent the democratic state
system.

Third, it is not part of my argument that national sovereignty today,
even in regions with intensive overlapping and divided political and
authority structures, has been wholly subverted – not at all. But it is part
of my argument that there are significant areas and regions marked by
criss-crossing loyalties, conflicting interpretations of rights and duties,
interconnected legal and authority structures etc., which displace notions
of sovereignty as an illimitable, indivisible and exclusive form of public

power. The operations of states in increasingly complex regional and global systems both affects their autonomy (by changing the balance between the costs and benefits of policies) and their sovereignty (by altering the balance between national, regional and international legal frameworks and administrative practices). While massive concentrations of power remain features of many states, these are frequently embedded in, and articulated with, fractured domains of political authority. Against this background it is not fanciful to imagine, as Bull once observed, the development of an international system which is a modern and secular counterpart to the kind of political organization found in Christian Europe in the Middle Ages, the essential characteristic of which was a system of overlapping authority and multiple loyalties (Bull 1977: 254–5).

Fourth, the late twentieth century is marked by a significant series of new types of 'boundary problem'. If it is accepted that we live in a world of overlapping communities of fate, where the trajectories of each and every country are more tightly entwined than ever before, then new types of boundary problem follow. In the past, of course, nation-states principally resolved their differences over boundary matters by pursuing reasons of state backed by coercive means. But this power logic is singularly inadequate and inappropriate to resolve the many complex issues, from economic regulation to resource depletion and environmental degradation, which engender an intermeshing of 'national fortunes'. In Zimbabwe, it is said, many villagers used to believe that weather patterns were due to 'acts of God' and, accordingly, climate shifts had to be accepted; today, the same people believe that their weather is affected by Western energy policy, patterns of pollution as well as some local practices and, of course, some bad luck. In a world where powerful states make decisions not just for their own peoples but for others as well, and where transnational actors and forces cut across the boundaries of national communities in diverse ways, the questions of who should be accountable to whom, and on what grounds, do not easily resolve themselves. Overlapping spheres of influence, interference and interest create fundamental problems at the centre of democratic thought, problems which ultimately concern the very basis of democratic authority.

Rethinking democracy in the context of globalization

In the liberal democracies, consent to government and legitimacy for governmental action are dependent upon electoral politics and the ballot box. Yet, the notion that consent legitimates government, and that the ballot box is the appropriate mechanism whereby the citizen body as a whole periodically confers authority on government to enact the law and regulate economic and social life, become problematic as soon as the nature of a 'relevant community' is contested. What is the proper constituency, and proper realm of jurisdiction, for developing and implementing policy with respect to health issues such as AIDS or BSE (Bovine Spongiform Encephalopathy), the use of nuclear energy, the management of nuclear waste, the harvesting of rain forests, the use of non-renewable resources, the instability of global financial markets or the reduction of the risks of chemical and nuclear warfare? National boundaries have demarcated traditionally the basis on which individuals are included and excluded from participation in decisions affecting their lives; but if many socio-economic processes, and the outcomes of decisions about them, stretch beyond national frontiers, then the implications of this are serious, not only for the categories of consent and legitimacy but for all the key ideas of democracy. At issue is the nature of a constituency (how should the proper boundaries of a constituency be drawn?), the meaning of representation (who should represent whom and on what basis?), and the proper form and scope of political participation (who should participate and in what way?). As fundamental processes of governance escape the categories of the nation-state, the traditional national resolutions of the key questions of democratic theory and practice are open to doubt.

Against this background, the nature and prospects of the democratic polity need re-examination. The idea of a democratic order can no longer be simply defended as an idea suitable to a particular closed political community or nation-state. We are compelled to recognize that we live in a complex interconnected world where the extent, intensity and impact of issues (economic, political or environmental) raises questions about where those issues are most appropriately addressed. Deliberative and decision-making centres beyond national territories are appropriately situated when those significantly affected by a public matter constitute a cross-border or transnational grouping, when 'lower' levels of decision-making cannot manage and discharge satisfactorily transnational or international policy questions, and when the principle of democratic legitimacy can only be properly redeemed in a transnational context (see Held 1995, ch. 10). If the most powerful geo-political interests are not to settle many pressing matters simply in terms of their objectives and by virtue of their power, then new institutions and mechanisms of accountability need to be established.

It would be easy to be pessimistic about the future of democracy. There are plenty of reasons for pessimism; they include the fact that the essential political units of the world are still based on nation-states while some of the most powerful socio-political forces of the world escape the boundaries of these units. In reaction to this, in part, new forms of fundamentalism have arisen along with new forms of tribalism – all asserting the *a priori* superiority of a particular religious, or cultural, or political identity over all others, and all asserting their sectional aims and interests. In addition, the reform of the UN that is currently contemplated by the most powerful countries is focused on efforts to include other powerful countries – above all, Germany and Japan. This would consolidate the power of certain geopolitical interests, but at the expense of many other countries which have some of the fastest rates of economic growth and some of the largest populations. I believe this position to be unsustainable in the long run.

But there are other forces at work which create the basis for a more optimistic reading of democratic prospects. An historical comparison might help to provide a context for this. In the sixteenth and seventeenth centuries, Europe was marked by civil conflict, religious strife and fragmented authority; the idea of a secular state, separate from ruler and ruled, and separate from the church, seemed an unlikely prospect. Parts of Europe were tearing themselves to pieces and yet, within 150–200 years, a new concept of politics became entrenched based around a new concept of the state. Today, we live at another fundamental point of transition, but now to a more transnational, global world. There are forces and pressures which are engendering a reshaping of political cultures, institutions and structures. First, one must obviously note the emergence, however hesitatingly, of regional and global institutions in the twentieth century. The UN is, of course, weak in many respects, but it is a relatively recent creation and it is an innovative structure which can be built upon. It is a normative resource which provides – for all its difficulties – an enduring example of how nations might (and sometimes do) cooperate better to resolve, and resolve fairly, common problems. In addition, the development of a powerful regional body such as the European Union is a remarkable state of affairs. Just over 50 years ago Europe was at the point of self-destruction. Since that moment Europe has created new mechanisms of collaboration, human rights enforcement and new political institutions, in order not only to hold member states to account across a broad range of issues, but to pool aspects of their sovereignty. Furthermore, there are, of course, new regional and global transnational actors contesting the terms of globalization – not just corporations but new social movements such as the environmental movement, the women's movement and so on. These are the 'new' voices of an emergent 'transnational civil society', heard, for instance, at the Rio Conference on the Environment, the Cairo Conference on Population Control and the Beijing Conference on Women. In short, there are tendencies at work seeking to create new forms of public life and new ways of debating regional and global issues. These are, of course, all in early stages of development, and there are *no* guarantees that the balance of the political contest will allow them to develop. But they point in the direction of establishing new modes of holding transnational power systems to account – that is, they help open up the possibility of what I call 'cosmopolitan democracy'.

If this possibility is to be consolidated, each citizen of a state must learn to become a cosmopolitan citizen – a person capable of mediating between national traditions, communities and alternative forms of life. Citizenship in a democratic polity of the future must increasingly involve a mediating role: a role which encompasses dialogue with the traditions and discourses of others with the aim of expanding the horizons of one's own framework of meaning and prejudice, and increasing the scope of mutual understanding. Political agents who can reason from the point of view of others are likely to be better equipped to resolve, and resolve fairly, the new and challenging transboundary issues that create overlapping communities of fate. Moreover, if many contemporary forms of power are to become accountable and if many of the complex issues that affect us all – locally, nationally, regionally and globally – are to be democratically regulated, people must have access to, and membership in, diverse political communities. Put differently, democracy for the new millennium should describe a world where citizens enjoy multiple citizenships. They should be citizens of their own communities, of the wider regions in which they live, and of a cosmopolitan, transnational community.

Against this background, democracy must be thought of as a 'double-sided process' (Held 1996). By a double-sided process I mean not just the deepening of democracy within a national community, but also the extension of democratic processes across territorial borders. Democracy for the new millennium must involve cosmopolitan citizens able to gain access to, and mediate between, and render accountable, the social, economic and political processes and flows which cut across and transform their traditional community boundaries. The notion of cosmopolitan democracy recognizes our complex, interconnected world. It recognizes, of course, certain problems and policies as appropriate for local governments and national states; but it also recognizes others as appropriate for specific regions, and still others – such as the environment, global security concerns, world health questions and economic regulation – that need new institutions to address them. Such political arrangements are not only a necessity but also a possibility in the light of the changing organization of regional and global processes, evolving political decision-making centres such as the European Union, and growing political demands for new forms of political deliberation, conflict resolution and decision-making.

Notes

1   This is a revised and abridged version of 'The transformation of political community', first prepared for publication in Shapiro and Hacker-Gordon (1999).
2   The conception of globalization, along with many of the examples in this section, are drawn from this joint volume. I should like to acknowledge my debt to my co-authors with whom I have collaborated over the last four years on these issues.
3   I am indebted to Anthony McGrew for this point.

References

Beetham, D. (1998) 'Human rights as a model for cosmopolitan democracy', in D. Archibugi, D. Held and M. Köhler (eds), *Re-imagining Political Community: Studies in Cosmopolitan Democracy*, Cambridge: Polity Press.

Bobbio, N. (1989) *Democracy and Dictatorship*, Cambridge: Polity Press.

Bull, H. (1977) *The Anarchical Society*, London: Macmillan.

Capotorti, F. (1983) 'Human rights: the hard road towards universality', in R. St J. Macdonald and D. M. Johnson (eds), *The Structure and Process of International Law*, The Hague: Martinus Nijhoff.

Cassese, A. (1986) *International Law in a Divided World*, Oxford: Clarendon Press.

Connolly, W. (1991) 'Democracy and territoriality', *Millennium* 20, 3.

Crawford, J. (1994) *Democracy in International Law*, inaugural lecture, Cambridge: Cambridge University Press.

Dahl, R. A. (1989) *Democracy and Its Critics*, New Haven, Conn.: Yale University Press.

Evans, T. (1997) 'Democratization and human rights', in McGrew (1997a).

Fernández-Armesto, F. (1995) *Millennium*, London: Bantam.

Giddens, A. (1990) *The Consequences of Modernity*, Cambridge: Polity Press.

Goldblatt, D., Held, D., McGrew, A. G. and Perraton, J. (1997) 'Economic globalization and the nation-state: shifting balances of power', *Soundings*, 7 (Autumn), 61–77.

Hayek, F. A. (1960) *The Constitution of Liberty*, London: Routledge and Kegan Paul.

Held, D. (1995) *Democracy and the Global Order: From the Modern State to Cosmopolitan Governance*, Cambridge: Polity Press.

——(1996) *Models of Democracy*, 2nd edn, Cambridge: Polity Press.

Held, D., McGrew, A. G., Goldblatt, D. and Perraton, J. (1999) *Global Transformations: Politics, Economics and Culture*, Cambridge: Polity Press.

Hirst, P. and Thompson, G. (1996) *Globalization in Question*, Cambridge: Polity Press.

Keohane, R. (1995) 'Hobbes's dilemma and institutional change in world politics: sovereignty in international society', in H. H. Holm and G. Sorensen (eds), *Whose World Order?*, Boulder, Col.: Westview Press.

McGrew, A. G. (ed.) (1997a) *The Transformation of Democracy?*, Cambridge: Polity Press.

McGrew, A. G. (1997b) 'Democracy beyond borders?: Globalization and the reconstruction of democratic theory and politics', in McGrew (1997a).

Mann, M. (1986) *The Sources of Social Power*, vol. I, Cambridge: Cambridge University Press.

Ohmae, K. (1990) *The Borderless World*, London: Collins.

Paine, T. (1987) *The Thomas Paine Reader*, Harmondsworth: Penguin.

Perraton, J., Goldblatt, D., Held, D. and McGrew, A. (1997) 'The globalization of economic activity', *New Political Economy*, 2, 2.

Reich, R. (1991) *The Work of Nations*, New York: Simon and Schuster.

Sabine, G. H. (1963) *A History of Political Theory*, London: Harrap.

Sandel, M. (1996) *Democracy's Discontent*, Cambridge, Mass.: Harvard University Press.

Shapiro, I. and Hacker-Cordon, C. (eds) (1999) *Democracy's Edges*, Cambridge: Cambridge University Press.

Walker, R. B. J. (1988) *One World, Many Worlds*, Boulder, Col.: Lynne Reiner.

2 A critique of Held

Michael Saward

Issues and problems spill beyond borders – more often, with more intensity, and with more significant consequences than before. National democratic systems alone cannot cope; we need new forms of representation, participation and accountability. In these terms, David Held raises the issue of political community in 'The Changing Contours of Political Community' (Chapter One of this volume) and other work (notably Held 1995). This 'critique' joins the conversation, questioning aspects of Held's argument while going with the spirit of his work in order to deal with a key issue of democracy today – how and where should democratic decisions now be made? The focus is less on 'globalization' or the substance of would-be cosmopolitan democracy, and more on how we might identify and explore the structures and mechanisms of cosmopolitan democracy. My aim is to illustrate some innovative possible mechanisms for cosmopolitan democracy, rather than to deal in great depth with any one of them.

Globalization

First, a point of clarification. Sifting through the justification for (or the importance of) potential cosmopolitan democratic mechanisms does not depend on the strength of arguments for 'globalization'. From Held's point of view, the main impetus for rethinking democracy is the evidence that globalizing trends tie together localities, nations and regions; and that the intensity and impact of cross-national issues has increased dramatically. On this view, it could be argued that, if the evidence for globalization is questionable, then the case for rethinking democracy along cosmopolitan lines diminishes accordingly.

There is indeed evidence that the impact of some elements of the strong globalization thesis are overstated – primarily economic and financial elements (Weiss 1998; Hirst and Thompson 1996 and Chapter Three of this volume). However that may be, the rethinking of democratic structures and processes within and beyond national boundaries – and entertaining the idea of cosmopolitan democracy – is a worthy goal and object of debate in its own right. The fact that many, troubling, undeniably important issues do affect peoples across borders, often highly distant ones, is enough for us to proceed seriously. How many such instances qualify as strong evidence for a trend towards 'globalization' will remain subjective and possibly circular; we can happily set that part of the argument to one side for present purposes. It is worth noting that Held himself can hardly be described as a 'hyper-globalist'.

Similarly, it makes sense to separate out the ideal, moral content of Held's conception of cosmopolitan democracy – centring on factors underpinning autonomy and a range of civic, political, social, economic and other rights – from my primary concern, the structure and mechanisms of cosmopolitan democracy. (Indeed, to complete the circle, to discuss the desirability of entrenching the principle of autonomy and the rights that flow from it, we need not enter into debates about the extent to which globalization may be occurring.) Autonomy and rights are about content, while the cosmopolitan model of democracy is about structures and mechanisms. In principle, those structures could defend and produce different content, still perhaps a 'common structure of political action', as Held puts it, but not necessarily the *particular* common structure defended in *Democracy and the Global Order*.

So much by way of preamble; I shall now proceed as follows. First, the possible shape of cosmopolitan democratic structures can be best explored by looking at where territorial communities meet, and overlap with, functional communities; and where more fixed or permanent decision centres overlap with more sporadic or temporary ones. Recognizing functional communities, and thinking through democratic mechanisms that can accommodate them, is a theme driven by the 'all-affected principle' – the principle that says that the constituency for a given collective decision ought to consist of those affected by the outcome. In 'Contours', Held seeks to shift the focus of democracy *towards* a system which embodies this principle more than existing structures, raising the question of how far this process could go in practice.

Building on the discussion of territorial and functional communities, I shall present a matrix which maps conceptually the menu of possibilities for structuring cosmopolitan democracy.[1] Some of the innovations in structure and process that Held advocates in *Democracy and the Global Order* can be located within this matrix; others not canvassed, or mentioned by him only in passing, can be generated from the matrix. These further innovations will be discussed in the final section of the chapter.

From territoriality to affectedness – how far can we go?

At the core of Held's analysis is the idea that the 'symmetry' or 'congruence' that we normally assume to exist between a given subject population and the decisions and powers of a particular government is being under-mined by the contemporary range, importance and intensity of cross-border issues. Accordingly, 'democracy within a single community and democratic relations among communities are deeply interconnected, and…new organisational and legal mechanisms must be established if democracy is to survive and prosper' (Held 1995: 237–8).

Essentially, Held seeks to adapt democracy so that new, cross-border 'constituencies' can be recognized and their members participate in deci-sion-making on issues the scope of which does not fall readily within the boundaries of a single national government. It is people *affected by* (for example) AIDS, acid rain, and the over-use of non-renewable resources who form a new sort of constituency and who embody together a new type of collective interest. In 'Contours', the presentation stresses examples of 'the global shift in organization and activity, creating some of the most fundamental pressures on the efficacy of the nation-state and state-centric democratic politics'. Talking merely about 'cross-border issues' seems to say something less than this, but I would suggest that the cited disjunctures between the formal and the actual authority and capacity of the nation-state can reasonably be understood in terms of 'issues' – some more self-contained and short-term, others more multi-faceted and longer-term – which states acting alone (or even a few states acting in concert) clearly cannot hope to resolve adequately.

The concern, then, is about people in different countries, drawn together in new forms of 'political community' by having a stake in the outcome of pressing cross-border issues. New democratic mechanisms are needed alongside, or perhaps instead of, the traditional machinery of national democracy. It is understandable that, when considering the need for and possible structure of cosmopolitan democracy, Held advocates shifting the emphasis of political representation, and the defining of polit-ical community and constituency, towards the use of the 'all-affected' principle, downgrading in the process more rigidly national–territorial (and to some degree also legal) definitions of political community (see May 1978).

I shall suggest shortly how we can go further towards institutionalizing the all-affected principle, while still recognizing the importance of the terri-torial basis of much political representation. For the moment, note that, for Held, shifting the emphasis towards the all-affected principle primarily takes the form of instituting new, permanent, territorial layers of govern-ment – adding regional (e.g., the European Union) and global (e.g., a reformed and democratized United Nations) to local and national layers. His cosmopolitan model would have us moving (so to speak) from state territoriality to multiple territoriality (with the multiple units formally nested rather than overlapping). This approach can be interpreted as jumping from the present democratic structures to a more extreme version of what might be needed; my view is that it is worth paying more attention to a number of intermediate and more fine-grained possibilities.

It is true that where cross-border issues become more fixed or permanent in character we are led to the stronger version of cosmopolitan democracy, where government structures corresponding to 'nested' layers of formal, territorial political communities like those proposed by Held take on issues most appropriate to 'their' respective levels. (And, of course, the very existence of political structures such as those of the European Union creates further 'European' issues.) But where such issues need be addressed in a more sporadic or fitful manner we need to consider carefully the *gradations* in structures for dealing with issues that require some sort of extra-national resolution. This I do in the next section.

Coping with cross-border issues

In general terms, we can set out four possible democratic responses to cross-border demands and issues, depending on the relatively temporary and sporadic or permanent nature of the issues.[2]

The first democratic response is to foster cooperation between democratic governments. This may involve cooperation between two or more sovereign authorities. The major problem with this response may be the lack of democratically governed units to start with. If government X faces demands from another government Y, where Y is pressured by (some of) its own citizens concerning the actions of X which affect them significantly in some way, X may not even be prepared to listen if it is not bothered about being seen to act democratically. Government Y, too, may perhaps ignore with impunity these demands from within its own citizen body, especially if it is not itself democratically constituted. Given these facts, note that instituting or deepening democracy in existing national political communities may be the primary appropriate response to demands and issues which cannot by their nature be readily dealt with within one country.

Where cross-border issues arise spasmodically and discretely, governmental cooperation between democratic states as and when problems arise is the first aim of the democrat. Where such problems persist over time, and involve perhaps a range of related issues rather than discrete, isolated issues, some semi-permanent or permanent structure which provides a framework for ongoing cooperation between democratic states will be more appropriate. The Framework Document, establishing a new political body with representatives from the United Kingdom, Northern Ireland within the United Kingdom, and the Republic of Ireland to deal with a selected set of issues pertaining to the future of Northern Ireland, is an example.

The third response deepens further this second approach. It involves a permanent process of more or less loose confederation between previously sovereign bodies or units to deal with a range of issues agreed by all, with each participating unit accepting the authority of the confederal structure in the areas of the latter's agreed legal competence. This approach may be accompanied by guiding rules which define which new issues are to be dealt with (a) by the confederal body, (b) by the independent states, and (c) by lower levels of government within the different states – perhaps some version of the principle of subsidiarity.

The fourth approach would be to institute a new, overarching and permanent framework of institutions and rules that, in effect, deprives previously sovereign national authorities of much of their former capacity to act independently. Held's cosmopolitan model of democracy is the primary example of such a framework. He would establish an extensive framework of democratic law explicitly recognizing that a wide range of pressing issues and problems will need to be addressed 'above' the level of existing national authorities. In his ideal structure of nested layers of governance – local, national, regional, global – no decision-making centre would be regarded as primary or sovereign. Within such a structure, which lies somewhere between federalism and confederalism, each issue or proposed action could be dealt with at the appropriate level (Held 1995: 235–6).

So, arguably, Held's hypothetical cosmopolitan model sets aside too quickly some intermediate possibilities, ones that fall short of full, permanent institutionalization of cosmopolitan democracy while potentially still adequate to the task. Further, in approaching matters in this way, Held opens up the debate to concerns about which level of government would deal with what sorts of issues. Held offers three criteria for distributing issues to different levels of government in which sovereign authority is not vested exclusively at any one level:

> [t]he test of extensiveness examines the range of peoples within and across delimited territories who are significantly affected by a collective problem and policy question. The test of intensity assesses the degree to which the latter impinges on a group of people(s) and, therefore, the degree to which national, regional or global legislation or other types of intervention are justified. The third test, the assessment of comparative efficiency, is concerned to provide a means of examining whether any proposed national, regional or global initiative is necessary in so far as the objectives it seeks to meet cannot be realised in an adequate way by those operating at 'lower' levels of decision-making.
>
> (Held 1995: 236)

But on the face of it this approach opens the way to endless disputes about what issues ought to be dealt with at which level. It seems more desirable, in democratic terms, to have a baseline unit (so to speak) which is sovereign, with demands and issues that sit uncomfortably within that framework moving up or down as appropriate. In my view, Held underestimates (a) the difficulties of abandoning the view that a single level of government ought to be the base or sovereign level, and (b) the difficulties of finding a more or less neutral and workable way of assigning issues to different levels of governance.

The necessity of territorial bases

So, there may be a more primary role to be played by more familiar levels of government within cosmopolitan democracy, even where the range and importance of cross-border issues is considerable. New mechanisms and structures may also help us to develop more fine-grained ways to deal with certain cross-border issues, almost regardless of the precise version of territorially-based political communities being considered. In order to explore this point further, let us now return directly to the issue of territoriality and the all-affected principle.

Within the ideal structure of Held's cosmopolitan model of democracy, there is little scope to take specific, sporadic intensities of affectedness into account. For example, the proposed global parliament would coordinate action with respect to the issue of global warming, since citizens of all nations and regions are 'affected', but the intensity of affectedness of the Association of Small Island States (AOSIS) – representing states that might literally disappear if some predictions about the effects of global warming are accurate – cannot be especially accommodated. Similarly, citizens in some member states of the European Union are more intensely affected by North Sea pollution than others. In short, territoriality would remain the basis of spatial political organization within Held's framework, at least within the primary structures of cosmopolitan democracy. This is the case despite the fact that, to reiterate, the 'nested' levels of territorial authority within Held's cosmopolitan model would owe the extent of their power (or domain) to an effort to incorporate the all-affected principle up to a point.

I do not question this basis of territoriality in itself – at the primary level it is surely right. In theory, we could dispense with the view that demarcating political communities for democracy has anything important to do with territorial boundaries. However, Whelan (1983: 18–19) for example is right to reject the view that the 'all-affected principle' provides an answer to the problem of delineating primary political communities. Historically, of course, the principle that those affected by decisions ought to have a say in their making has played a central role in progressive extensions of the franchise to middle-class men, working-class men, women and younger men and women; to that extent, it remains a key principle in the general democratic armoury. Once more-or-less-universal suffrage is achieved securely, however, the usefulness of the principle is less clear. On the face of things at least, it would appear to sanction *restricting* constituencies within political units to those who can be said to be 'affected' with respect to a discrete issue. Further, it falls down in seeming to require a different constituency – in effect, a new political unit – each time a collective decision needs to be made.

The defects of the all-affected principle as the *primary* guide to delineating political communities go further than finding constituencies for votes. Presumably, if the constituency can and must change for each decision, then the rights of 'members' are not fixed, or immutable, from one decision to the next. What of democratic rights, which are owed equally to all as members of a democratic polity? The protection of democratic rights, like justice on the account of Walzer (1983), depends upon secure and equal membership of a given unit. Membership is only secure, because the grounds of citizenship and rightful political participation can only be clear, in a territorial entity.

Despite these points, I have suggested that we can go further than Held does in shifting the balance more towards the all-affected principle. Ironically, perhaps, innovative efforts to institutionalize the all-affected principle beyond what Held suggests become more attractive once territorially-based mechanisms are conceded at the primary level. 'Restricting' constituencies to capture smaller groups united by their common 'affectedness' is democratically attractive so long as membership of all within some larger, permanent democratic community is firmly in place. While the all-affected principle has fatal flaws as the primary means of delineating political communities, it has great attractions as an important supplementary guide to mechanisms and institutions.

In short, taking on board the all-affected principle as a multi-faceted supplementary device opens up the possibility of taking on board a fuller range of mechanisms and structures than Held does. It can also help us to think through some of the implications of their interrelationships, locating ways of more effectively blending territorial and functional modes of political representation – and, in turn, clarifying more fully the range of alternative conceptions of political community that might inform cosmopolitan democratic practice. To show how this is the case, I turn now to a conceptual map of potential democratic structures.

Democratic mechanisms

In Figure 2.1, the vertical axis accounts for whether decision mechanisms are (or need to be) permanent or temporary; the horizontal axis for whether the mechanism concerned is primarily private/informal (non-governmental) or public/formal (governmental). This generates a four-part typology in which specific proposals for using mechanisms can be located. For example, the referendum mechanism could be employed as a type B or a type D mechanism, depending on the scope and domain of the issue(s) it is hoped it might help to resolve.

There are some key thoughts behind this matrix. First, communities of fate may take a great variety of forms. People within different national communities can (fatefully) be thrown together by cross-border issues, which may be permanent or temporary, barely felt or intense. Communities of fate can and do overlap; some come and stay, others come and go. Which democratic mechanisms might be versatile enough to cope with such an array of possibilities?

Second, we need to rethink the basic reason why we have 'sovereign' territorial decision-making centres (be they state, global, or whatever). Although (as discussed above) some such centres must always form the core of democratic practice, 'sovereignty' need not (and should not) be about full, or near-complete, control over the inhabitants of the relevant territory; rather, sovereign territorial entities are functionally required for dealing with cross-border as well as 'internal' issues. We have become used to thinking of sovereignty as control; we need to think of it more as a functional, fluid requirement for dealing with disparate issues that create and divide multiple 'political communities'. Sometimes, 'sovereign' entities may not be required for purposes beyond a guarantor role for agreements reached within other legitimate decision-making centres.

Mechanisms for cosmopolitan democracy

As my use of the example of the referendum in the previous section suggests, specific democratic mechanisms may be located in more than one of the categories generated from the matrix. We normally think of democratic mechanisms as 'Box B' mechanisms. National elections to national

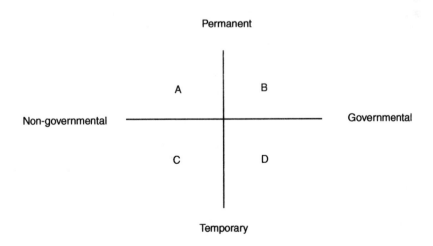

Figure 2.1   Characterizing democratic mechanisms

parliaments fit here, and also the proposed institutions of Held's cosmopolitan model of democracy – regional and global democratic parliaments, and regional and global courts, for example. These mechanisms are conceived as permanent structures of government. Referendums and deliberative forums, for example, may also fit here – as permanently available mechanisms to deal with issues pertinent to the established political community more or less in isolation.

The point is that these more familiar ways of conceiving of democratic mechanisms are familiar because we think in relatively fixed, territorial terms. The really interesting points begin to emerge when we think of which of these mechanisms – and, perhaps, which new mechanisms – might be used to cope with issues that are temporary, sporadic, and which by their nature create new 'political communities' across established political boundaries. In other words, the use of mechanisms in a 'Box D' sense could be much more extensive, extending the range of ways in which the all-affected principle might more fully be satisfied in practice.

Existing examples of Box D mechanisms may be the Rio, Cairo and Beijing conferences on (respectively) the environment and development, population and development, and women's rights – though note that these examples begin to blend into Box C (and even A), since extensive involvement of national and international non-governmental organizations is a key ingredient of such gatherings.

There are at least five forms of mechanism that could in principle (a) be employed as temporary, governmental devices, (b) enshrine the all-affected principle further than Held envisages, and (c) provide a potentially effective and democratic way of coping with challenging and unpredictable cross-border issues. These are: the deliberative forum, the cross-border referendum, reciprocal representation, functional representation and complex accountability. This list is illustrative rather than exhaustive.

Deliberative forums (according to the dominant versions – Cohen 1989; Fishkin 1991; Benhabib 1996) involve a microcosm of a larger political community meeting to deliberate in depth on issues, and having at least some formal say in the resolution of those issues. For example, randomly-picked samples of citizens from different national constituencies linked by the effects of acid rain could deliberate and (depending on the precise status of the forum) recommend policy solutions. The key idea of such forums is that these deliberators will be able to inform themselves more fully, and be more aware of the reasons behind the positions of others affected, through participating in such a way. At best, the considered views of the deliberative forum can be taken as the informed view of the larger community from which it is drawn. The deliberative forum lends itself to sporadic, cross-border issues because it creates the possibility of actually bringing together representatives from a 'political community' of fate to consider its interests with respect to a discrete issue. Its probable flexibility in the face of the distinctive difficulties of dealing with cross-border issues demonstrates promise in theory at least.

Much would depend, of course, on how such deliberative forums could be brought into being, and how much formal and informal authority they would have with respect to other, more traditional decision-making centres. For many issues, locating the 'boundaries' of the relevant community of fate would be a fraught business. It would presumably be more straightforward, though still very difficult, for cross-border 'communities' who occupy continuous territory. The possibilities in terms of the authority of such forums would range from the purely advisory to the final decision-making body. Without exploring these complex issues in anything like the depth required, a maximalist view of the potential for deliberative forums would see them as putting forward collective views which could only be overridden by national and/or regional governments in exceptional circumstances.

Reciprocal representation, as advocated by Dobson (1996) and the inventor of the term, Schmitter (1997), would involve (for example) British parliamentarians having seats (and voting rights on relevant issues) in the French national assembly. It could, of course, be used as either a permanent or temporary governmental mechanism to cope with an array of actual and potential cross-border issues. As with the possible use of deliberative forums, a real danger of reciprocal representation could be tokenism. Certainly it would be difficult to conceive of reciprocal representatives having anything akin to veto powers; nevertheless, serious consideration of its use may represent a step towards recognizing the need to deal democratically with the complex interdependencies created by many cross-border issues.

Useful mechanisms may also include other forms of representation that are not primarily territorial, but instead functional – for example, language-based forms of functional representation such as that operating in the Brussels region within Belgium's distinctive federal system. In principle, what might be considered here are formal and governmentally protected forms of autonomy for democratic forums arising from cultural groups whose membership stretches across national or other fixed territorial boundaries. The communities concerned may, for example, be based on religious adherence as well as (or apart from) language and other shared cultural attributes. Issues that such forums might normally address could include, for example, how religious communities wish to conduct the education of their children. There may be scope for limited, specialized mandates for representatives of cross-border cultural communities to take charge of their affairs in a manner that is formally recognized by more traditional political forums like national parliaments – who, recall, remain the primary democratic forums, and must act as guarantors for these potentially more fine-grained devices.

With respect to complex accountability, the key idea is that multiple forms of accountability of powerful governmental actors and organizations can compensate for the imperfections of single lines of accountability. Note here that, as part of his thoughts about the shape of cosmopolitan democracy, Held seeks more accountability for public and private suprastatal bodies. Sometimes he expresses this in terms of the need to enhance participation in the decisions of such bodies. But popular participation in the IMF and NATO and Shell and Nestlé sounds quite unfeasible and utopian. However, fortunately, participation and accountability can be separated to a degree. There are various mechanisms for achieving accountability of organizations which do not require enhanced participation within them and which are compatible with organizational independence. In terms of independent public bodies, for example, Giandomenico Majone writes:

> What is required to reconcile independence and accountability are richer and more flexible forms of control than the traditional methods of political and administrative oversight. Statutory objectives, procedural requirements, judicial review, budgetary discipline, professionalism, expertise, monitoring by interests groups, even inter-agency rivalry, can all be elements of a pervasive system of control which only needs to be activated. When the system works properly no one controls an independent agency, yet the agency is 'under control'.
>
> (Majone 1995: 118)

One might add that, if deliberative forums, forms of cultural group autonomy, and reciprocal representation were in place in more than a tokenistic manner, then more specific and special forums would exist outside traditional political structures to hold decision-makers to account on issues that affect in particular quite specific cross-border constituencies.

Discussing the idea of the cross-border referendum allows us to focus on that part of Held's (1995) argument where he does explicitly promote a more radical extension of the all-affected principle, within the primary framework of nested territorial levels of government. He cites, as a short-term goal of the cosmopolitan model of democracy, 'the use of transnational referenda' (Held 1995: 279). For this device, as for others, the problems of *defining* constituencies are considerable. Indeed, the practical difficulties of defining constituencies according to who is affected by discrete issues across borders normally leads to the rejection of the idea (Whelan 1983: 18–19). In principle, there are two possible resolutions. First, the one Held uses, is the 'objective' approach – in Held's words: '...issue-boundary forums or courts will have to be created to hear cases concerning where and how a "significant interest" in a public question should be explored and resolved' (Held 1995: 237). (The primary role of such forums or courts would be, according to Held, to allocate issues to territorial levels of government.) Given the enormous powers this approach would vest in unelected authorities requiring inhuman levels of knowledge and wisdom (and we know that agenda-setting is a primary means to power), thought should be given to a 'subjective' way of locating issue-based subject populations. By this token, the use of cross-border initiatives could be considered. Cross-border initiatives would not only relieve the proposed courts or forums of their most difficult tasks, but put the initiative literally in the hands of ordinary citizens, thus dealing to some extent with the problem of intensity of affectedness at the same time. Held writes approvingly of Ian Budge's (1996) work on referendums and initiatives; he could, it seems to me, call on this work in a more central way to support his arguments. Likewise, the 'international civil society', corresponding to types A and C in Figure 2.1, could facilitate the 'triggering' of this and other devices (like deliberative forums) in a bottom-up manner. This in turn implies the importance of having such devices constitutionally available on a clear and widely-understood basis, say at the level of the European Union (or the equivalent elsewhere).

If cross-border referendums are workable, there would be a case for using them more than Held suggests. He would have them used 'in the case of contested priorities concerning the implementation of democratic law and the balance of public expenditure' (Held 1995: 272). But contested priorities may or may not be the important issues. This reminds one of a long-standing criticism of the British cabinet – that it deals with those issues that cannot be resolved elsewhere, rather than the most important issues.

So, on the face of it there is a case for using cross-border referendums more often, and in a more democratic, bottom-up manner, than Held's elaboration of the cosmopolitan model of democracy would suggest. The same is true for the other mechanisms I have canvassed briefly. It is worth noting that, in all likelihood, each of these innovative mechanisms could work more effectively if the others were in place. Deliberative forums could be used to clarify issues as part of a process involving a cross-border referendum, for example. Taken together, such mechanisms would operate as supplementary devices to more traditional, territorial forms of organization, perhaps along the lines of Held's preferred array of nested levels of government structures. Nevertheless, one can imagine a dynamic series of forums, groups and formal decision mechanisms, reflecting 'political communities' or constituencies which are the product of cross-border issues of various kinds, having a formal say in government decisions at local, national, regional and even global levels. Further, such an array of mechanisms could begin to draw upon the energies of increasingly dynamic non-governmental activity across national and regional boundaries.

Much more needs to be said, of course, on all of the points I have raised. But the key point is that we do not have to conceive of cosmopolitan democracy, in terms of mechanisms and structures at least, in overly blunt territorial terms. The menu of possibilities is larger, with more nuances, than that. There may be more, and more democratic, ways of dealing with cross-border issues than have so far been canvassed. Certainly, traditional democratic institutions that are permanent and governmental are best suited to dealing with permanent interests and permanent issues, especially as they affect a relatively fixed and territorially-based group of people (such as within a nation-state, of course). There are strong reasons for believing, however, that temporary governmental mechanisms and devices might be better suited in principle to dealing with issues that are more sporadic, which encompass the interests of more scattered cross-border political communities of people not necessarily united by direct territorial links. They can in principle deal with 'affected' interests in a more fine-grained and responsive way than conventional democratic devices.

Political community?

How might these ideas lead us to think about the changing contours of political community? Institutions understood in terms of Figure 2.1's Box B can be designed and used to represent existing, clearly delineated (even if disputed) territorial political communities or constituencies, national, regional or global. They may reflect pre-existing such communities (if, for example, 'nation' is prior to 'state'), or in part or in whole be efforts to create such communities (where, for example, state forges nation): in short, they can be bottom-up or top-down in character. They reflect or establish territorial communities of fate, characterized by the mechanisms of government involved having some share in a monopoly of the legitimate use of force on a permanent basis over inhabitants of the relevant territory.

Institutions understood in terms of Box D can be designed or used to represent communities of fate, but more temporary ones; fateful, fragile communities thrown together across borders by, for example, the drift of pollutants across boundaries. These political communities are more shifting, depending on the nature of the issue that more-or-less-temporarily unites what are otherwise separate political communities.

The various mechanisms located within Box D – less permanent, and in principle usable for discrete and sporadic issues that arise with no simple territorial basis – can form a key ingredient within structures designed to foster cosmopolitan democracy. We may be missing something important if we insist on territorial arrangements above the level of the nation-state which, in essence, mirror the territorial rationale and indirect democratic basis of conventional national political organization in the contemporary world. Not all supra-statal issues are permanent, requiring state-mirroring permanent policy machinery. There are mechanisms that can in principle provide a more responsive, fine-grained way of dealing with awkward issues that spill across borders. It may be the case that even to discuss such mechanisms is to be quite idealistic; international politics is still dominated by state-centred interests. But political change has been breathtakingly rapid in recent years; it would be no great surprise if today's idealism becomes tomorrow's prominent, practical proposal.

It is interesting to speculate on the links between issues and institutions in the matrix. I make two points in particular. First, the greater use of Box D mechanisms could usefully enhance the legitimacy of more indirect Box B mechanisms. For example, decisions made by national or regional governments could have enhanced credibility if more fine-grained mechanisms were used to locate and consult the more sporadic political communities brought together across borders by a particular problem or issue. Of course, the use of such innovative mechanisms above the level of the nation-state may also legitimize their use within nation-states, thus enhancing internal democracy as well by promoting, among other things, greater citizen participation and deliberation and by fostering greater formal accountability.

Second, and relatedly, the boundaries between 'community of fate' and 'community of choice' can usefully be broken down. Inter-societal non-governmental networks (communities of choice) could have an impact on actual governmental choices by sponsoring the constitutional triggering of mechanisms like the initiative for a cross-border referendum. Relatedly, the formal or governmental use of innovative democratic mechanisms may well foster the positive participation of non-governmental organizations, blurring the boundaries (represented in Figure 2.1) between non-governmental and governmental mechanisms.

Conclusion

'The Changing Contours of Political Community', like other statements of Held's distinctive position, rightly provokes us to rethink standard democratic categories in the light of major events which have destabilized our notions of political community. I have suggested that Held's vision of nested levels of democratic authorities brings the all-affected principle into a revised, innovative territorial framework of government more weakly than it need do. This is understandable, perhaps, given the immense practical difficulties of defining constituencies according to the scope of individual issues. However, below this, when he considers more fine-grained ways to bring in the all-affected principle (notably via cross-border referendums), there are further possible innovations, such as the use of the initiative, reciprocal representation, deliberative forums, complex accountability and forms of functional representation, which at least deserve further attention in the relevant debates.

Notes

1   Of course, the character of a political culture will qualify the structures and mechanisms that could be adopted, and which might work, in a given context. For the sake of focus, I simply bracket this issue for the present discussion. On the importance of factoring it in for a full-blooded account of democratic innovation, see Dryzek (1996).
2   This section draws in part on the discussion in Chapter 7 of the author's *The Terms of Democracy* (Saward 1998).

References

Benhabib, S. (1996) 'Toward a Deliberative Model of Democratic Legitimacy', in S. Benhabib (ed.), *Democracy and Difference*, Princeton: Princeton University Press.

Budge, I. (1996) *The New Challenge of Direct Democracy*, Cambridge: Polity Press.

Cohen, J. (1989) 'Deliberation on Democratic Legitimacy', in A. Hamlin and P. Pettit (eds), *The Good Polity*, Oxford: Blackwell.

——(1996) 'Procedure and Substance in Deliberative Democracy', in S. Benhabib (ed.) *Democracy and Difference*, Princeton: Princeton University Press.

Dobson, A. (1996) 'Representative Democracy and the Environment', in W. Lafferty and J. Meadowcroft (eds), *Democracy and the Environment*, Cheltenham and Brookfield, VT: Edward Elgar.

Dryzek, J. (1996) 'The Informal Logic of Institutional Design', in R. E. Goodin (ed.), *The Theory of Institutional Design*, Cambridge: Cambridge University Press.

Fishkin, J. (1991) *Democracy and Deliberation*, New Haven, Conn.: Yale University Press.

Held, D. (1995) *Democracy and the Global Order*, Cambridge: Polity Press.

Hirst, P. and Thompson, G. (1996) *Globalization in Question*, Cambridge: Polity Press.

Majone, G. (1995) 'Independence Versus Accountability? Non-majoritarian Institutions and Democratic Government in Europe', in J. J. Hesse and T. A. J. Toonen (eds), *The European Yearbook of Comparative Government and Public Administration* (vol. 1, 1994), Baden-Baden: Nomos Verlagsgesellschaft; and Boulder, Col.: Westview Press.

May, J. D. (1978) 'Defining Democracy', *Political Studies* 26, 1: 1–14.

Saward, M. (1998) *The Terms of Democracy*, Cambridge: Polity Press.

Schmitter, P. (1997) 'Exploring the Problematic Triumph of Liberal Democracy and Concluding with a Modest Proposal for Improving its International Impact', in A. Hadenius (ed.), *Democracy's Victory and Crisis*, Cambridge: Cambridge University Press.

Walzer, M. (1983) *Spheres of Justice: A Defence of Pluralism and Equality*, Oxford: Martin Robertson.

Weiss, L. (1998) *The Myth of the Powerless State*, Cambridge: Polity Press.

Whelan, F. (1983) 'Prologue: Democratic Theory and the Boundary Problem', in J. R. Pennock and R. W. Chapman (eds), *Nomos XXV: Liberal Democracy*, New York and London: New York University Press.

3 Global myths and national policies

Paul Hirst and Grahame Thompson

The notion that an integrated global economy has developed in recent decades has become part of a new conventional wisdom. It is widely believed that distinct national economies with their own dynamics have dissolved into the world system. Not only have competitive pressures now become predominantly international, but national public policies are now so constrained by global market forces that there is little room for manoeuvre, let alone for radical alternatives. The new global system is driven by uncontrollable international financial market forces and dominated by large transnational companies that invest, produce and sell wherever their own economic advantage dictates. Capital is becoming increasingly international capital, without consideration for national origins. States cannot singly or collectively govern world markets. They have to accept, if they are not to act against the interests of their societies, that the only roles remaining to them are to promote the competitiveness of local economic actors and to make their territory as attractive as they can to inward investment by internationally mobile capital.

If the new conventional wisdom is true, then we are facing not just the 'end of the geography' but also the end of the left. In a moment we shall try to assess the distinctive features of a global economy and see whether the evidence supports the currently popular thesis of globalization. But before we do, we need to spell out the implications of a truly global system for national politics and, in particular, for those policies of social solidarity, equality and fairness that have distinguished the social democratic European left.

Governance and the market

Global market forces are held to be beyond governance. This means that states have no effective role in macro-economic policy other than to adjust to what world markets dictate. They cannot alter the rate of growth or the level of employment by national manipulation of macro-economic aggregates. Social policy is also directly affected and constrained by globalization. Welfare rights and benefits, tax levels and labour market policies that deviate from the minimum level that is acceptable to international capital will render the society in question uncompetitive and lead to capital flight.

The only way a society can reverse unfavourable macro-economic circumstances such as high unemployment and low growth is to get the micro-economic fundamentals right. Limited investments in training and infrastructure that attract business will be accepted by global markets; as will policies to make the unemployed more employable – i.e., more skilled and more enterprising. Thus the roles remaining to national public policy are to promote 'sound money', to keep inflation low, and to make markets work better. Macro-economic circumstances can only be altered in the long run by the natural workings of capital and labour markets. Public policy should follow the needs of international capital rather than trying to alter the economic environment by changing the behaviour of local economic actors.

Keynes and Beveridge are both dead if this is true. The only way to survive is to compete, whether as nation, firm or individual. Social solidarity and collective reinsurance against economic shocks are obsolete; international capital will only accept a minimum safety net and the barest of intervention consistent with market-led efficiency. Social democracy in any meaningful sense is dead. The project of humanizing and civilizing capitalism, so that a market society without losers could be created and sustained, is obsolete when self-interested corporate elites and global markets call the tune.

Tax-aversion would thus become a rational strategy for all successful economic actors. In a volatile and ultra-competitive system one must protect one's marketability and one's own assets. Resources must be concentrated on privately insuring oneself against the risks one can afford to cover and on maintaining one's own skills. Long-term loyalty to society or to the firm is out of the question, and will not be repaid anyway. One must carve out a career, and if that involves leaving company or country, so be it. Those who fail in this system are either unlucky or lazy, but we cannot sacrifice resources to help them.

Solidarity will thus collapse. Society will be divided not only by income and wealth but also by marketability and mobility. A successful highly skilled elite can move on international labour markets. Increasingly they will be not only self-interested but also supranational in their outlook and ambitions. They will neither identify with nor defer to a nationally rooted mass of the less skilled, whose jobs are easily replicable anywhere in the globe with cheap local labour. The whole world will become like a quasi-colony for the business class. They will enjoy virtual extra-territoriality and move between major world cities in their transnational corporate careers. The old claims that national labour could make on its economic elites, that they shared a community of fate and must work together, are now gone. The communist threat has vanished and the need to mobilize the population for major wars has ceased in the advanced states. Thus local social democrats have much less to bargain with when offering the loyalty of the national working class. Capital can move, and its elites with it; labour cannot.

Approaches from right to left

For the Anglo-Saxon right, the idea of a globalized economy is a godsend. The idea took root in the late 1980s. It arrived just in time to rescue the New Right project from the debacle that its adventurist monetarist policies of macro-economic management had created by the end of that decade. It could now claim that labour must accept that its wages and social standards are dictated by competition in the Far East, that it is Hong Kong and not Sweden from which we must now learn. In the USA, the Republican right openly advocates liquidating as much of the state that is not of direct benefit to the rich and to its own constituencies as possible. In Britain, the Conservative right has argued against further economic and political integration of the European Union, citing over-regulation and excessive social costs that are leading to a progressive loss of international competitiveness in Europe. The right thus needs globalization for its self-interested and anti-labour policies.

How can the moderate left respond? With difficulty, if it believes that the process of globalization described above really has taken place. So far the left has tried to argue that only fairer, longer-term public policies will enable countries to restore and retain international competitiveness. For example, Robert Reich, the former US Secretary of Labour, argues that protection of 'American' firms is irrelevant, and that Japanese subsidiaries are actually producers of US output and employers of American labour (Reich 1993). He sees the key remaining roles for national policy as promoting training, thereby ensuring an effective and attractive workforce, and investing in the infrastructure business requires. These policies will attract and retain capital, and thus promote employment and output.

The problem with this argument is that, in a truly globalized economy, mainstream political parties competing to control the policies of the nation-state would matter less. In a world beyond sovereignty, political projects that have relied on it, like the democratic left, would be all-but beached. It will be difficult for the left to mobilize enthusiastic national action for an alternative politics that amounts to making the country an attractive location for international business but with a slightly fairer social dimension, because it is more efficient in the long run. This may be necessary, but national politics will seem and sound like municipal politics, providing essential collective services in the way local authorities deliver street lighting and rubbish collection. Global rhetoric actually undercuts the political energy needed, even for moderate reform.

Actually the evidence does not sustain the extreme globalist thesis. We have an open international economy in which the national economic bases of the major advanced countries and regional trade blocs, like the EU, remain significant, and in which the scope for national and bloc policy (and therefore for active reform) is far greater than the pessimists who believe in the dominance of world market forces allow.

The first indicator of this is evidence on the long-term trends in the international openness of major economies. The first thing one would expect to find if there had been a rapid shift toward globalization is much greater economic openness of national economies, as evidenced by ratios of external exchanges (imports and exports) to total GDP. In fact the evidence available demonstrates nothing like this. Table 3.1, and most subsequent evidence, are drawn from the first edition of our book *Globalization in Question* (Hirst and Thompson 1996). What it shows is a dramatic decline in international openness caused by the First World War and the Great Crash of 1929, substantial recovery in the period 1945–73 as the new multilateral economy based on fixed exchange rates and free trade rules boosted world trade growth, and only modest change there-after.[1]

The figures demonstrate that, in terms of *trade*, the world has not changed markedly since 1913, let alone since 1973. Keynes was one of the chief architects of the economic settlement following the Second World War, and the current open international economy is one of the great achievements of the 'Keynesian' era, not a sharp deviation from it. Too often the period before the 1980s is presented as if it were a time of quasi-closed national economies rather than an international regime in which trade was relatively free but capital movements regulated. In the period 1950–73, world trade grew at an average annual rate of 9.4 per cent – twice world output – but world output also grew at the historically hith-erto unprecedented rate of 5.3 per cent annual average. Thus, in terms of the 'globalization' of trade, the key period in the twentieth century is the long postwar boom.

Table 3.1 Ratio of merchandise trade to GDP at current prices (exports and imports combined) 1913–93[2]

	1913	1950	1973	1993	1995
France	35.4	21.2	29.0	32.4	36.6
Germany	35.1	20.1	35.2	38.3	38.7
Japan	31.4	16.9	18.3	14.4	14.1
Netherlands	103.6	70.2	80.1	84.5	83.4
UK	44.7	36.0	39.3	40.5	42.6*
US	11.2	7.0	10.5	16.8	19.0

Source: Hirst and Thompson (1996: 27) – revised and updated.

Note: *1994

The response to such evidence may well be to say that what is really crucial is the new capital mobility made possible by the relaxation of exchange controls in the 1980s. To some extent the picture for merchandise trade might be held to be misleading because of the growth in trade by investment in the form of foreign direct investment (FDI). The issue here is complicated; world trade continues to grow faster than output (at about 9 per cent p.a.) but in the period 1983–90 FDI grew much faster than trade, at an average annual rate of 34 per cent. The striking fact about FDI, however, is that it remains a game played by the rich countries. In 1981–90, 75 per cent of investment flows were accounted for by the USA and Canada, the EC, EFTA and Japan – representing 14 per cent of the world's population in 1990. If one adds to this the nine most important developing countries as recipients of FDI, plus China's eight coastal provinces and Beijing, then they amounted to another 14 per cent of the world's population in 1990 and took 16.5 per cent of FDI. Thus, in the period in question, 28 per cent of the world's population took 91.5 per cent of FDI. In the period 1991–96, on the same basis, 30 per cent of the world's population received 84 per cent of the FDI flows. After the crisis of 1997–98, the substantial flows to developing countries of the early 1990s will be reversed, probably restoring the ratios to something like that of the 1980s.[3] FDI is not stripping the advanced world of its capital.

Moreover, FDI is not the main source of capital in either the developed or the rapidly industrializing countries. Most developed countries still source over 90 per cent of their investment from domestic capital, and the most rapidly developing countries of Asia have had very high ratios of domestic saving to national income, some 30–35 per cent.[4]

When one looks at figures showing where companies have the bulk of their sales and maintain the bulk of their assets, it will be clear that FDI is not creating footloose transnational companies. Most major companies are *multinational*; they produce in more than one location, and sell in a wide variety of markets, but they have a distinct national origin and a clear national productive base. Very few companies are *transnational* – i.e., without a clear national identity and so tied into global markets that their sales and assets are widely spread across the globe. Tables 3.2 and 3.3 show average figures of about two-thirds of both sales and assets are in the 'home' country or region: US manufacturing multinational companies (MNCs), for example, had 70 per cent of sales in North America in 1987.

Table 3.2 Percentage distribution of MNC sales to home region/country, 1987 and 1992–93

Country	Manufacturing		Services	
	1987	1992–93	1987	1992–93
Germany	72	75	na	na
Japan	64	75	89	77
UK	66	65	74	77
USA	70	67	93	79

Source: Hirst and Thompson (1996: 96, table 4.1).

Table 3.3 Percentage distribution of MNC assets to home region/country, 1987 and 1992–93

Country	Manufacturing		Services	
	1987	1992–93	1987	1992–93
Japan	–	97	74	92
UK	52	62	–	69
USA	67	73	81	77

Source: Hirst and Thompson (1996: 96, table 4.2).

These figures are taken from limited surveys and they are not exhaustive, but the pattern across the different sources of data remains similar.[5] In 1994, the gross product of the foreign affiliates of MNCs as a proportion of world GDP was 6 per cent, up from 5.2 per cent in 1982 but down from 6.7 per cent in 1990 (Hirst and Thompson 1998: 13, table 4) – hardly a massive trend towards the internationalization of production in recent decades, and far less than in the 1950s and 1960s. Companies trade and produce predominantly in their countries of origin, and their management is mainly made up of nationals from these countries. Companies are not thus able to cut loose from their home bases at will. The fact that most major MNCs have a base in one of the regions of the Triad, made up of Japan, the North Atlantic Free Trade Association (NAFTA) and the EU, does not mean that they are easy to regulate. Domestic capital has always bullied national governments when policies have deviated from its interests. It simply means that a regime of regulating MNCs through country of origin is possible in principle, whereas with true transnational companies (TNCs) it could only be achieved through supranational agencies.

It might be argued that all this is true, for trade, for FDI and for the character of companies, but the big difference since the 1970s is in the scale and integration of world financial markets. These really can sanction national policies of which they disapprove, selling nationally quoted equities and undermining the exchange rate. How far is this true? The financial crisis that began in Southeast Asia seems to prove the point. We will consider that crisis in a moment. But let us stay with the apparent major example of markets overwhelming public policy – the Exchange Rate Mechanism (ERM) crisis of 1992. The role of the market here seems to have been less to sanction incautious policies in advance or at their inception, but to create a *fait accompli* once policy has clearly failed. Dealers and company treasurers start to act when they wake up to the fact that they will suffer a substantial loss unless they exit, and the fixed exchange rate enables them to do so up to the extent of the available foreign exchange reserves. If anything, recent history seems to prove that the markets are able to tolerate stupid and destructive national policies without complaint, until it becomes glaringly obvious that there has to be a radical change of direction. In the UK, the markets responded well to Chancellor Nigel Lawson's disastrously inflationary 1988 budget and to Prime Minister John Major's entry into the ERM at an unsustainably over-valued target rate of 2.95DM in 1990. The macro-economic adventurism of the UK since 1979 is remarkable, but hardly evidence that distinct and ambitious national policies cannot be pursued.

International currency and bond markets are highly integrated. The volume of international currency trading – one trillion dollars per day – dwarfs the real flows of international trade and direct investment. It also means that central banks do not have the muscle to maintain exchange rates if the markets are convinced that these rates will move in the opposite direction. But it is foolish to pretend that the national governments of the advanced countries have been 'sovereign' in relation to exchange rates in the past. The UK laboured throughout the 1950s and 1960s under a 'balance of payments' constraint; it was part of an international monetary system and had to obey its rules. Modern governments can easily tolerate modest balance of payments deficits, but in that case they do not have autonomy in relation to interest rates. In essence, external constraints have changed and shifted but the degree of national autonomy for medium-sized nation-states in the supposed 'Keynesian' era is often talked up as much as the powerlessness of national policy is now talked down.

Following the collapse of the Bretton Woods system in 1971, there had been a seesaw struggle between the regulation of exchange rates and periods of intense volatility. The oil crisis intensified the problems created by the American decision to suspend convertibility. No system of managed exchange rates could have survived the inflationary pressures imposed by OPEC in 1973 and 1979. States struggled as best they could to contain inflation, and accepted a floating rate regime. The capacity of the advanced states to respond to the policy-induced inflationary pressures of the 1970s was impressive (OPEC, after all, was a cartel of states, not a market). This hardly shows that national policies have to be ineffective in a period of intense volatility. With the Plaza Accord of 1985 and the

Louvre Accord of 1987, some degree of stability was introduced after the period of floating exchange rates. Similarly, the European Monetary System (EMS) served to stabilize exchange rates in Europe until the consequences of German unification began to undermine it. The UK's position in relation to the EMS was always close to suicidal; it joined at the wrong rate at the wrong time, when it was struggling to contain a level of inflation way above Germany's, and it then refused the option of an orderly devaluation within the system. Idiocy is hardly an index of globalization. Of course, when it became clear that the position was unsustainable, 'speculators' moved in to force the issue.

Short-term financial movements are either predominantly attempts by financial institutions to generate revenue by making small percentage gains on small variations between markets by churning large volumes (as Nick Leeson proved so inept at doing), and/or they are attempts to hedge against volatility. Most economic actors in all three internationally active sectors – financial assets, manufactured goods and tradable services – have an interest in a minimum degree of calculability and stability. Incalculable risks undermine expectations; extreme volatility is an investment and growth killer (Hirst 1994).

The Asian financial crisis made this evident. The commercial banks once again made huge losses by incautious investments in emerging markets, as they did in Latin America in the 1970s. The IMF mobilized something like $100 billion to meet the effects of the Mexican and Asian crises, plus the collateral damage to Russia and Brazil. Such experiences show that the theory of efficient capital markets, on which the advocacy of financial liberalization in developing economies was based, is naive in the extreme. Countries like Thailand, Indonesia and South Korea liberalized their domestic financial systems and external capital accounts. The result was a massive and unsustainable inflow of foreign short-term funds, exacerbating domestic asset price bubbles. The combination of such major flows into relatively shallow financial systems and the defence of a pegged exchange rate was disastrous, capital flight causing the collapse of both asset markets and the exchange rate and thereby severely dislocating economic activity. Yet in fact none of those countries needed such short-term inflows, even if certain types of FDI in real assets could have been beneficial. Given very high domestic savings ratios, the only possible benefits of external liberalization would have been to enable foreign investors to participate in above-average rates of return. Yet their intervention has led to the opposite: in the case of Indonesia a contraction of something like 20 per cent of GDP during 1998 is projected.[6]

The best option would have been more cautious domestic financial liberalization and continued controls on the external capital account, plus floating exchange rates. This would have promoted domestic growth, while containing foreign flows. Some difficulties were inevitable as export growth and GDP growth contracted sharply in Southeast Asia, partly as a result of the falling value of the yen against the dollar. This could perhaps have been coped with, had not commercial bank funds flowed into the Asian economies to a total of some $129 billion in 1994–96 and then flowed out again in 1997 to a net total of some $21 billion.[7] In most cases, Southeast Asian national economic policy-makers were neither incompetent nor consequentially corrupt. 'Cronyism' is an excuse by Western economic liberals to cover market failure on a colossal scale. The Asian crisis was in large measure not the effect of some autonomous process of 'globalization' but of ill-conceived policies pressed upon Asian governments by international elites. The principal actors are familiar, the commercial banks. Developing countries do have national policy options, and the chief one is to avoid excessive external financial liberalization while supporting a regime of free trade. Policies to promote beneficial FDI and constrain unproductive short-term flows, like those adopted in Chile after the crisis of the early 1980s, can be more widely adopted. Financial markets are not all-powerful and can be constrained by national policy, even in the developing countries.

In the case of dealing in financial derivatives, clearly the secondary effects of the 1998 crisis show the need for re-regulation. Derivatives are not just a hedge against market fluctuations, controlling risk. Developed into a speculative instrument, they are a potential source of systemic risk, as the failure of the Long Term Capital Management fund demonstrated. International conventions to limit the players to recognized banks, to limit the rise of their positions relative to assets, and to limit or abolish the over-the-counter trade, are perfectly possible. Perhaps the 1998 crisis may stimulate re-regulation and a new international regime of supervision between the main financial centres. Containment of this nature would promote a measure of stability and certainty, and hence reduce volatility. Such markets are not inherently beyond control.

Competitiveness and state policies

A calculable framework for international economic relations would benefit the vast majority of international economic actors, and be in the long-term interest of labour and capital (most of which is generated by the financial assets of labour and re-cycled through institutions like banks, pension funds and insurance companies). It will be difficult to construct such a framework, although it is vital to long-term growth. The problem, above all, is the perceived and genuine differences of interest between national states. Paradoxically, because the international economy is still dominated by the big advanced nation-states, agreements to control the relations between them are difficult. Governance problems stem from conflicting national interests much more than they do from 'global' market forces. The chief obstacle to a new international monetary regime is not the markets, but the contradictory interests of Japan and the USA with respect to the respective values of the dollar and the yen. The world economy is minimally governed. States need to act to set ground rules for financial markets, to regulate the micro operations of those markets rather than to control outcomes, and to try to prevent excessive volatility that could produce meltdown. The extreme fears about globalization are false. But we are still far from the creation of a new international financial and trade governance regime directed towards employment and growth – that is, a new Bretton Woods agreement – which is still just talk among intellectuals and a few liberal central bankers (Uzan 1996; Grieve-Smith forthcoming).

Ambitious stand-alone national macro-economic policies to promote employment and growth through boosting demand are not currently possible. The constraints are domestic more than they are international. Most policy-makers and central banks remain concerned with the inflationary fears generated by the 1970s. Despite the current talk of deflation and falling commodity prices, domestic prices in the major industrial economies are not yet falling in the way they were in the 1930s when Keynes first advocated his policies. Equally, in countries like the UK that have suffered de-industrialization and rationalization, there is little 'excess capacity' that can quickly generate new output if there were a substantial domestic stimulus to demand. Beyond a certain modest level of stimulus, new jobs require new investment, even in the labour-intensive public sector. Inevitably, therefore, a strong stimulus to domestic demand will prove inflationary and will suck in imports. We should not blame this on 'globalization', but on a changed conjuncture in which skilled labour shortages and time lags in investment condition the short-term responsiveness of the economy. This feature helps to explain why ambitious national policies, like those of the French government in the early 1980s, fail.

Social policy has much greater autonomy than macro-economic policy at the national level. Some of the wealthiest societies, like the USA, seem to have persuaded themselves that they cannot afford a proper welfare state. The constraints here are domestic, and depend on the political culture, not global markets. *The Economist*, not noted for its hostility to globalization, recognizes that there are wide variations in the percentage of GDP devoted to public spending: 20 per cent in Singapore, 33 per cent in the USA, 49 per cent in Germany and 68 per cent in Sweden.[8] Global economic pressures are not reducing these differences. If anything, the distinct national 'styles' in the division of national income between public and private spending are becoming more pronounced.

Provided an economy remains competitive in the goods and services it trades internationally, its population can choose high levels of social spending, and it does not have to be 'competitive' or drive down wages in the non-internationally-traded sectors. Denmark is a good example of a country that has managed to combine high internationalization, an extensive welfare state and successful economic performance. The same is true of The Netherlands. Indeed, the evidence points to the fact that small, highly internationalized advanced countries have had higher-than-average levels of public expenditure and extensive welfare states (Katzenstein 1985; Rodrick 1997). Public spending and welfare have served to cushion the domestic economy against internationally induced shocks and have enabled domestic economic actors to remain competitive by giving them aid and time to adapt. The experience to date seems to indicate that high levels of international exposure typically have led to greater, rather than less, welfare and public intervention. The question is whether such regimes can survive in an era when capital controls have been removed. Space prohibits an extensive answer here; we have argued elsewhere that the process of welfare reform and economic adaptation in countries like The Netherlands and Italy shows that it can indeed survive (Hirst 1998; Hirst and Thompson 1999, ch. 6).

However, other advanced countries have followed very different strategies. Until recently both the USA and Japan have combined relatively low levels of internationalization with relatively low levels of public spending relative to GDP and either very imperfect welfare systems in the American case, or vestigial ones in the case of Japan. Japan has had such a dual economy: highly competitive in certain manufacturing sectors; its financial institutions and its labour intensive service sectors have both been highly 'inefficient'. Yet they have provided cheap capital for the manufacturing sector and served to absorb labour.[9] Japan has had a social settlement in which economic growth and full employment has compensated for the absence of a welfare state in the European sense.

This settlement is now coming apart. Japan's system has relied on a very low level of imports and a modest level of exports relative to GDP (8–10 per cent), heavily concentrated in certain sectors. Japan's domestic economy was thus relatively disengaged from international shocks as far as labour markets and social protection are concerned. It adjusted to the 1973 and 1979 Oil Price crises by energy efficiency and productivity-enhancing measures coordinated through the system of administrative guidance. Japan is now facing a crisis stemming from its asset price inflationary boom of the 1980s and the subsequent effects of the collapse of the bubble economy on its financial system. In the absence of a welfare state, Japanese citizens have responded to the crisis by boosting their already high savings ratios. This response to uncertainty creates a vicious circle in which falling consumption breeds further insecurity. In this crisis of underconsumption and excessive saving the government has few conventional Keynesian levers, interest rates being low and tax-to-GDP ratios also low. Japan seems to offer the lesson that mature industrial economies actually benefit from welfare spending as a stabilizing factor.

Unlike Japan, the UK does not have such a broadly competitive manufacturing sector. Indeed, it still has large numbers of poorly managed firms that continue to underinvest and underperform by international standards. It has highly developed capital markets, profitable financial institutions, a highly developed and well-capitalized marketed services sector – *and* mass unemployment, continuing balance of trade deficits, and poor public services. These patterns are not imposed by globalization, but by distinct paths of domestic institutional development.

Nevertheless, Britain is a relatively rich country whose governments over the past twenty years have tried hard to convince people they should accept standards of public transport and health care that are no longer really consistent with advanced-nation status. Britain is not so poor that it has to suffer crumbling schools and a dearth of decent public housing. The problem, in the short term, is that the present Labour government is boxed in by the consequences of Conservative macro-economic recklessness and a long period of both neglect and profligate waste in the public sector. Two deep policy-induced recessions in the early 1980s and early 1990s have left a legacy of massive real unemployment – 25 per cent of men of working age are 'economically inactive' – and consequent high social security spending. Recklessly undervalued privatizations, the Poll Tax, Black Wednesday and the NHS reorganization, have all depleted the public purse to no great purpose. These constraints are domestic; most of them originate in Westminster and Whitehall. Globalization has little to do with them. Yet the concept of globalization has been used to undermine any attempt to maintain or improve domestic public services and welfare standards, in the belief that they will render UK private employers uncompetitive. Labour is still in thrall to the concept and has an over-diminished set of expectations about the possibilities of national policy.

Globalization is thus a concept with dangerous political side effects. Whatever the long-term prospects for international governance of financial markets or of coordinated action to combat environmental degradation, the key issue at the moment is to restore confidence in the governance capacities of the nation-state and of trade blocs like the EU. Without such capacities there can be no effective foundations on which to build and to control forms of international governance. We can begin to resist these potentially destructive arguments about the emergence of a global economy dominated by ungovernable market forces, which is at variance with the evidence.

Notes

1   This is confirmed by data cited by Martin Wolf in 'Globalisation and the State', *Financial Times*, 18 September 1995, p. 24.
2   This is not the place to argue the relative merits of using current or constant prices. We discuss this and other contentious matters of evidence in the second edition of *Globalization in Question* (Hirst and Thompson 1999). Suffice it to say that constant prices understate the effects of new technologies and production innovations in reducing the costs of commodities and, therefore, tend to overstate trade-to-GDP ratios.
3   Source for 1981–90, Hirst and Thompson (1996: 68, table 3.2), for 1991–96, Hirst and Thompson (1999: table 3.2).

4 See David Miles, 'Globalisation: the Facts Behind the Myth', *Independent*, 22 December 1997, for the localization of most capital investment.
5 Other studies confirm this overall picture – see Pauly and Reich (1997) and van Tulder (1995).
6 On the Asian crisis, see Hirst and Thompson (1999, ch. 5), and Montes (1998).
7 See data cited by Martin Wolf, *Financial Times*, 3 March 1998, p. 22.
8 'The Myth of the Powerless State', *The Economist*, 7 October 1995, pp. 15–16.
9 For a perceptive critique of the inefficiency of Japanese institutions that foretold the current crisis, see Reading (1992).

References

Grieve-Smith, J. (ed.) (forthcoming) *Global Instability and World Economic Governance*.
Hirst, P. (1994) 'Why the National Still Matters', *Renewal* 2: 4.
——(1998) 'Can the Welfare State Survive Globalization?', *Working Papers on European Studies*, 2: 1 (International Institute University of Wisconsin–Madison).
Hirst, P. and Thompson G. (1996) *Globalization in Question*, Cambridge: Polity Press.
——(1998) 'The Tyranny of Globalization: Myth or Reality', paper for University of Antwerp conference on 'Globalization and the Nation State'.
——(1999) *Globalization in Question*, 2nd edn, Cambridge: Polity Press.
Katzenstein, P. (1985) *Small States in World Markets*, Ithaca, NY: Cornell University Press.
Montes, M. F. (1999) *The Currency Crisis in South East Asia*, Singapore: ISEAS.
Pauly, L. and Reich, S. (1997) 'National structures and multinational corporate behaviour: enduring differences in an age of globalization', *International Organization* 51: 1: 1–30.
Reading, B. (1992) *Japan: The Coming Collapse*, London: Weidenfeld and Nicolson.
Reich, R. B. (1993) *The Work of Nations*, London: Simon and Schuster.
Rodrick, D. (1997) *Has Globalization Gone Too Far?*, Washington, DC: Institute of International Economics.
Ruigruk, W. and van Tulder, R. (1995) *The Logic of International Restructuring*, London: Routledge.
Uzan, M. (ed.) (1996) *The Financial System Under Stress; An Architecture for the New World Economy*, London: Routledge.

4 Hirst and Thompson's 'Global myths and national policies'

A reply[1]

Jonathan Perraton

Introduction

The hype surrounding globalization has attracted an important coun-
terblast; despite the often iconoclastic tone of their writings, the
globalization sceptics' arguments from Hirst and Thompson (among
others) are fast becoming orthodox in some circles. There is certainly
plenty to challenge in the extreme or 'hyper-globalization' arguments, be
they neo-liberal business literature or radical prophesies of the total eclipse
of any space for progressive politics. Such writers do indeed cite evidence
selectively, use this evidence in loose theoretical frameworks, and consequently draw highly questionable conclusions. However, the
counter-evidence cited by the sceptics is often problematic itself and does
not necessarily lead to the conclusions they propose. Above all, both these
approaches in effect share much of the same framework: they both presup-
pose a unique end-point to globalization processes. Having set up this
end-state as the concept of globalization, albeit by reference to the hyper-
globalization literature, it is relatively easy for Hirst and Thompson to find
this conception wanting as a description of reality. But this approach is
problematic. It is unclear what benchmarks could be used to decide how
close is close enough to such an end-point. More fundamentally it seems
highly unlikely that social processes have one end-point: historical forms
of globalization – both as a general social phenomenon and in their
specific forms – have multiple causes and, given the likelihood of multiple
equilibria, are unlikely to have a single even implied end-point. End-point
analysis obscures the processes at work here. Rather, globalization is more
appropriately conceived as an historical process which engenders a shift in
the spatial reach of networks and systems of social relations to transcontinental (or inter-regional) patterns of human organization, activity and the
exercise of social power. Ultimately Hirst and Thompson cite evidence
which may refute hyper-globalization claims but which does not simply
support their contention that nothing substantive has changed; however,
their framework leaves them stuck between these two choices. Examining
globalization as a process instead allows for multiple possible outcomes.

Politically the end-point conception of globalization is influential, but damaging. It promotes the view of globalization moving us inexorably to a particular outcome, producing either a fatalism or voluntarism in respect of political action. Like Hirst and Thompson I regard this as unwarranted and undesirable, but from a different conceptual analysis. Even here there are elements of caricature in Hirst and Thompson's reading of the hyper-globalist position. They charge this position as claiming that power has irrevocably shifted from national polities to firms and markets; where they can point to possibilities for states regaining power, sometimes by acting in consort, they take this as evidence against globalization. Neo-liberal versions of the position may claim that states have lost power irrevocably, but, as I argue below, the neo-liberal position maintains that government intervention is ineffective and counter-productive anyway, irrespective of globalization. Radical hyper-globalist theorists such as Greider (1997) do, however, admit some potential for states reclaiming power. They remain, though, rather less sanguine about these possibilities.

There are many points in Hirst and Thompson's chapter I have no quarrel with, and I would concur with their assessment that hyper-globalist claims are inducing an unnecessary paralysis in public policy. Nevertheless, several of Hirst and Thompson's claims and conclusions are highly debatable. The first parts of this response deal with Hirst and Thompson's specific claims on international trade, multinational production and finance; the latter part draws together analysis to indicate what policy space remains.

International trade

As trade barriers have fallen, often to negligible levels, and trade has grown faster than income, markets for goods, and increasingly services, have been stretched from national or regional levels to the global. This has meant the fortunes of different groups within nations are increasingly determined in world markets. For sceptics like Hirst and Thompson this is too much, but their objections are partly based on some empirical quibbles dealt with in this chapter and partly on objections to the hyper-globalization claim that global trade renders countries as firms competing in the global economy and will act to reduce wages and standards to the lowest common denominator. Hirst and Thompson are basically correct in rejecting this latter claim on theoretical and empirical grounds, but their analysis misses key developments. Their claim that trade is no higher, relative to national income, than in earlier periods is misleading. Even using current price data, recent estimates indicate that world trade-to-GDP ratios are higher today than ever before (Krugman, 1995). Such comparisons are for trade in goods only – including trade in services increases the contrast. Netting out government activity, as virtually entirely non-traded, shows a clear rise in the proportion of private output traded (see Held *et al.* 1999, ch. 3). Further, using current price data is also misleading – prices of tradables tend to rise less rapidly than those of non-tradables due to the greater competition they face and higher potential for technical progress. It is therefore more appropriate to make the comparison using constant price data. This clearly shows a rise in trade-to-GDP ratios from the 1970s (see Table 4.1). Far from there being only 'modest change' since 1973, more sophisticated analysis bears out the evidence here that there was a struc- tural break in countries' trade-to-GDP ratios after 1973 (Ben-David and Pappell 1997). Qualitatively the world has changed, too. Whereas earlier periods, including the time before the First World War, were marked by protectionism, from the 1980s there has been a marked trend towards free trade among developing as well as developed countries, so that now a clear majority of the world's economies – by GDP and by population – operate under something like free trade (Sachs and Warner 1995). With on-going liberalization programmes in developing and transition economies, this is likely to continue.

Notions that trade renders countries as competitive firms and will reduce wages and standards to the lowest common denominator are typi- cally based on basic misunderstandings of trade theory. However, while it remains the case that specialization still develops so that countries cannot have a relative advantage in everything or nothing, trade can still have a major impact on the fortunes of groups within a country. Even if trade ratios had simply returned to pre-First World War levels, it is not clear that this would help Hirst and Thompson's argument in view of recent evidence that there was substantial convergence in wage levels (and other incomes) through trade over the period 1870–1914 (Williamson 1996). Similar trends can be discerned today for labour of different skill levels. While there is an important debate over how far trends in employment and wages for groups in developed countries can be attributed to international trade, the evidence indicates that it is significant.[2] Increased trade, and changing patterns of trade, lead to major structural change in national economies. Overall, national economies should gain from increased trade, but some groups within them stand to gain and others to lose even though

Table 4.1 Trade–GDP ratios for developed countries in constant prices (percentages)

	1913	1950	1973	1985	
Exports–GDP	11.2	8.3	18.0	23.1	
	1880–1990	*1901–1913*	*1948–1959*	*1959–1972*	*1973–1987*
Imports–GDP	12.4	13.3	10.1	15.4	21.7

Sources: Maddison (1991: 327); McKeown (1991: 158).

in principle the gainers could fully compensate the losers and still be better off. This puts questions of whether the welfare state makes countries 'uncompetitive' into perspective. As Hirst and Thompson note, countries with high trade shares actually tend to have larger welfare states; this may work crudely to ensure that gainers from structural change at least partially compensate the losers. However, the decline of low-skilled employment in developed countries and the apparent end of full employment place increasing demands on the welfare state. Increasing trade with developing countries in particular tends to heighten the income redistribution effects. Thus, although a country can decide to maintain (or increase) welfare provision, the costs of doing this have risen. Heightened competition from global trade has made it harder to pass on cost increases and therefore has made it increasingly difficult to raise taxes on business and employers' social security contributions. Tilting at the unsustainable positions advanced by hyper-globalization theorists allows Hirst and Thompson to understate the impact of global trade. Further, their account ignores institutional arrangements for global trade. Although it may change, the current remit of the World Trade Organization is to work against barriers to trade generally. There is very little in its current set-up that allows for exceptions to this on grounds of, for example, environmental or labour standards. As such it limits possibilities for ensuring that international goods are priced to reflect their full social costs. Further, it limits policies to support industrialization that historically have been used by many of today's developed economies. Some of the industrial policy measures that Hirst and Thompson seem to have in mind might well be in breach of WTO regulations.

Multinational corporations

On foreign direct investment (FDI) by multinational corporations (MNCs), it is certainly true that the majority of FDI flows are to developed countries, while flows to developing countries are concentrated on a small number of states. Even in its own terms, though, this is somewhat misleading: FDI flows to developing countries have grown rapidly since the mid-1980s and this can be important to their investment. For example, FDI accounts for a large proportion of many transition economies' total investment (World Bank 1996). More fundamentally, such distribution only contradicts globalization if globalization is taken to imply that activity would flow to the lowest wage countries. As with trade, this contradicts basic principles of comparative advantage. Where low wage countries do have a relative advantage, MNCs often are important in developing their production. More sustainably here, globalization implies international movement of capital for international production, not that it must be evenly distributed worldwide or flow systematically to developing countries. On the contrary, unevenness is quite consistent with globalization and a common feature of its contemporary forms.

Hirst and Thompson effectively set up a model of frictionless international capital movement and find that reality falls short; they cannot, though, simply leap from this and claim that MNCs are essentially national companies. Their figures indicate that around a third of multinationals' activity takes place overseas: this is hardly secondary, let alone marginal, to their operations. The leading 100 (non-financial) MNCs by foreign assets, which control around a third of FDI stocks, in 1994 had 55.3 per cent of their sales overseas and (for those companies for which data was available) 49.5 per cent of their assets and 46.9 per cent of their employment overseas (calculated from UNCTAD 1996: 30–2). International operations of MNCs have increased, and, while it is not costless to shift activity internationally, it has become substantially easier to do so. Evidence indicates that this has significant effects on wages and the allocation of investment funds (Cowling and Sugden 1996; Hatzius 1997a; 1997b).

Further, focusing on individual MNCs ignores the extent to which, overall, the effect of MNCs is to create global competition (cf. Baily and Gersbach 1995); although any one MNC may not be able to serve all markets or source from any location, overall MNCs serve markets worldwide and link up to production locations across the globe. It is not clear what claims are being made when MNCs are said to have a distinctive national base, for example why the nationality of their leading personnel is supposed to matter. In the first place, it is in the very nature of MNCs that technological advantages developed in the home country can be diffused internationally. Studies of national R&D indicate that a significant proportion of it diffuses overseas through various channels (Coe and Helpman 1995; Verspagen 1997). Second, the nature of global competition is now such that MNCs increasingly invest in R&D ventures abroad and often engage in strategic alliances with other firms to develop technology, around a half of such alliances being with firms in other continents (OECD 1996). Thus, not only are MNCs able to diffuse technological advantages generated at home to locations overseas, they also tap into foreign innovation networks as increasingly the national base is becoming insufficient to generate their technological advantage. These changes make it harder to tie firms into national economic relations with the state and other stakeholders. MNCs have played an important role in shifting formal and informal social bargains, both directly though their wages and investment policy and politically through lobbying for neo-liberal policies (Kurzer 1993; McCann 1995). Simultaneously, countries – and regional agencies within them – compete to attract internationally mobile capital through fiscal incentives. The economic justification for this is quite unclear, and collectively this is an irrational approach for nation states; that much of industrial policy has come down to such measures, which effectively transfer taxpayers income to MNCs, is indicative of the shift in power towards firms relative to states. There is nothing inevitable about this: countries could negotiate international treaties to limit the extent of fiscal competition for international capital.

Hirst and Thompson appear to set great store by the notion that because they see MNCs as still essentially national companies they are amenable to national policy, but it is not clear what this entails and it presupposes a high degree of effectiveness of state intervention. It is increasingly hard to find examples of pervasively successful industrial policy, and more generally there has been a decline in broadly social corporatist policies which tie capital into national economic arrangements. This is hardly surprising when it is precisely those companies that are most important in technology generation that are also the most mobile internationally. As MNCs have become less dependent on their home base and their exit options have increased, it has become increasingly difficult to tie them into national arrangements. Further, the trend has been towards less regulation of MNCs, even if, thus far, attempts to negotiate the Multilateral Agreement on Investment – which would effectively preclude any regulation of MNCs – have foundered.

International finance

Effectively Hirst and Thompson concede much of the power of international finance. They note, not just the awesome scale of current international financial activity, but also that key economic variables are effectively determined in private global markets. They accept that, although national governments regulate their activities and act as lenders of last resort, these regulations set the very liberal framework for international finance to operate rather than determine its activities. Combined with the elimination of capital controls, key economic variables, particularly interest rates, are now determined in global markets.

As Hirst and Thompson also accept, financial markets have at times supported policies by favoured governments, before rapidly and heavily turning against them. On the other hand, governments of the left in particular recently have often pursued financially orthodox policies with paltry gains in terms of lower interest rates. This matters: tight monetary policy can easily produce unemployment and Europe's poor unemployment record from the 1980s may partly be attributed to high interest rates (Heylen *et al.* 1996). Hirst and Thompson do claim that the level of national autonomy in macroeconomic policy during the Bretton Woods era has been overstated. (Parenthetically, to reiterate, they still appear to assume a high degree of potential effectiveness for national industrial policy.) Here their British example is probably exceptional: the evidence indicates that international flows only had a secondary impact on most developed countries' macroeconomic policies during Bretton Woods (Webb

1995: chs 3 and 4). The high level of capital flows since the end of Bretton Woods have qualitatively transformed macroeconomic policy so that exchange rates and interest rates have become highly sensitive to international financial flows (Webb 1995: chs 5 and 6). The upshot of this is that countries have very limited room for manoeuvre in their macroeconomic policies without differences in their stance producing significant movements in exchange rates and interest rates. As markets attach risk premia to different countries' interest rates, effectively they set costs for different policy packages. Here the form of contemporary globalization is important. If global financial markets worked in textbook fashion then, although national autonomy would be limited, governments would still have clear policy options for targeting domestic variables. However, it is not simply that international financial flows are highly sensitive to global flows, but their movements are unpredictable. Financial innovations and the unpredictability of market response has made it increasingly difficult to target macroeconomic policy for domestic objectives. Floating exchange rates did not provide countries with the expected level of policy autonomy in the 1970s, and fixed exchange rate systems have become increasingly difficult to maintain. A key aspect of this is that speculative activity in global financial markets can move macroeconomic variables to values that are inappropriate for the real economy. Overall, these changes substantially reduce the effectiveness and reliability of national macroeconomic policy instruments. It is not simply that markets can impose significant costs on different policy packages; their response is unpredictable and liable to change. In the most extreme cases this takes the form of strong capital inflows being suddenly reversed in a speculative attack.

Although Hirst and Thompson effectively concede much of this, they remain sanguine about the effects of global finance in practice and regard regulation of markets to reduce instability as not merely desirable but straightforward in principle; that such regulations have not been agreed they attribute largely to conflict between the US and Japan. This perspective leads them to some odd and questionable judgements over recent episodes. They attribute the failure of the French radical Keynesian experiment during 1981–83 to supply-side constraints. However, there is strong evidence of Keynesian unemployment in France at the time, and the level of reflation entailed was more modest than is often supposed (Muet and Fonteneau 1990; Halimi *et al.* 1994). The speculative attacks against the franc meant that, not only did pursuing the package become impossible within the European Monetary System, but floating the franc would probably have led to it plummeting. Hirst and Thompson tout the Plaza–Louvre episode as bringing greater stability to exchange rates, but this is against the background of extraordinary volatility in the early 1980s. As a one-off attempt to manage the dollar, it hardly signalled the emergence of a new exchange rate regime. Ironically, it fits their perspective of the importance of major power politics, as the continued international power of the US enabled it to enlist the help of other countries to manage dollar movements that were largely driven by its own policy imbalances. Again Hirst and Thompson's perspective on the European currency crisis of 1992–93 is unduly influenced by the British case. A range of currencies was attacked despite strong inflation and policy convergence and without clear evidence of deteriorating competitiveness (even in the UK case); this episode thus suggests the markets' ability to shift macroeconomic policy by launching a speculative attack (cf. Eichengreen 1996, ch. 5). In 1997, financial markets suddenly changed from regarding East Asia as a leading growth pole to seeing it as a corrupt and inefficient disaster area. Although they attribute this to international capital flows rather than a crisis of domestic 'crony capitalism', Hirst and Thompson claim the crisis is 'not the effect of some autonomous process of "globalization" but of ill-conceived policies pressed upon Asian governments by international elites'. This is a strained distinction. The effects of the East Asian crisis on economic activity, trade, exchange rates and stock markets across the world powerfully demonstrates the limits to their claims that economic activity is essentially nationally-based or largely contained within regional 'Triads'. Whatever imbalances there were in these economies, the subsequent falls in their currencies far exceed any appropriate adjustment. Hirst and Thompson claim that, for these economies, 'the best option would have been more cautious domestic financial liberalization and continued controls on the external capital account, plus floating exchange rates'. On the contrary, developing countries, in particular, find it optimal to operate fixed exchange rates since appropriate rates provide stability for exporters and a macroeconomic anchor (Helleiner 1994, ch. 1). Floating exchange rates have been tested and found wanting for many countries; their apparent appropriateness reflects the ability of speculative finance to disrupt any arrangement. There is merit in Hirst and Thompson's argument that excessive financial liberalization in these countries contributed to the crisis, while they recognize the disruptive role of private international finance in this crisis. Their view of the crisis reflects their wider view that disruptive financial flows can be readily controlled and that the failure to do so is essentially political. Limits on disruptive flows may be desirable and are increasingly on the agenda in the aftermath of the East Asian crisis. Nevertheless, Hirst and Thompson's account ignores the practical difficulties of controlling financial flows and the way in which financial innovations have meant that financial authorities play catch-up with regulating these. Even those who explain financial deregulation in terms of domestic politics, rather than international market pressure, recognize that one cannot simply reverse earlier policies (Sobel 1994).

It is increasingly difficult to maintain the sanguine view that markets simply deliver appropriate values for macroeconomic variables, reward good policies and precipitate inevitable crises when inappropriate ones are pursued. Hirst and Thompson recognize the instability that this produces and the harmful effects it can have on investment and growth.

Policy

Hirst and Thompson effectively set up a case where governments have irrevocably lost almost all power to private markets and firms. However, even some hyperglobalist authors would not argue that private actors are necessarily beyond regulation in principle. The policy implications of the changes sketched in the previous section are not that national governments have lost all power to firms or markets, but that their power has diminished substantially relative to these institutions. The costs of various policy options have changed, in some cases dramatically. Further, the uncertainty of market responses to policy packages, and the changes in their responses, means that governments themselves do not have a clear picture of what the costs of any particular policy may be and how this may change over time.

Taken together, trade and international diffusion of technology through various channels have similar effects. In this sense globalization arguments do not depend on how much of the decline in demand for low-skill employment is attributed to trade with developing countries and how much to technical change. Both act to increase differentials between groups in developed economies, with the consequences for the welfare state we have discussed. Technology has diffused internationally so that these changes have occurred across developed countries. The international diffusion of technology, both among developed countries and also to developing ones, means that income levels and trade advantages in economies are increasingly determined by relative human capital supplies rather than by particular national technological advantages. Again, this is more a matter of degree than absolute change, but it does have important distributional consequences. The generality of these shifts across developed countries is indicative of the international spread of technology and the limits to national political economies in delivering bargains favourable to the traditional interests of the left.

It is important to note that the neo-liberal arguments for the ineffectiveness of government intervention – macroeconomic demand management or supply-side interventions – have virtually nothing to do with globalization *per se*. If markets worked in perfect textbook fashion then these policies would be ineffective, largely irrespective of how open the national economy is to international flows. Limited international economic flows and national restrictions on them would not make Keynesian or interventionist policies effective under new classical economics or neo-liberal analysis; at most they would change the nature or timing of the perverse effects such policies would have. Thus, Hirst and Thompson find themselves querying pieces of evidence which are largely irrelevant to the policy conclusions they wish to refute.

For government intervention to be effective, Hirst and Thompson must assume a different framework. This raises difficulties for their arguments. Rather than questioning whether multinationals' power of exit is total, they need to address its increased power. A broadly Keynesian approach to economic policy entails a Keynesian perspective. Keynes was adamant that financial markets should be controlled and, in particular, that there should be limits on private international finance to ensure national macroeconomic autonomy. The astronomic rise of private global finance and ending of national restrictions has indeed sharply diminished national policy autonomy. As basic macroeconomic variables are determined in these markets they can be and often are driven to levels inconsistent with high levels of output and employment. Hirst and Thompson's response to this is unclear, but there appear to be three arguments. The first is to claim that little has really changed. Beyond citing some misleading statistics, this argument is based on claiming that macroeconomic policy autonomy was never absolute during the Bretton Woods era and has not totally vanished today. Both propositions are valid, but they are also consistent with a major decline in national policy autonomy. Their second argument is to suggest that markets largely penalize unsustainable policies. But even they acknowledge that markets sometimes support such policies for years before turning against them; and, as already argued, this sanguine view is hard to sustain now. Their third argument is that the shifts in economic policy are largely ideological as governments have become in thrall to the 'necessary myth' of globalization. This argument has some merit, and governments probably do have more room for manoeuvre than the current risk-averse stance of many suggests. Many arguments that particular policies would make a country 'uncompetitive' are simply wrong. But it is hard to attribute it all to ideology, one that business has been busy espousing since the nineteenth century. Again the problem is the way they set up the globalization argument. It is easy to refute arguments that any progressive measure is bound to lead to MNCs relocating and/or adverse movements on the money markets. Tilting at this argument allows Hirst and Thompson to ignore the increased relative, not absolute, power of these agents.

When it comes to specifics, Hirst and Thompson's arguments are actually close to the hyper-globalization school they criticize. They do deny hyper-globalization claims that national economic policy has been reduced to developing human capital and making countries market-friendly, arguing that if true this would herald the end of the left. But when discussing specific cases such as that of France in the early 1980s, or of contemporary Britain, Hirst and Thompson emphasize supply-side constraints, particularly human capital. Whatever the effectiveness of governments in influencing long-term growth rates, a central task is to manage short-term fluctuations; but the uncertainties and deflationary bias of private global finance makes this increasingly difficult. The best-laid plans to develop skills will founder if macroeconomic conditions are too tight so that the jobs are simply not there.

Hirst and Thompson are correct to say that it is still open to nations to decide levels of public expenditure, notably on welfare, and to tax accordingly. However, even some hyper-globalists like Reich concede this.[3] Simply to note that nations have that autonomy, though, is to ignore the difficulties of doing so. Business can and does resist taxation to pay for this. Human capital policies may or may not be effective on welfare and efficiency grounds, but the business community's apparent support for them typically evaporates when it is suggested that they contribute to it. Even where government expenditure packages are covered by receipts, the markets may still penalize them with a premium on interest rates. However, it is almost inevitable that, periodically at least, governments will run deficits and, even where these are likely to be sustainable, markets are likely to impose risk premia on the interest rates. Although globalization makes it harder to tie elites into national arrangements, this does not necessarily entail, *pace* Hirst and Thompson's assertions, the end of social solidarity. It does, however, imply that more than ever the welfare state will be financed by non-elite members of society. There is a wider point. Social democratic arrangements have entailed tying business into national relationships with other stakeholders. The effects of globalization here are not simply, or even mainly, on the financing of the welfare state but on the wider sustainability of social democratic arrangement. Even when these are backed politically, implementing public expenditure packages is likely to face difficulties from business resistance and adverse response on the money markets. Although this does not make such packages impossible, it may well raise their costs.

Conclusions

Hirst and Thompson set up an extreme hyper-globalization, admittedly one proposed by some authors, and find it easy to knock down. Much of the evidence they cite speaks past these arguments, which are often logically faulty in themselves. But Hirst and Thompson's alternative is largely to suggest that little has really changed, a claim the figures do not, under closer examination, bear out. As a result their interpretations of many recent episodes are questionable. It is certainly unhelpful, both analytically and politically, to argue that globalization has one end-point and that either the world is moving inexorably towards it or this can only be reversed by an unlikely coalition of groups deemed to be 'anti-systemic'. But Hirst and Thompson's rejection of this simplistic analysis simply substitutes social democratic complacency for this. They take rejection of the hyper-globalization claims as allowing them to claim, improbably, that the world hasn't really changed. The multiple possibilities of globalization matter politically. Examining how the world economy has changed and what possibilities remain for governments is a more important and useful task than scoring easy points off sloppy hyper-globalization authors. This would help identify areas for effective international cooperation and governance of the world economy. I have already suggested that measures to limit competition for FDI would be appropriate. In the aftermath of the East Asian crisis the appropriate forms of international governance are being debated with new urgency. The globalization debate needs to move on to address these concerns.

Notes

1 This paper is based on my work for the project 'Globalization and the Advanced Industrial State' at the Open University, funded by Economic and Social Research Council Research Grant R000233391. Further details of the economic arguments are in Perraton *et al.* (1997); further details of the general argument are in Held *et al.* (1999).
2 See Minford *et al.* (1997), Wood (1994; 1995), and the Policy Forum in the *Economic Journal* of September 1998.
3 See interview with Robert Reich, *New Statesman*, 14 November 1997.

References

Baily, M. and Gersbach, H. (1995) 'Efficiency in manufacturing and the need for global competition', *Brookings Papers on Economic Activity*, Microeconomics Issue: 307–47.

Ben-David, D. and Pappell, D. (1997) 'International trade and structural change', Working Paper No. 6096, Cambridge, Mass.: National Bureau of Economic Research.

Coe, D. and Helpman, E. (1995) 'International R&D spillovers', *European Economic Review* 39, 5: 859–87.

Cowling, K. and Sugden, R. (1996) 'Capacity, transnationals and industrial strategy', in J. Michie and J. Grieve Smith (eds), *Creating Industrial Capacity*, Oxford: Oxford University Press.

Eichengreen, B. (1996) *Globalizing Capital: A History of the International Monetary System*, Princeton, NJ: Princeton University Press.

Greider, W. (1997) *One World, Ready or Not: The Manic Logic of Global Capitalism*, London: Penguin Books.

Halimi, S., Michie, J. and Milne, S. (1994) 'The Mitterand experience', in J. Michie and J. Grieve Smith (eds), *Unemployment in Europe*, Aldershot: Academic Press.

Hatzius, J. (1997a) 'Domestic jobs and foreign wages: labour demand in Swedish multinationals', Discussion Paper No. 337, London: LSE Centre for Economic Performance.

——(1997b) 'Foreign direct investment, capital formation and labour costs: evidence from Britain and Germany', Discussion Paper No. 336, London: LSE Centre for Economic Performance.

Held, D., McGrew, A., Goldblatt, D., and Perraton, J. (1999) *Global Transformations: Politics, Economics and Culture*, Cambridge: Polity Press.

Helleiner, G. (1994) *Trade Policy and Industrialisation in Turbulent Times*, London: Routledge.

Heylen, F., Goubert, L. and Omey, E. (1996) 'Unemployment in Europe: a problem of relative or aggregate demand for labour?', *International Labour Review* 135, 1: 17–36.

Krugman, P. (1995) 'Growing world trade: causes and consequences', *Brookings Papers on Economic Activity*, I: 327–62.

Kurzer, P. (1993) *Business and Banking: Political Change and Economic Integration in Western Europe*, Ithaca: Cornell University Press.

McCann, D. (1995) *Small States, Open Markets and the Organization of Business Interests*, Aldershot: Dartmouth Press.

McKeown, T. (1991) 'A liberal trade order? The long-run pattern of imports to the advanced capitalist states', *International Studies Quarterly* 35: 151–72.

Maddison, A. (1991) *Dynamic Forces in Capitalist Development*, Oxford: Oxford University Press.

Minford, P., Riley, J. and Nowell, E. (1997) 'Trade, technology and labour markets in the world economy', *Journal of Development Studies* 34, 2: 1–34.

Muet, P. A. and Fonteneau, A. (1990) *Reflation and Austerity: Economic Policy Under Mitterand*, Oxford: Berg.

OECD (1996) *Globalisation of Industry: Overview and Sector Reports*, Paris: Organisation for Economic Co-operation and Development.

Perraton, J., Goldblatt, D., Held, D. and McGrew, A. (1997) 'The globalisation of economic activity', *New Political Economy* 2, 2: 257–77.

Reich, R. (1991) *The Work of Nations*, London: Simon and Schuster.

Sachs, J. and Warner, A. (1995) 'Economic reform and the process of global integration', *Brookings Papers on Economic Activity*, I: 1–95.

Sobel, A. (1994) *Domestic Choices, International Markets: Dismantling National Barriers and Liberalising Securities Markets*, Ann Arbor: University of Michigan Press.

UNCTAD (1996) *World Investment Report 1996*, New York: United Nations.

Verspagen, B. (1997) 'Estimating international technology spillovers using technology flow matrices', *Weltwirtschaftliches Archiv* 133, 2: 226–48.

Webb, M. (1995) *The Political Economy of Policy Coordination: International Adjustment Since 1945*, Ithaca: Cornell University Press.

Williamson, J. (1996) 'Globalization, convergence, and history', *Journal of Economic History* 56, 2: 277–306.

Wood, A. (1994) *North–South Trade Employment and Inequality*, Oxford: Oxford University Press.

—— (1995) 'How trade hurt unskilled workers', *Journal of Economic Perspectives* 9, 3: 59–80.

World Bank (1996) *World Development Report 1996*, New York: Oxford University Press.

5 The lords of peace
From the Holy Alliance to the new international criminal tribunals[1]

Danilo Zolo

A modern political Cosmopolis?

Among Western jurists and political philosophers – Richard Falk, Antonio Cassese, Norberto Bobbio, David Held and Jürgen Habermas for instance[2] – the opinion is gaining ground that the achievement of a stable international order relies on an essential precondition: it is necessary, they maintain, to overcome the international anarchy which has been inherited from seventeenth-century Europe.

A gradual dismantling is proposed of the system of sovereign states which was established by the Peace of Westphalia (1648) and which, by the end of the nineteenth century, had become universal. As is well known, it was a system which affirmed the right of the nation-state to exercise exclusive power within its own boundaries and to claim absolute independence from any external authority. In place of this 'Westphalian model', it is argued that a new political and legal structure of international power is necessary. The establishment of a kind of modern Cosmopolis – in Kelsen's lexicon a new *civitas maxima* – is therefore presented as the sole alternative, not simply to war and international disorder but to the planet's destruction and the extinction of human species.

Even democratic writers who have declared themselves opposed to military intervention by the great powers in countries such as Iraq, Somalia, Haiti or Bosnia see 'world government' as the means of realizing a more peaceful and just international order. For this reason they declare their support for a 'democratic reform' of the United Nations which aims to legitimize it as a provider of compulsory worldwide justice and an international police force.

In the wake of this political cosmopolitanism, there has recently and successfully developed something I suggest should be called 'legal globalism'. I am referring to the theoretical and juridical school of thought that is derived from the Kantian idea of *Weltbürgerrecht* or 'cosmopolitan law'. Through the mediation of neo-Kantian theories of the Marburg school this line of thought led, during the present century, first to Hans Kelsen's great theoretical construction and then, in Italy, to Norberto Bobbio's political theory and philosophy of law. I am referring in particular to Bobbio's proposal of a 'legal pacifism'.[3] The line of thought also led, in Germany, to such important developments as Jürgen Habermas's recent philosophy of international law (cf. Habermas 1995).

'Legal globalism' finds its philosophical basis in the Kantian idea of the moral unity of humankind. This idea, based on the theories of natural law, and on the Enlightenment, was articulated by Kelsen in juridical theses which were both radical and innovative. These were: the unity and objectivity of the legal system, the primacy of international law, the 'partial' nature of national legal systems, and, last but not least, the need to ban the idea of sovereignty as the main obstacle to a universal and durable peace (cf. Kelsen 1920, 1944).

At the normative level, Kantian universalism is currently identified with the need for the globalization of law as one legal system which, on the one hand, would be binding for all humankind and, on the other, would absorb all other legal systems. Law should be shaped as universal legislation, a sort of modern *lex mundialis* – law which is applicable globally and to everybody, and which is based on the gradual harmonization of both political and cultural differences at world level, and consuetudes and normative traditions at national level.

The idea is that the unification of the planet should, first, involve a mechanism for the creation of law, with a central organization in charge. Second, the process of globalization should embrace the interpretation and the application of law, in particular the criminal law. This twofold function should be performed by a universal judiciary, with binding authority, in charge of judging not only the responsibilities of states but also the behaviour of individuals. In this normative context Kelsen, and in particular Habermas, attach to the 1948 'Universal Declaration of Human Rights' the importance of a kind of 'fundamental norm': a core of juridical and political principles that supply the legitimation of the *civitas maxima*, whose creation is the main objective of their project.

A theorem of general system theory .

Contrary to the cosmopolitan proposals, I shall attempt to argue that this is a view which the growing complexity of international relations is rendering increasingly facile and dangerous. I will suggest that we should distinguish very clearly between: (a) the 'global' character of some crucial problems that currently assail the international agenda; and (b) the thesis which argues that such problems are soluble only 'globally', that is, by resorting to a supranational political and legal authority. To say that 'global' problems require an intense activity of cooperation between states is quite different – this is my contention – from belief in the thaumaturgic effects of a cosmopolitan concentration of international power.

In maintaining this general thesis I refer to a classical systemic proposition: within an environment of increasing complexity, interdependence and turbulence, the only possible order is an order emerging 'spontaneously' from disorder. Of course, it would be an imperfect, partial and precarious form of order, always calling for a rational 'organization of complexity', namely for an intentional, normative intervention. But this intervention should be 'weak' in nature: aiming, in other words, at a flexible, polycentric, essentially non-hierarchical kind of order. In contrast a monocentric, hierarchical structure of power can, over the long term, have the effect of inhibiting the development of factors of systemic equilibrium and thereby bring about more serious functional tensions and conflicts. Hence there is considerable reason to wonder whether, in the presence of a high level of complexity and turbulence in the international environment, a certain dose of political indeterminacy and normative disorder might not be preferable to the quest for a universal political and legal order.

Cultural globalization: homologation without integration

Contemporary 'Western globalists' – in particular Richard Falk and David Held – propose the use at international level of a classical category of the European theoretical–political lexicon: that of 'civil society'. Recently Ralf Dahrendorf has made use of the term 'global civil society', and indeed this expression now also appears in official documents of the United Nations. This notion is meant to refer to the complex of movements and associations which, especially during the 1980s, has developed on an international scale. More generally, reference is made to the increasing awareness of the global character of the problems that today crowd the international agenda. It is the growth of this cosmopolitan philosophy, together with the processes of the globalization of politics, economics, finance and communications, that in the judgement of Falk, Held and their followers will gradually point the way towards planetary social integration and thereby constitute the premise for the construction of a world constitutional state and a transnational democracy (see Archibugi and Held 1995).

These authors take for granted the 'domestic analogy' (Suganami 1989), which in their theoretical elaboration is a sort of general enthymeme. The idea is that, since political and legal centralization proved successful in the reduction of violence in nation-states, then the centralization of power in the hands of a supranational supreme authority should also lead to the creation of a safer and more peaceful world. The implicit assumption is that, between a 'civil society' (within a Western nation-state) and the so-called contemporary 'global society', there is a relationship of analogy. This assumption is far from being straightforward and is currently extremely controversial: one only has to refer to the ideas of Samuel Huntington (1996) and Kenichi Ohmae (1995), even though they are very different. These authors claim that there is no such thing as a 'global civil society', and that there are processes under way which have a highly subversive potential and which aim at differentiating, fragmenting and possibly uprooting the supposed unity of the 'global village'.

Other Western authors, including globalization sociologists, are likewise sceptical: Mike Featherstone and Bryan S. Turner, for instance, see the compression of the world as producing frames of cultural reference which can hardly be called 'global culture' (Featherstone 1991; Turner 1990). What is happening on a world scale is rather a process of 'creolization'; i.e., the adoption by a large number of 'indigenous populations' of a foreign, which is to say technical–scientific–industrial, culture which does not result in order and communitarian integration, but on the contrary produces contamination, resistance and disorder. In short, globalization does not produce a cultural homogenization of the world. Quite the opposite, it promotes particularistic reactions that assert the identity of cultural codes rooted in nations and ethnic groups.

Serge Latouche, for his part, has stated that the cultural globalization induced by the hegemony of the West produces no integration of world society (Latouche 1989). On the contrary, it brings about deculturation and the uprooting of peoples and social groups. Countries like Singapore, Taiwan, Hong Kong and South Korea are exemplary from this point of view. Throughout the world the West operates like a 'technical–scientific megamachine' wrenching populations from their homelands, disrupting their social bonds and hurling them into the wasteland of metropolitan urbanization. This machine achieves an increase in functional differentiation in terms of the growing international division of labour and an increase of technical–scientific specialization, but it does so without constructing an authentic cultural universalism, a core of shared values to generate a new form of popular imagination.

Globalization and 'global development'

One assumption implicit in political cosmopolitanism is that the processes of globalization of the international economy tend to reduce the gap between the economies of the rich countries – to which have recently been added the so-called NICs (Newly Industrializing Countries) – and the economies of the poor countries, which form the vast majority. This assumption is necessary because there is a close correlation between economic development and 'human development', and it is inconceivable that a 'global civil society' will be formed as long as a billion individuals remain below a minimum level of literacy. It is likewise a necessary assumption because neither peace nor the advent of a 'transnational democracy' is conceivable without a reduction in the potentiality for conflict which originates from an overall asymmetry in economic development.

Let us consider the facts.

At the beginning of the 1960s, the richest 20 per cent of the world population had an income thirty times greater than the poorest 20 per cent. Today, after some three decades, the richest 20 per cent enjoys an income sixty times greater than the poorest section of the world population. If distributive inequalities within each country are also taken into account, then the global disparity increases still further: the richest 20 per cent of the total world population receives a share of wealth 150 times that of the poorest 20 per cent. In thirty years the distance between the poorer and the richer countries, calculated in terms of GNP, has more than doubled.[4]

These data are largely beyond dispute and already represent, in my opinion, a form of objective confutation of the idea of an emerging 'global civil society'. More controversial are the theoretical interpretations of 'unbalanced development' and the ensuing attempts to propose economic policies which, it is hoped, will prove capable of reversing the ever-widening gap between strong and weak economies. In the long term – economic liberals claim – a solution to the gap between the rich and poor countries can be found within the global framework of a competitive economy: an economy freed from the residues of mercantilism and protectionism and from the new practices of economic nationalism.

There is obviously some truth in these positions. The Third World no longer exists, just as the vertical geopolitical contraposition between North and South no longer exists. In the span of another few decades countries like China and India could exploit their 'comparative advantages' so intensely as to overtake the present major economic powers and recover the position of absolute pre-eminence in world manufacturing markets that they held 250 years ago.

Yet cosmopolitan optimism can draw no comfort from the 'end of the Third World', since in many respects the differentiation of the rate of economic development among the poor countries seems destined to multiply the disparities, increase competition and, potentially, to provoke new conflicts. In short, globalization of production factors can in no way be equated with the socio-economic integration of the planet. The highest costs of ever-more differentiated and fragmented development run the risk of falling on the poorest of the poor countries, representing a sizeable majority of the population of the world, living in Southern Asia, most of Africa, the more backward countries of Latin America and also countries like Brazil and Mexico (southern Mexico in particular).

Despite their profession of faith in liberal principles, the major industrial powers practise complex strategies which, as Robert Gilpin has written, combine mercantilistic competition between states, economic regionalism and sectorial protectionism (Gilpin 1987). The opening up of markets is greatest in sectors where global competition is all to the advantage of the strongest. By contrast, in the labour-intensive manufacturing sector, or in that of exported unskilled labour, the 'new protectionism' reigns supreme and discriminates against weaker countries.

Globalization and the process of concentration of political and legal power

The cultural and economic aspects of globalization are paralleled by a gradual concentration of international power that set in after the collapse of the Soviet empire and the end of the Western/Eastern bloc system. Once this equilibrium between the two nuclear superpowers had been removed, the international power-sharing mechanisms began to function in an even more asymmetric manner. Today the whole planet is gravitating around a single political, economic and cultural orbit comprising the industrial powers, with the United States as their focal point.

Literally following the hierarchical model of the Holy Alliance, a restricted number of military powers engage increasingly in 'humanitarian' interventionism, by which I mean the propensity to use force to regulate the internal conflicts of the weaker countries on the basis of a highly controversial theory of the 'implicit powers' of the Security Council. It is sufficient to think of the peace-enforcing armed interventions in Somalia, Rwanda, Haiti and Bosnia. Blue-beret interventions have proliferated, accompanied by a soaring rise in United Nations military expenditure.

Following the end of the cold war and the collapse of the Soviet empire, 'global security', it is argued, is now threatened by the explosion of nationalism and ethnic conflicts. Defensive military strategies, developed in accordance with a previous minimalist conception of collective security and international regulation, now appear inadequate. Indeed the situation of increased economic and technological interdependence requires the political stability of the planet to be guaranteed by intervention of a kind which will meet quickly and flexibly the needs of collective security.

An even more important success has been attained by 'legal globalism' which now tends to change into a kind of 'judicial internationalism'. On the initiative of the UN Security Council, new International War Tribunals have been created for former Yugoslavia and Rwanda, while the first UN prison has been built in The Hague. Recently, NATO troops sent to Bosnia for the IFOR and SFOR operation were entrusted with the task of arresting those indicted by the Hague Court (the vast majority of whom are of Serbian nationality).

A yet more important and far-reaching development is going to take place over the next few years. Thanks to the initiative of international public agencies and private Western foundations, the statutory charter of a new International Criminal Tribunal was decided during the international meeting which took place in Rome in June 1998 (however, the normative and organizing procedures will be rather lengthy). Unlike all other previous international tribunals, the new one will not be temporary and special, but will be permanently and universally in charge of the punishment of genocide, crimes against humanity and war crimes committed by any inhabitant of the planet. It is important to point out that the new

Tribunal will base its verdicts on an International Criminal Code promulgated by a supranational legislative authority.

Towards an alternative philosophy of international law

The Western doctrine of 'legal globalism' has gained great importance during the last decade, after the collapse of the Soviet empire and the end of the bipolar division of the world; and this should not be understated. The international relevance of this doctrine surely depends on the increased economic and military hegemony of the West, and on the influence of the globalization process which seems to entail the unification at planetary level of all normative and judicial structures. It also depends on the fact that this philosophy points to the legitimation of present international institutions and particularly of their most recent 'humanitarian' and judicial lines of development.

This undeniable success of legal globalism does not counterbalance its weak points. Despite its cosmopolitan aspirations, this theory remains firmly linked to the philosophy of old Europe, namely to the classic Christian doctrine of natural law. It implies a theological and metaphysical idea of international law, which bases the international legal community on two beliefs: the moral quality of man, and the moral unity of humankind.

This philosophy of law is based on the Kantian idea according to which humankind can develop only if a few ethical principles are shared by all men and enacted by a supranational authority. This should go beyond the 'polytheism' of current ethical beliefs and normative systems. It is not by chance that the liberal–individualistic theory of human rights, which, as Kelsen claimed, bears some characteristics typical of natural law doctrine, is today obsessively presented to non-Western countries as the paradigm of the political constitution of the world.

An alternative philosophy to the political and legal globalism I have been describing so far could be articulated with reference to the neo-Grotian and realistic line of thought, developed by Martin Wight, Hedley Bull and partly also by Andrew Hurrell. In the 1970s this line of thought achieved its most authoritative formulation in Hedley Bull's *The Anarchical Society* (1977), which in my opinion retains great theoretical value. What I mean is that a modern and realistic philosophy of international law could be developed, organizing in a systematic way the intuitions and the general proposals formulated by this non-globalist school of thought. In other words, a modern philosophy of international law should be able to put forward alternative institutional and legal schemes, different to the hierarchical and centralist model of the Holy Alliance, whose most typical example is the United Nations Charter.[5]

First of all the rationalist and normative concept of law, to which globalists refer, should be criticized. This philosophy of law puts aside the close connection between international law, political conflict and military power in the name of an ideal vision of international justice. It also undervalues the complex interaction between normative structures on the one hand, and cultural and economic processes on the other. Thus, this philosophy attributes to law a regulatory power concerning social phenomena, including civil war and international war, which history constantly rejects.

Second, there is the ethnocentric prejudice of this juridical culture: on the one hand it is trying to unify the world, but on the other, it is noticeable, it shows indifference towards non-Western political and juridical traditions. I am referring here to cultures and civilizations – one only has to think of the examples of China and India – which are worlds away from natural law doctrine, individualism and the technical and scientific efficiency typical of Western civilization; in fact they are often in open ideological conflict with it. The human rights doctrine is, above all, an example of this cultural tension: it can be considered universal only within the Western juridical and political community.

Third, and of extreme importance, there is the question concerning the structural differentiation of legal systems. I believe that the tendency to measure the historical evolution of international law according to the 'evolutionary steps' made by states should be criticized. Even leaving aside all possible doubts about the existence of evolutionary laws changing the structure of legal systems, the very (Kelsenian) idea that international law is a 'primitive system', because of the decentralized character of its coercive functions, lacks theoretical basis. Likewise, the idea according to which international law should evolve towards a centralization of its coercive functions and towards making its criminal jurisdiction binding, in order to overcome its structural primitiveness, is certainly questionable.

A final point deals with the problem of the sources of international law. Global legal normativism emphasizes the need to have a central and specialized organ in charge of the law-making process. A realistic approach would not in principle deny the need for an explicit production of norms; however, it would stress the function performed by consuetudes, pacts and consensual processes in the creation of international law. This is a process that has been extremely lengthy, especially in the sectors in which modern international law is more effective such as diplomatic and consular protocols, mutual protection of citizens abroad and political asylum. As Friedrich von Hayek claimed, in direct opposition to Kelsen (Hayek 1976: passim), *ius gentium* has been created not by the passing of laws but thanks to ancient consuetudes regarding commerce, consolidated through the centuries in ports and fairs.

Therefore, instead of supporting the idea of a *lex mundialis* regulating international relations from above in a monolithic normative hierarchy – a sort of planetary *Stufenbau* – what is needed is a doctrine of the sources of law which could include and generalize the theory of the 'international regimes'. This theory has been recently reformulated in realist terms by

Robert Keohane and Stephen Krasner.[6] The idea is to propose the Grotian objective of an international 'legal society' or, better, a constellation of 'international regimes' capable of coordinating the subjects of international politics according to a systemic logic: namely the adoption of diffuse and polycentric normative structures and forms of leadership.

The new international criminal tribunals

As far as the supranational judicial institutions are concerned – from the Nuremberg and Tokyo Tribunals to the more recent criminal Tribunals established for trials relating to the former Yugoslavia and Rwanda – I believe that Hedley Bull's criticism of this kind of institution is still relevant (Bull 1977: 89). In fact, nothing guarantees that the activity of judicial institutions, which are able to apply even the severest sanctions to individuals who commit international crimes, could reduce the structural dimensions of war. In other words it could not influence the deep reasons for human aggressiveness, violent conflicts and war. One could also raise doubts about the quality of this kind of supranational justice; indeed, such justice would inevitably be far removed from the cultural, social and economic context in which those to be judged live and committed their crimes.

One could also add a general remark: what is really surprising today is the lack of any kind of theoretical debate concerning the philosophy of punishment which lies behind the judicial activity of the new judicial organs. The creation of the Nuremberg and Tokyo Tribunals clearly resulted from a desire for political revenge, despite the fact that it was done in the name of international justice, and even Kelsen could not but denounce it. By contrast, the new International Tribunals are based on the idea that by sentencing a few dozen people to severe punishment – although in the future their number may rise to a few hundreds – a kind of 'humanitarian criminal jurisdiction' could be created to promote human rights and guarantee world peace.

One of the slogans most used by the supporters of these new International Criminal Tribunals is: 'There cannot be peace without justice'. I believe that, propaganda aside, this shows an oversimplified notion of the relationship between justice and world peace, justice being considered only from a judicial point of view. But there is something else to consider. The slogan shows a sort of criminal fetishism, naively applied to international relations, which ignores centuries of theoretical debate on the problem of the 'preventive efficiency' of criminal sentences – and in particular of prison sentences – and the doubts raised about the effectiveness as a rehabilitation process of a stay in prison.

The most ardent supporters of this unprecedented judicial and penitentiary internationalism seem to ignore the conclusion reached by theoretical and sociological research on modern penal structures, according to which their real significance remains retributive and vindictive, according to an archaic logic of the sacrifice of a victim. This is the logic that the modern juridical rationalists tried on the one hand to oppose, while on the other putting it forward again in a slightly different form. The 'judicial globalists' should at least try to claim that the pessimistic conclusions regarding domestic penitentiary structures are not relevant at the international level. In the absence of even such a basic attempt to provide a more profound analysis, one must believe that the new supranational jurisdiction, which is about to be created, is not based on any serious philosophy of punishment. This strengthens the belief that the new institutions will play one role only – i.e., thanks to their halo of impartiality, the attribution of more symbolic legitimacy to the existing international institutions. Moreover, it has not yet been proved that the safeguarding of civil rights at the international level – which in the Continental European and Anglo-Saxon traditions needs to be ensured by structures of the rule of law – would be improved if transferred to supranational organizations. The main obstacle to this vision is the absence – both at the level of the United Nations and at the level of regional organizations such as the European Union – of any kind of constitutional structure of the supranational institutions comparable to the order of constitutional powers involved in the rule of law.

The attribution of the function of safeguarding of civil rights exclusively – or even just mainly – to international judicial institutions would then be contradictory and risky, even when contemplating the circumstance of citizens' rights being violated by the political or the judicial institutions of their own state. Actually, it is unacceptable even to think that it is possible to guarantee the safeguarding of human rights at the international level, when the domestic institutions of the rule of law are not able to do it at the domestic level. This argument can be applied also to international criminal tribunals, and the justice they administer.

Towards a weak international interventionism and a weak pacifism

As far as the general problem of the maintenance of world order and peace is concerned I will very briefly suggest the following five points in opposition to the theses put forward by political and legal globalists:

1   *A minimal international order.* Expressions such as 'global civil society', 'universal citizenship' and 'world constitutionalism' may be said to belong to a normative vocabulary which draws strongly on wishful thinking. Furthermore, not only are the objectives they refer to almost certainly not realizable in the near future – huge political and economic powers oppose them – they are also of limited desirability.

    For it is hard to see wherein lies the attraction of a world authority whose scope of action is not limited to guaranteeing a 'minimal political order' – to use the expression owed to Hedley Bull – but aims instead to establish an 'optimal political order': in other words a guarantee of stable and universal peace, distributive justice, the definition and protection of rights, the ecological integrity of the planet, and the determination of the proper weighting between available resources and demographic growth. A cosmopolitan authority of this type could not fail to be pervasive and intensely interventionist, thereby giving rise to a political system inclined towards drastic reduction in the complexity and differentiation of the international system.

2   *Governance without government.* The growing complexity of the international environment tends to produce a systemic situation which James Rosenau (1992) has defined as 'governance without government'. It is a situation in which the absence of a government possessing formal authority (government) co-occurs with a context of extensive phenomena of self-regulative aggregation (governance) of international agents. It is therefore a situation that contradicts the logic of centralized and universal jurisdiction advocated by Kelsenian jurists. In conditions of high complexity, systemic dynamics tend to give rise to a polycentric normative matrix, which arises from widespread processes of strategic interaction and multilateral negotiation. This matrix has more the structure of a series of webs than the pyramidal structure of the celebrated Kelsenian *Stufenbau*.

3   *Weak peacekeeping interventionism.* A 'minimal' international order – namely an order able to coordinate the strategies of individual states within a network of 'international regimes' – would require only 'weak interventionism'. This should hold for the entire gamut of international issues, including the attempt to curb the destructive aggression of war by 'weak' means. In order to make progress towards this goal, there would be a need for international institutions capable of carrying out non-coercive, preventive diplomacy and guaranteeing permanent monitoring of political, economic and territorial claims emerging in the international arena.

4   *Weak peacemaking institutions.* In order to contain the destructive effects of already existing armed conflicts, 'weak' peace-making institutions will be required. These should offer contenders all necessary operational tools, knowledge and international connections, as well as the protected physical areas needed for prompt and effective diplomacy. Furthermore, these institutions should be in a position to act as mediators, and, upon request by the parties involved, provide arbitration and the consensual interposition of peace-keeping forces equipped solely with light arms, along the lines of the model adopted in the post-war period by Dag Hammarskjöld.

5   *Territorial decentralization.* My last point concerns the location of the 'weak' international institutions. They should be decentralized, with strong local roots, coordinated within homogeneous regional or conti-

84 *Danilo Zolo*

nental areas and linked together through a weak 'subsidiary' centralization of a federal type. The fact that current international
institutions are concentrated in the West is certainly one of the reasons
determining their failure. By contrast, a strong local base for alternative institutions could be assured by embedding them in the cultural
and social fabric of the world's great urban areas.

Naturally, 'weak' international institutions would not succeed in achieving
a rapid cessation of armed conflict. Contenders would not be willing to
alter their warmongering mentality or to lay down their arms and face
each other across a diplomatic table. What is minimally required, however,
is that the international community should make no attempt to use military force in order to prevent the continuation of the conflict. The
intervention of the international community should be restricted to
isolating the contenders politically, thereby putting them under a form of
guard from the outside, in the attempt to compel them to accept a negoti-
ated solution to the conflict. In short: the international community should
not wage war on the contenders, in other words it should not, as it did in
the Gulf War, overlay with further violence, however internationally legitimized, the violence it professes to be either repressing or subjecting to
sanctions.

All this may well appear to be too weak a form of pacifism. I may
perhaps be accused of advocating inertia on the part of the international
community in the face of violence, destruction and genocide. However, the
realistic assumption on which my proposal rests is that only in and
through conflict can peace be achieved. Only by overcoming the underlying reasons of conflict can the need for peace, and hence peace itself,
take root among the warring parties. In other words, peace cannot be
'exported', any more than can democracy. The fallacy of all peace-
enforcing strategies should be clear to all after the recent lessons of
Somalia, Rwanda and, signally, the war between the peoples of former
Yugoslavia. After more than three years of war, at long last peace has been
achieved in the Balkans. But it can safely be predicted that it will be a
peace of reconciliation only if the deep-seated reasons underlying the
conflict have been finally overcome – paradoxically, in part through the
conflict itself – and have not simply been removed or repressed by military
intervention from the outside. If this hypothesis is well founded, no such
outcome is to be expected from the *pax cosmopolitica* imposed in the
Persian Gulf in 1991.

Notes

1 On the subjects of this essay, see Zolo (1997).
2 See Falk (1995), Cassese (1988), Bobbio (1979), Held (1995) and Habermas
(1988).
3 On Kelsen's and Bobbio's legal pacifism, see Zolo (1998).

4 See the Annual *Reports* of the United Nations Development Programme (UNDP), UNDP 1990: 9–16; UNDP 1992: 12–25; UNDP 1994: 90–101.
5 Hegel was the first to maintain ironically that the Holy Alliance was akin to the Kantian proposal of an international league of states for the maintenance of peace (Hegel 1964: 434–7): 'Thus, Kant proposed a league of sovereigns to settle disputes between states, and the Holy Alliance was meant to be an institution more or less of this kind'. And Hans Morgenthau was the first to note sarcastically that the United Nations conform to the model of the Holy Alliance (Morgenthau 1960: 480): 'The international government of the United Nations is identical with the international government of the Security Council. The Security Council appears, as it were, as the Holy Alliance of our time. And the five permanent members of the Security Council are as it were, a Holy Alliance within a Holy Alliance'.
6 Cf. J. G. Ruggie (1975). For the neo-realistic elaboration, see R. O. Keohane (1983: 141–71).

References

Archibugi, D. and Held, D. (1995) *Cosmopolitan Democracy: An Agenda for a New World Order*, Cambridge: Polity Press.
Bobbio, N. (1979) *Il problema della guerra e le vie della pace*, Bologna: il Mulino.
Bull, H. (1977) *The Anarchical Society*, London: Macmillan.
Cassese, A. (1988) *I diritti umani nel mondo contemporaneo*, Rome-Bari: Laterza (English translation 1990), Cambridge: Polity Press.
Falk, R. A. (1995) *On Humane Governance: Towards a New Global Politics*, Cambridge: Polity Press.
Featherstone, M. (ed.) (1991) *Global Culture, Nationalism, Globalization and Modernity*, London: Sage Publications.
Gilpin, R. (1987) *The Political Economy of International Relations*, Princeton: Princeton University Press.
Habermas, J. (1988) 'Law and Morality', in S. M. McMurrin (ed.), *The Tanner Lectures on Human Values*, vol. 8, Salt Lake City: University of Utah Press.
——(1995) 'Kants Idee des ewigen Friedens – aus dem historischen Abstand von 200 Jahren', *Kritische Justiz*, 28: 293–319 (now in J. Habermas, 1996, *Die Einbeziehung des Anderen*, Frankfurt a.M.: Suhrkamp).
Hayek, F. A. (1976) *Law, Legislation and Liberty*, Vol. 2: *The Mirage of Social Justice*, London: Routledge.
Hegel, G. W. F. (1964) *Grundlinien der Philosophie des Rechts* (first published 1821), E. Gans (ed.), Stuttgart: Friedrich Frommann Verlag.
Held, D. (1995) *Democracy and The Global Order*, Cambridge: Polity Press.
Huntington, S. P. (1996) *The Clash of Civilizations and the Remaking of the World Order*, New York: Simon and Schuster.
Kelsen, H. (1920) *Das Problem der Souveränität und die Theorie des Völkerrechts. Beitrag zu einer reinen Rechstlehre*, Tübingen: Mohr.
——(1944) *Peace through Law*, Chapel Hill: The University of North Carolina Press (2nd edn, 1973, New York: Garland Publishing).
Keohane, R. O. (1983) 'The demand for international regimes', in S. D. Krasner (ed.), *International Regimes*, New York: Cornell University Press.

Latouche, S. (1989) *L'occidentalisation du monde. Essai sur la signification, la portée et les limits de l'uniformisation planétaire*, Paris: Editions La Découverte.

Morgenthau, H. J. (1960) *Politics Among Nations*, New York: Knopf.

Ohmae, K. (1995) *The End of the Nation State. The Rise of Regional Economies*, New York: The Free Press.

Rosenau, J. N. (1992) 'Governance, Order and Change in World Politics', in J. N. Rosenau and E.-O. Czempiel (eds), *Governance without Government: Order and Change in World Politics*, Cambridge: Cambridge University Press.

Ruggie, J. G. (1975) 'International responses to technology: concepts and trends', *International Organization*, 29, 3: 557–84.

Suganami, H. (1989) *The Domestic Analogy and World Order Proposals*, Cambridge: Cambridge University Press.

Turner, B. S. (1990) *Theories of Modernity and Postmodernity*, London: Sage Publications.

UNDP (1990, 1992, 1994) Annual *Reports* of the United Nations Development Program, New York: Oxford University Press.

Zolo, D. (1997) *Cosmopolis. Prospects for World Government*, Cambridge: Polity Press.

——(1998) *I signori: della pace. Una critica del globalismo giuridico*, Rome: Carocci.

6 Neither cosmopolitanism nor realism

A response to Danilo Zolo

Tony Coates

The thesis of Danilo Zolo's chapter (Chapter Five) is a highly condensed version of his book *Cosmopolis* (1997). The argument of both sources is wide-ranging, complex and elusive. Its elusiveness is worth stressing. It is certainly not easy to pigeonhole Zolo's views, and they are of course all the more interesting for that. His work has a paradoxical character often appearing to combine positions that, in more conventional guise, are commonly thought to be mutually exclusive. Here, for example, is a writer who dons the mantle of pacifism while upholding the necessity and the value of war.

His work is openly polemical. He characterizes *Cosmopolis* as 'a work of iconoclasm...a matter of breaking an image – that of the moral, legal and political rationality of world government – which, despite its entirely regressive nature...has come to assume for us all the overbearing dominance of an idol' (Zolo 1997: xiv), and many other criticisms are swept up in this criticism of the cosmopolitan image (it leads, for example, to a general denunciation of all attempts to apply ethical criteria to international relations). *Cosmopolis* is a passionate work, a work of conviction, imbued with a sense of urgency: cosmopolitanism is both 'facile *and* dangerous'.

'A work of iconoclasm'. Is there any need for 'iconoclasm'? Do the 'icons' really exist? Though there is no denying its contemporary presence and influence in the theory as well as in the practice of international relations, it is arguable whether the 'cosmopolitan' image *has* achieved the 'overbearing dominance' ascribed to it here.

At the theoretical level certainly, there is no cosmopolitan consensus, and criticisms of cosmopolitanism are rife (as the growth of the contemporary communitarian tradition exemplifies). Perhaps the reason why the cosmopolitan phenomenon is seen to be more widespread than in fact it is is that Zolo's critical net is often cast too widely, cosmopolitan assumptions being attributed to positions or schools of thought to which they are fundamentally alien. This tendency is most evident in his chapter in its treatment and criticism of the tradition of natural law, a tradition which Zolo associates closely with cosmopolitanism (it is claimed to be the movement's philosophical foundation). The criticism takes no account of the important distinction (crucial so far as the argument itself is concerned) between that part of the tradition which grew out of the Enlightenment and which, as a result, became imbued with enlightenment values (including cosmopolitan ones) and an earlier but still flourishing variant of the tradition which has always been fundamentally at odds with cosmopolitanism. However, even if 'overbearing dominance' is putting it too strongly, the more modest claim of the chapter that cosmopolitanism is gaining ground among jurists and political philosophers seems indisputable.[1]

At the practical level at least some of the evidence advanced in both book and chapter appears too mixed to be convincing. In the book, for example, much is made of the case of the Gulf War (a whole chapter is devoted to it). In many respects its analysis structures the argument of the book which has, it seems, its point of origin in the author's reaction to the war. Similarly, his chapter's closing reference to the war and its *'pax cosmopolitica'* suggests that it continues to play a key role in Zolo's analysis. In his view the war was an event of great historical importance, even perhaps of epochal significance: this 'first cosmopolitan war' has had a transformative impact on the subsequent perception and conduct of international relations, encouraging the major powers (with the connivance of the UN) to play a much more interventionist role in international affairs than in the past via an appeal to humanitarian intervention and global security.

But was the Gulf War a 'cosmopolitan' war? For realists like Henry Kissinger (a supporter of the war) there was nothing especially new about it (not even about the heightened moral rhetoric which accompanied it). This was a war which, for all the rhetoric, conformed with realist principles. It was fought, not with the cosmopolitan aim of establishing a 'new world order' in which war would be progressively eliminated, but with the realist aim of restoring and maintaining a fragile, imperfect and uneasy peace. Its object was to uphold, not to undermine, the principle of state sovereignty (to uphold that principle without regard to the internal, and thoroughly undemocratic, nature of the state whose sovereignty had been infringed), and to protect strategic and economic interests through the maintenance of the regional balance of power.

The conduct of the war and the manner in which it was concluded were governed by similar concerns. The decisive military defeat of Iraq was not followed by the takeover and reconstitution of the Iraqi state, though that lay within the power of the coalition. Iraqi sovereignty, though impaired by 'safe havens' and 'no fly zones', was left fundamentally intact and an internal rather than an imposed solution to the problem (a policy preference which Zolo recommends) was sought. The fear of a power vacuum and a consequent loss of the regional equilibrium or balance of power, along with other prudential considerations, were arguably far more dominant in the minds of coalition leaders than any more radical and ambitious project.

However, even if the Gulf War's own cosmopolitan credentials are suspect, it does seem to have marked the emergence of a new way of thinking about war and international relations. One of Britain's foremost military historians, John Keegan, detected 'a profound change in civilization's attitude to war' along with 'the emerging outline of a world without war'. 'The elements of a new world resolution to suppress the cruelties of disorder are', he claimed, 'clearly visible' (Keegan 1993: 58).

Whatever the truth about the war itself, those of a cosmopolitan persuasion have been keen to use it to advance their cause. As one advocate has urged: '[T]he experience of the Gulf Crisis showed that it was eminently possible to build a UN consensus against violations of international law. That experience needs to be generalised as soon as possible to ensure that all UN resolutions seeking to remedy such violations are acted on with comparable vigour' (Ekins 1992: 61). The frequent expression of such sentiments lends support to Zolo's analysis: the war (along with the termination of the Cold War which made it possible) gave a fresh impetus to the cosmopolitan movement and to the emergence of what some aspirants saw as nascent forms of world government.

This, it seems, is the context (practical at least as much as theoretical) in which to place Danilo Zolo's criticism of cosmopolitan philosophy. Of course, given the terms of Zolo's argument, we can expect all such cosmopolitan initiatives to fail, and not just to fail but to fail dangerously or disastrously, threatening rather than enhancing the prospects of a more peaceful world. Typically, the grounds of this 'realist' criticism are, in very large measure, prudential.

On this reading, the cosmopolitan movement is seen to play into the hands of the hegemonic states, giving 'theoretical justification to the new strategy of the industrial powers'. In the absence of global social integration (a well founded scepticism about the reach of globalization is an essential part of the criticism), and in the presence of the overwhelming power and influence of the industrialized states, the promotion of a cosmopolitan agenda leads inevitably not to the fulfilment of a global common good but to the reinforcement of the hegemony of the dominant industrial states, to a form of imperial rule in accordance with Western values and interests.

Opposition to cosmopolitanism is, however, more radical than this (with good reason). It rests on much more than the contingent grounds of the temporary infeasibility of the cosmopolitan agenda; the differences are more than strategic. It is not simply that present circumstances are seen to conspire against the promotion of a worthy and shared long-term goal or aspiration. The real argument is about ends rather than means, about the very concept of world order that ought to inform and guide the present and future conduct of international relations. At the same time, of course, it is impossible to divorce ends and means. The two hang together, for the manner in which the end is conceived will dictate the choice of means. The means *are* the end in the making, its real prefigurement.

The fundamental question which the criticism poses (to which a resounding and negative reply is ultimately, and it seems rightly, given) is this: '*Can any cosmopolitan project ever be anything other than an inherently hegemonic and violent undertaking?*' (Zolo 1997: 15; added emphasis). It is the end itself, the very concept of unity or universality which informs and guides cosmopolitanism, that is seen to be radically deficient. It is a concept which is incapable of doing justice to, can only do violence to, non-hegemonic values and interests. It is a concept of unity which is imperialistic through and through and which, as such, can only lead to the impoverishment rather than to the enrichment of humanity.

The source of that 'imperialism' can be seen to lie in the rationalist spirit that is part of the cosmopolitan movement's Enlightenment heritage.[2] That spirit is manifested in the reliance on 'reason' (and the distrust of particular and affective ties);[3] in the assumption of progress (identified with the triumph of rationalist values);[4] in the contempt for a 'pre-modern' past (or present);[5] in the antipathy to tradition, custom and inherited institutions (particularly religion);[6] in the faith in the enlightened and self-sufficient individual (the 'cosmopolitan citizen' who transcends particular or group loyalties);[7] and in the confident pursuit of a 'rational' (and, therefore, uniform[8]) solution to the most complex and intractable problems of international relations.[9]

Zolo argues that the spirit of Enlightenment rationalism informs and guides the project of global democracy. His objection to that project is in part 'methodological', sharing a close affinity with Hayek's well-known criticism of 'constructivism' (though Zolo's inspiration is closer to home, as his acknowledgement of a debt to Pareto makes clear). At the heart of both critiques is a rejection of the view that social order is always the result of conscious design. In opposition to this view, both Hayek and Zolo proclaim the reality and the worth of a 'spontaneous' or 'evolved' order, of an order or pattern of human association (of an *objective* rationality) that is the product of human interaction and yet not of human design (an assumption which, as Hayek suggests, seems fundamental to any satisfactory social theory).

In both cases the view is taken that the more total and complex the social reality in question (and what could be more total or more complex than 'international society'?) the more prudent (and rational) it is to rely on the processes of spontaneous order.[10] Not to do so is to pretend to a knowledge and a capacity that we do not in fact possess (a limitation which the 'lords of peace', in true rationalist fashion, are unable or reluctant to recognize). The imposition of some rational scheme (the possibilities or permutations of which are endless given the studied indifference to particular circumstances), by its abstract simplicity, does violence to the variety and complexity of the reality which it attempts to order. In so doing it undermines the natural or spontaneous regulatory process, putting at risk an imperfect but real order for the sake of a perfect but illusory one.

To take a familiar example, and one which figures prominently in Hayek's work, such a complex social reality as the 'market' must (in the interests of good order or, for that matter, of the ends which intervention itself is intended to promote, such as the wider distribution of goods and resources) be left, in the main, to regulate itself. Attempts to organize or plan the economy, in its totality and along so-called rational lines, will lead to the disruption of its internal mechanisms of self-regulation and control, to an economic *disorder* far worse than any which prompted intervention in the first place. The only kind of intervention which is acceptable is that aimed at the removal of obstacles to the operation of those internal mechanisms which generate spontaneous order (for example, the preservation of competition through restrictive monopoly laws).

Zolo approaches international relations in a similar 'systemic' fashion. The danger of cosmopolitanism is seen to lie in its faith in 'a monocentric, hierarchical structure of power [that] can over the long term have the effect of inhibiting the development of factors of systemic equilibrium and thereby bring about more serious functional tensions and conflicts' (this volume: Chapter Five). This is *not* an argument for laissez-faire. The real need is for a 'weak intervention', or an 'organization of complexity', that does nothing to impair and everything to assist the processes of spontaneous ordering.

The objection, however, is not merely functional. Deep down the dispute is about values. Critics like Hayek (and, it seems, Zolo) object to rationalist politics (of which cosmopolitanism is a prime example) not simply because of their alleged dysfunction, but because they are seen to be intrinsically authoritarian, involving (as they inevitably do) the imposition of ends on the agents whose behaviour they seek to regulate. The objection to this is more than pragmatic, and it springs from a concern for the whole as well as for the agents themselves. Not only are the agents seen as having a right to their integrity, but the acknowledgement and securing of that right is seen as the precondition of a more total human good. In the case of international relations, it is through the interaction of diverse and particular moral communities that real human progress and enrichment are seen to take place – not through the imperial rule of the particular moral culture that happens to be dominant at any one time.

The imperialistic tendencies of cosmopolitanism are, of course, implicit rather than explicit, covert rather than open. This is, after all, a movement which prides itself on its humanitarianism. The rational and universal pretensions of cosmopolitanism effectively conceal (not least perhaps from the advocates themselves) the reality and the extent of its imposition. In the first place, the empirical universality of cosmopolitan values (if not of cosmopolitan practice), of human rights and democracy, is greatly exaggerated; second, the normative authority and moral superiority of those values are everywhere assumed. The 'rational' character ascribed to cosmopolitan values is sufficient to convince adherents of their universality and practicality: their appeal to the 'rational' or 'enlightened' individual everywhere is thought to be irresistible, and to their intrinsic authority all particular norms are expected to yield. Liberated from the parochialism of particular moral cultures, enlightened individuals will come together in a community of the wise and the virtuous.[11]

Of course, both empirically and normatively cosmopolitan values are less than universal. Their 'rational' appearance belies their particular origins and their own parochial status. A system of values that cannot even command assent in its own (predominantly Western) moral culture struggles to lay claim to a universal or global authority. As one recent critic suggests: 'The attempt to convince Third World societies to accept the Western canon of human rights...seems like an invitation for them to govern themselves by precisely those norms that make Western societies so devoid of a sense of the common good and that create the social space for so much of what is most squalid in them' (Boyle 1996: 177).

The blindspot which conceals from view the specific cultural origins and particular limitations of cosmopolitan values (their excessive individualism, for example) facilitates imperialism. The values of a particular moral culture (or even sub-culture) are readily identified with the universal moral law. The reason why cultural determination is overlooked and universal status assumed is because those values (unlike other, 'irrational', values) are regarded as the products of pure reason. As Hayek has suggested, a Cartesian dualism posits 'an independently existing mind substance...[obscuring] [t]he fact [that] mind is as much the product of the social environment in which it has grown up' (Hayek 1973: 17). As a result, cosmopolitanism, its own particularity effectively disguised, is invested with a universal authority over all other particular moral traditions.

In defence of cosmopolitanism it will perhaps be argued that, because of its democratic form, the cosmopolitan project is free of the authoritarian or imperialist tendencies attributed to it.[12] How could a system of global governance which upheld the claims of cosmopolitan *democracy* ever be 'authoritarian' or 'imperialist'? The unity of cosmopolitan democracy would be a formal or procedural unity, not a substantive one. The democratic principle itself, therefore, would safeguard the right of each people or state to define its own substantive agenda. In short, the integrity of each moral community or culture would be left unimpaired by the introduction of global democracy.

The response is unconvincing. There is more to this project than meets the eye. Its intrusiveness, the threat which it poses to particular moral communities, is not to be underestimated. 'Cosmopolitan democracy' has a much fuller agenda than this defence implies. It stands for a *system* of values embracing much more than a set of formal procedural norms: form and substance are inseparable. Without reference to certain historically and culturally specific values (such as that of individual autonomy or subjective freedom), values which are, perhaps for good reasons, still far from being universally accepted, democracy and human rights are meaningless. From a Western liberal and individualist standpoint, for example, the practice of arranged marriage looks like a moral anomaly, an infringement of a basic human right, whereas in more traditional and communal cultures this institution is often regarded as an essential constituent of social order and human well-being. In a world where the legitimacy of a state and its inclusion in the global polity is to be made dependent upon its acceptance of democracy and human rights, what fate awaits those states which reject that liberal democratic agenda, not for the sake of some tyrannical abuse of power, but simply because that agenda conflicts with the received and preferred norms of the community in question?

Rejecting cosmopolitanism's monistic concept of unity ('according to which humankind can develop only if a few ethical principles are shared by all men and enacted by a supranational authority'), Zolo opts for a normative realism or relativism which upholds the value of 'political indeterminacy and normative disorder' (the ' "polytheism" of current ethical beliefs and normative systems'). The reason for doing so, it seems, is that *all* forms of universalism are assumed to be antagonistic to particular moral communities or cultures. By the terms of the argument, we are required to choose between moral universalism and moral particularism. But are all forms of universalism as hostile to the principle of particularity as cosmopolitanism? Is the idea of the moral unity of mankind an intrinsically 'totalitarian' one, as Zolo has suggested?

It was argued at the beginning of this criticism that Zolo's tendency to overestimate the influence of cosmopolitanism sprang, partly, from an attribution to the whole of the natural law tradition of something which belonged only to a part of it. It seems clear that Zolo's delineation of the tradition is (in effect, if not in intention) confined to its Enlightenment variant. This is most evident in his attribution to it of rationalism, individualism and ethnocentrism ('an indifference towards non-Western political and juridical traditions') and a preference for a *lex mundialis* over *ius gentium*. His argument takes no account of the important differences that exist within the natural law tradition itself. In fact, the traits which Zolo rightly detects in a cosmopolitanism born out of the Enlightenment are not present in the conceptions of the unity of mankind and of natural law which pre-date (and survive) that movement of thought.

The older tradition, for example, displays little of the rationalism to which, with good reason, Zolo takes such exception. This essential point of difference is something which Hayek's criticism of rationalism *does* take into account. According to Hayek, the rationalist spirit was alien to the older tradition of natural law, imbued as it was with a sense of the limits and fallibility of human reason.[13] With the rise of 'constructive rationalism', however, 'both the term "reason" and the term "natural law" completely changed their meaning'. What emerged was the 'new rationalist law of nature of Grotius and his successors' with its 'conception that all law was made by reason or could at least be fully justified by it' (Hayek 1973: 21).[14] Without supplanting the older tradition, this utterly transformed version of natural law became the dominant tradition and the one to which modern cosmopolitanism is most indebted.

In like manner, the older tradition displays none of the hostility to the particular so evident in the revised version. The reverse is the case. The traditional natural law ethic, while advancing the idea of the unity of mankind and maintaining the ethical subordination of the state to a universal moral law and common good (a subordination which excludes the maximal or absolutist idea of state sovereignty), consistently upholds the view, inherited from Aristotle, of the state as a 'perfect community' with its own common good. There is here no hint of the 'anti-statism' which is such a prominent feature of cosmopolitanism.[15]

Similarly (and relatedly), the individualism of the Enlightenment tradition, to which Zolo and other critics take such exception, is not shared by the older, more communitarian tradition of natural law. The Thomist–Aristotelian principles of the tradition focus on the political community as the essential context of moral growth and human fulfilment. The *political* nature of man is unequivocally proclaimed. In this way the law of nature is not set at odds with the state or the political community, as it is in the individualist and contractarian account favoured by the later Enlightenment tradition of natural law.

Far from being antagonistic to particular states and moral communities, the older tradition's understanding of the moral unity of mankind demands such differentiation. As a result, that tradition – unlike its rival – has the resources to resist the imperialist tendency. The resilience of the tradition in this regard is well illustrated by the reaction of the Spanish Neoscholastics of the sixteenth century to the discovery of the Americas. The discovery forced those thinkers to develop the concept of the moral community of mankind which they had inherited from a natural law tradition informed by Thomist–Aristotelian principles. The ideas which they advanced sought to reconcile the normative unity of mankind with the facts of cultural and moral diversity, so startlingly revealed in the New World.

They firmly resisted the imperial temptation to which so many of their contemporaries succumbed: men like Sepúlveda, who argued that the savage and chaotic state of Indian society justified its subjection 'to the imperium of nations or princes more humane and virtuous' (quoted in Fernández-Santamaria: 223); or like those who argued that it was the right and duty of Christian states to take upon themselves the governance of pagan or non-Christian societies which lacked true or rightful dominion by virtue of their infidelity. This easy identification of the universal moral community with the dominant Christian and European culture, and its investment with universal gubernatorial authority, met with Neoscholastic resistance, most prominently in the work of Francisco de Vitoria.

Vitoria's anti-imperial concept of unity or of global order was founded on a fundamental recognition of, and respect for, societies vastly different from his own. Where others reacted fearfully and hostilely to the challenge which these exotic and seemingly primitive cultures posed to basic European values and assumptions, he adopted a posture of relative open-ness and sympathy. In true 'anthropological' fashion, he affirmed the integrity and fundamental rationality of Indian society: '[T]hey have some order in their affairs: they have properly organized cities, proper marriages, magistrates and overlords, laws, industries and commerce, all of which require the use of reason' (Pagden and Lawrence 1991: 250). This was no savage and disordered world awaiting rational reconstruction by the imperial and Christian power but a society with an equal, legal and moral, status. Vitoria, therefore, was forced to conclude that 'the barbar-ians undoubtedly possessed as true dominion, both public and private, as any Christians' (Pagden and Lawrence 1991: 250).

It was not just generosity of spirit but philosophical principle that led Vitoria to this conclusion. His Thomist–Aristotelian heritage inclined him to recognize and to uphold the worth of particular moral and political communities different from his own. His concept of the unity of mankind (his universalism) was not only consistent with vigorous support for such communities – it demanded it. The 'state' (whether Christian or non-Christian, simple or complex, 'civilised' or 'barbaric') was a 'perfect community', not in the sense that it was without blemish or beyond improvement (no state, his own included, could ever be that), but in the sense that it was 'complete in itself...not part of another common-wealth...[having] its own laws, its own independent policy, and its own magistrates' (Pagden and Lawrence 1991: 301). In his view, the Indian states possessed a fundamental wholeness or integrity, the recognition of which precluded their absorption into an imperial unity (whether of Spain *or* of Rome).

Vitoria, of course, was no moral relativist. In line with the natural law principles of his thought, the state was seen as a subordinate part of the moral community of mankind. His universalism, however, kept faith with the particular. It was not based on the assumed moral superiority, and certainly not on the global hegemony, of his own culture and society. It did not prevent him from recognizing and valuing social structures and cultural and moral values at variance with his own. His idea of the unity of mankind was not hostile to such variety; rather, it presupposed it. Our common humanity was to be explored and advanced, not through the tyranny of one culture, but through the creative interplay of many. His view of his own society was sceptical enough and his view of humanity large enough not to confuse the fullness either of natural law or of the Christian gospel with contemporary European practice.

These ideas indicate that Zolo's attack on cosmopolitanism, and the philosophy of natural law which underpins it, is wide of the mark so far as the *non*-Enlightenment tradition of natural law (to which Vitoria's work belongs) is concerned. That tradition is 'universalist' without being 'cosmopolitan' (and 'particularist' without being 'realist'). It is, in fact, consistent with an 'anarchical society' and with the positive recognition of diverse moral and political communities. In this version of natural law the pivotal idea of the community of mankind does not lead inexorably to a system of world government with its own *lex mundialis*.

What reflection on this tradition suggests, therefore, is that Zolo's formulation of the argument is too restrictive, enabling us to avoid one pitfall only to fall victim to another. His counter to cosmopolitanism's abstract universalism is a form of moral particularism, but his moral particularism and cosmopolitan universalism *both* run to extremes and *both* are dangerously one-sided in their exclusiveness. Such polarization of the argument is not uncommon, but it needs to be resisted.[16]

At the heart of the debate are issues of war and peace. Behind Zolo's criticism of cosmopolitan theory are fears about its bellicose tendencies. This is ironic. After all, the supreme gift which the realization of cosmopolitan goals is thought to bestow is permanent peace: global democratization and political unification are expected to lead to global pacification. The peacemaking potential of cosmopolitanism is thought, by its adherents, to be its major strength and reason for support. Yet Zolo's fears appear far from groundless.

From this critical standpoint it is not the pacific but the war-making potential of cosmopolitanism which is to the fore. The criticism reverses cosmopolitan expectations: the zealous pursuit of a cosmopolitan agenda seems likely to multiply the causes of war; to increase the scale and incidence of war; to intensify and to prolong the prosecution of war. A 'militant humanitarianism'[17] is something to be feared rather than welcomed. As Waltz very plausibly suggests: 'The prospect of world government would be an invitation to prepare for world civil war' (Waltz 1979: 112).

Zolo's scepticism about the pacific potential of cosmopolitanism is not baseless,[18] but its generalized form and wider application are more questionable. The criticism of humanitarian interventionism, for example, a criticism which is certainly timely, leads to the sweeping exclusion of *all* armed intervention by the international community in the affairs of a member state. That there should be no moral presumption in favour of intervention is one thing, but that the principle of non-intervention should be applied without exception is quite another. In cases of extreme need (say, the threat of genocide), when non-military means of resolving conflict have been effectively exhausted, military intervention appears not only permissible but, perhaps, even obligatory. Of course, even here, circumstances (such as the sheer complexity and intractability of the conflict in question) and the prospects of success should still determine whether intervention takes place. The common moralistic impulse to intervene without regard to consequences needs to be resisted. In some cases the prospects of a successful intervention may be so remote (and its negative potential so real) as to rule it out. But this need not apply in all cases. The problems (insuperable or otherwise) of military intervention in Bosnia or Rwanda, for example, seem of a different order from those in the Gulf (though it is significant that, in Zolo's argument, these cases are treated indiscriminately).

The argument that a lasting peace cannot be exported or imposed from without is a persuasive one in many respects. The point is important, not least because it tends so often to be overlooked. Yet cases may arise (they are certainly conceivable) where military intervention is the *conditio sine qua non* of an *internal* settlement. Why should it be assumed that intervention must always obstruct rather than facilitate an internal resolution of conflict? That said, the need for an internal resolution *is* fundamental, not simply in the interest of an enduring peace. An authentically humanitarian intervention (based on the idea of the international community as a plural or diversified unity) must respect the integrity (moral, cultural, social, political) of the state in question. Intervention may be (as Zolo justifiably fears it will be) an exercise in hegemonic control and a pretext for the advancement of a dominant interest, but it does not have to be. While it is right to be sceptical about some of the more extravagant claims made for humanitarian intervention, its absolute proscription seems unjustified.

From an ethical standpoint the alternative to intervention which Zolo proposes is cause for grave concern. '[T]he realistic assumption on which my proposal [of non-intervention] rests,' he writes, 'is that only in and through conflict can peace be achieved' (this volume: Chapter Five). To that, appropriate responses might be: 'What *kind* of peace?' and 'Is it a peace worth having?' Leaving the controversial issue of a 'just' peace aside, in some extreme, but sadly not uncommon, cases the peace which a policy of non-intervention helps to bring about may be no better than the 'peace of the dead', the peace which follows a war of annihilation. To avoid that kind of peace military intervention might well be justified. Even if it did leave the underlying causes of the conflict unresolved, at least it would keep open the possibility of some future reconciliation.

What Zolo's criticism of interventionism seems to reveal is the moral ambiguity of his theory of war. The self-proclaimed 'pacifist' orientation of his thinking, his obvious concern to restrain and limit war and to advance the cause of peace, are combined with a disturbing endorsement of war, worryingly permissive in its implications. War is seen to be rooted in the human condition. It is an 'inevitable choice' for a given social group, and that inevitability demonstrates the folly, the 'grotesqueness', of *any* attempt (moralistic or otherwise) to subject war to moral regulation. More than that, the very development of the human species is bound up with war. From this 'evolutionary' perspective the aim of permanent peace is not only a hopelessly utopian ideal, it is a regressive one too: 'aggression and reconciliation (together with conflict and pacification) are evolutionary constants of the human species that rule out the cosmopolitan project for a stable and universal peace' (Zolo 1997: 129). These are sentiments more often associated with militarism than with pacifism. Nowhere is the paradoxical nature of Zolo's argument more evident than in its teaching on war. Nowhere, perhaps, is the need for a more inclusive appraisal of the issues, avoiding the extremes of 'cosmopolitanism' *and* 'realism', more acutely felt.

Notes

1   This may have something to do with the crisis which has overtaken Marxism since the collapse of communism. The 'domestic' failure of Marxist-inspired communist movements appears to have encouraged some Marxists to focus more sharply on Marxian cosmopolitanism.
2   For critical accounts of modern rationalism, see Oakeshott (1962) and Hayek (1973).
3   A prime example (and a formative influence) is the systematic separation of duty and inclination in Kant's moral philosophy. The moral purism of the Kantian school breeds hostility to the particular. As one critic has argued: 'The Kantian has...the "cosmopolitan agenda" of detaching people little by little from their local attachments and replacing these with universalist commitments to all rational agents as such...local attachments and loyalties come under the heading of "pathological love", they do not have moral worth in themselves' (Hare 1996: 84; see also Lumsdaine's essay in the same volume).
4   The progressivist tone often borders on triumphalism (as in the view that liberal democracy is the culmination or completion of the world historical process).
5   From this standpoint the past has been not only unproductive but obstructive, so that a break with the past is seen as a condition of progress. The rational organization of society must not be impeded by any indebtedness to the past – hence the readiness to deal cavalierly with inherited institutions, no matter how long-lived. In fact the longer-lived the institution the greater the hostility to it tends to be: here, longevity is a mark of the worthlessness rather than the value of an institution.
6   An antipathy to religion is manifested in several contributions to this volume, but nowhere more than in Richard Falk's chapter which has as one of its professed aims: 'to weaken the political appeal of resurgent organized religion' (Chapter Ten). Secularism seems to be an article of faith among cosmopolitans, religion being seen as a major threat to cosmopolitan values. Given the universal claims of both, it is perhaps inevitable that cosmopolitanism should see religion in such adversarial terms.
7   The objection to cosmopolitanism being advanced here is not to the fostering of transnational ties, loyalties and responsibilities (far from it) but rather to their abstraction from the particular moral communities to which moral agents are seen essentially to belong and in which transnational values must take root.

Richard Falk, for example, laments the way in which, at present, 'the transnational referent tends to root the identity of the actors in the subsoil of national consciousness' (this volume: p. 162). Far from being a weakness and an obstacle to progress, which is how Falk regards it, this is seen here as a fundamental strength: a rooted transnationalism is worth more than a rootless cosmopolitanism.

8 'The rational solution of any problem', wrote Oakeshott, 'is, in its nature, the perfect solution. There is no place in this scheme for a "best in the circumstances"...the function of reason is precisely to surmount circumstances...from this politics of perfection springs the politics of uniformity; a scheme which does not recognize circumstance can have no place for variety...Political activity is recognized as the imposition of a uniform condition of perfection upon human conduct' (Oakeshott 1962: 5–6).

   David Held furnishes an example of the approach Oakeshott criticized when he cites (clearly with approval, since a similar view underpins his own project of 'cosmopolitan democracy') James Mill's view of representative government as 'the grand discovery of modern times [in which] the solution of all difficulties, both speculative and practical, would be found' (this volume: Chapter One).

   Compare this disposition and approach, which evinces such indifference or even hostility to circumstance and such supreme confidence in a rational solution, with that of Edmund Burke. Reflecting in 1777 on the problems of governing an empire composed of parts as disparate as India and North America, Burke was led to the following conclusion: '[I]t was our duty, in all soberness, to conform our Government to the character and circumstances of the several people who compose this mighty and strangely diversified mass. I never was wild enough to conceive, that one method would serve for the whole...I was persuaded that Government was a practical thing, made for the happiness of mankind, and not to furnish out a spectacle of uniformity, to gratify the schemes of visionary politicians' (Letter to the Sheriffs of Bristol, in Elofson with Woods 1996: 316–17).

9 That confidence is manifest in what might be seen as the ease with which cosmopolitan theorists move beyond the articulation of general principles to the construction of elaborate models of global government (see, for example, Chapter Nine in this volume, by Johan Galtung).

10 Such a preference is, of course, wholly consistent with the application of reason to more specific or particular problems. There the specific focus diminishes the rationalist threat. It is in this light, perhaps, that Zolo's distinction between the cooperative search for solutions to specific 'global' problems and the cosmopolitan search for global governance is to be understood.

11 Since the Stoic age, cosmopolitanism has been associated with an intellectual elite's sense of moral superiority and universal fellowship. This is an 'heroic' rather than 'common' morality which engages the critical faculties of moral *individuals* who possess the power of moral initiative and the strength to resist particular or traditional social norms.

12 In response to Zolo's criticism, David Held argued along these lines at the Reading conference.

13 The primacy of reason in the rationalist version of natural law is out of place in the older tradition. As a modern exponent of that tradition has argued: '[H]uman reason does not discover the regulations of natural law in an abstract and theoretical manner, as a series of geometrical theorems...it does not discover them through the conceptual exercise of the intellect, or by way of rational knowledge...the very mode or manner in which human reason knows natural law is not rational knowledge, but knowledge *through inclination*...our

knowledge of it is no work of free conceptualization...it develops in proportion to the degree of moral experience and self-reflection, and of social experience also, of which man is capable in the various ages of his history' (Maritain 1951: 91–4).

14 It seems that this revised tradition of natural law was not averse to imperialism. According to Richard Tuck, Grotius 'urged the prosecution of the Dutch imperial mission' and his 'theory of aristocratic, imperialist republicanism...helped to underpin' the growing Dutch empire (Miller 1987: 186).

15 Ekins, for example, describes states as 'awkward, artificial political entities with absolute power over the people within their boundaries', the consequence of which 'has been disastrous for hundreds of millions of their citizens [with] peoples who have lived largely free from outside interference for millennia...now feeling the oppressive, often genocidal, impact of state power' (Ekins 1992: 206–7). The diagnosis (as well as the remedy) is, of course, disputable. Often it seems that it is the *absence* of the state (in everything but name) that accounts for the misery and suffering to which Ekins alludes. In such cases it is not liberation from the state but the presence of the rule of law which, at its best, the state provides that the oppressed stand in need of most.

16 One of the main strengths of the conception of international relations yielded by the non-Enlightenment (Thomist–Aristotelian) tradition of natural law is its capacity to resist polarization. Yet this version of the natural law tradition is commonly neglected. Much contemporary international political theory appears to be conducted in the light of the three normative conceptions of international relations popularized by Charles Beitz (1979): 'international moral scepticism'; the 'morality of states'; and 'cosmopolitan morality'. None of these conceptions fits the concept of international relations adumbrated here (Beitz recognizes the natural law tradition only in its so-called 'modern' form), and none shares its concern to do justice to the claims of both the universal moral community of mankind and the particular historic communities into which humanity is divided.

17 The phrase is Webster's (see note 18). For further discussion of the concept, see Coates (1997), ch. 2.

18 For the expression of a similar concern, see the essays by Hare and Webster in Lugo (1996); also Coates (1996).

References

Beitz, C. R. (1979) *Political Theory and International Relations*, Princeton: Princeton University Press.

Boyle, J. (1996) 'On the Importance of Natural Rights', in Lugo (1996).

Coates, A. J. (1996) 'The New World Order and the Ethics of War', in B. Holden (ed.), *The Ethical Dimensions of Global Change*, Basingstoke: Macmillan.

—— (1997) *The Ethics of War*, Manchester: Manchester University Press.

Ekins, P. (1992) *A New World Order*, London: Routledge.

Elofson, W. M. with Woods, J. A. (eds) (1996) *The Writings and Speeches of Edmund Burke*, vol. III, Oxford: Clarendon Press.

Fernández-Santamaría, J. A. (1977) *The State, War and Peace*, Cambridge: Cambridge University Press.

Hare, J. (1996) 'Kantian Ethics, International Politics, and the Enlargement of the *Foedus Pacificum*', in Lugo (1996).

Hayek, F. A. (1973) *Law, Legislation and Liberty*, vol. I, London: Routledge & Kegan Paul.

Keegan, J. (1993) *A History of Warfare*, London: Hutchinson.

Lugo, L. E. (ed.) (1996) *Sovereignty at the Crossroads?*, Lanham: Rowman & Littlefield.

Maritain, J. (1951) *Man and the State*, Chicago: Chicago University Press.

Miller, D. (ed.) (1987) *The Blackwell Encyclopaedia of Political Thought*, Oxford: Blackwell.

Oakeshott, M. (1962) *Rationalism in Politics*, London: Methuen.

Pagden, A. and Lawrence, J. (eds) (1991) *Francisco de Vitoria: Political Writings*, Cambridge: Cambridge University Press.

Waltz, K. N. (1979) *Theory of International Politics*, Reading, Mass.: Addison-Wesley.

Zolo, D. (1997) *Cosmopolis*, Cambridge: Polity Press.

Part II
Structures and processes

7 An agenda for democratization[1]

Democratization at the international level

Boutros Boutros-Ghali

V DEMOCRATIZATION AT THE INTERNATIONAL LEVEL

Democratization internationally is necessary on three interrelated fronts. The established system of the United Nations itself has far to go before fulfilling to the extent possible the democratic potential of its present design, and in transforming those structures which are insufficiently democratic. The participation of new actors on the international scene is an acknowledged fact; providing them with agreed means of participation in the formal system, heretofore primarily the province of States, is a new task of our time. A third challenge will be to achieve a culture of democracy internationally. This will not only require a society of States committed to democratic principles and processes; it will also demand an enlarged international civil society deeply involved in democratic institutions, whether State, inter-State or supra-State, private or quasi-private; committed to democratic practices, procedures and political pluralism; and composed of peoples ingrained with those habits of openness, fairness and tolerance that have been associated with democracy since ancient times.

There are of course substantial differences between democratization at the international level and democratization within States. At the international level there are international organizations and institutions, and international decision-making and international law, but there is no international structure equivalent to that of State government. International society is both a society of States and a society of individual persons. None the less, the concept of democratization as a process which can create a more open, more participatory, less authoritarian society applies both nationally and internationally.

There are likewise substantial differences between the ideas of national democracy and international democracy. Growing recognition of the practical importance of democracy within States has nevertheless contributed to growing recognition of the practical importance of democracy among States, and generated increased demand for democratization internationally.

Individual involvement in the political process enhances the accountability and responsiveness of government. Governments which are responsive and accountable are likely to be stable and to promote peace. Many internal conflicts stem from the belief, justified or not, that the State does not represent all groups in society or that it seeks to impose an exclusive ideology. Democracy is the way to mediate the various social interests in a particular community. In the international community, it is the way to promote the participation of all actors and to provide a possibility to solve conflicts by dialogue rather than by force of arms. The process of democratization internationally can therefore help promote peaceful relations among states.

With participation, economic and social development become meaningful and establish deeper roots. Building democratic institutions at the state level helps to ensure that the priorities of diverse social groups are considered in the formulation of development strategies. In the international economic system, democracy can mean that the relationship between developed and developing States is one not of assistance but of cooperation. Instead of chronic reliance on emergency relief, the concerns of developed and developing States can be mediated in conferences and other United Nations intergovernmental consultations, which also engage relevant non-State actors. Democratization, therefore, can help guarantee that, through the United Nations, the poorest countries will have an ever growing voice in the international system. It can help ensure that the international system does not leave a vast portion of the world to fend for itself but truly promotes the integration and participation of all peoples.

If democratization is the most reliable way to legitimize and improve national governance, it is also the most reliable way to legitimize and improve international organization, making it more open and responsive by increasing participation, more efficient by allowing for burden-sharing, and more effective by allowing for comparative advantage and greater creativity. Moreover, just like democratization within States, democratization at the international level is based on and aims to promote the dignity and worth of the individual human being and the fundamental equality of all persons and of all peoples.

The new world environment has strengthened this fundamental link between democratization nationally and internationally. Once, decision-making in global affairs could have only a limited effect on the internal affairs of States and the daily lives of their peoples. Today, decisions concerning global matters carry with them far-reaching domestic consequences, blurring the lines between international and domestic policy. In this way, unrepresentative decisions on global issues can run counter to democratization within a State and undermine a people's commitment to it. Thus, democratization within States may fail to take root unless democratization extends to the international arena.

Decisions at the global level are going to increase because the problems which can only be solved globally are going to multiply. Already, States everywhere increasingly confront forces far beyond the control of any one state or even group of States. Some of these forces are irresistible, such as the globalization of economic activity and communications. These forces, although predominantly positive in effect, affect societies unevenly, can seem accountable to no one and are creating opportunities for a host of transnational criminal activities, from illegal arms transfers to the laundering of profits from the narcotic trade. Environmental pressures are similarly irresistible and create global problems. States can also be substantially affected by another State's domestic decisions in regard to finance or the environment and by the decisions of local authorities and private actors. It is not the forces themselves that are new but their increasing scale and level of influence upon the State.

These global forces can feed and interact with forces exerted upon States from below. Increased access to communications media, particularly radio, television and film, raises awareness of problems and opportunities and leads people everywhere to demand more accountability, more representation and more participation in governance – more control over their future and more say in the decisions that affect their lives. Global forces can also be a source of individual insecurity, social disarray and dangerous fragmentation, creating fertile ground for fanaticism, ethnocentrism and isolationism.

All this means that the requirements of political governance are extending beyond State borders, even as States feel new pressures from below. Democracy within the State will diminish in importance if the process of democratization does not move forward at the international level. For if a State today is to acquire or retain the capacity to provide an enabling environment for its citizens, it must extend its influence to those factors beyond its unilateral control which help to determine the conditions of life within it. Such an extension of sovereignty will be possible and legitimate only to the extent that it rests upon mechanisms of democratic accountability. For all States, democratization at the international level has become an indispensable mechanism for global problem-solving in a way that is accountable and acceptable to all and with the participation of all concerned. Dominance by one country or group of countries must over time evolve into a democratic international system in which all countries can participate, along with new non-State actors involved in international affairs.

There are signs that such a process is already taking place. As States have confronted popular demands to deal with economic, security and environmental issues that evade effective action on a strictly national basis, they have increasingly found themselves seeking solutions through cooperative arrangements and participation in regional and international intergovernmental organizations. Such organizations are proliferating and the scope of their activities is broadening, thereby fostering democratic principles and participation at the international level. At the same time, new channels of political expression and activity for individual citizens are developing outside governmental structures but inside the public sphere once considered the virtually exclusive province of government; the proliferation of non-governmental organizations from the local to the global and the expansion of activity through international political associations, or 'political internationals', both make clear the deficiencies of existing governmental structures in the face of global change. The overall result is that globalization is creating chains of interlocking decisions and political associations which link different levels of political representation. In other words, what is emerging are *de facto* linkages extending from individual citizens all the way to international organizations, grappling with global problems and prospects. The forces at work in the world today are thus demanding and enabling an unprecedented democratization of international politics and decision-making.

The United Nations has recognized and supported this process of democratization internationally. Its advancement deserves to become a leading priority in world affairs. But before discussing how the United Nations and others can further this process, it is essential to be clear about the nature of the political 'system' that is to be democratized.

The 'system' in which the world operates is by its very name 'international'. However, as observed above, the States which are its basic components increasingly must operate in the midst of global as well as internal forces. Moreover, 'international relations' – not relations among nations but relations among sovereign States – are increasingly shaped not only by the States themselves but also by an expanding array of non-State actors on the 'international' scene, ranging all the way from individual persons to civic associations, non-governmental organizations, local authorities, private multinational business, academia, the media, parliamentarians and regional and international intergovernmental organizations.

These changes have come to the fore largely because of the quick succession of historical events which the world has witnessed in recent years. The fall of the Berlin Wall and the end of the cold war and of East–West antagonism shattered the ideological screen which concealed the complex reality of international relations and precipitated the collapse of the bipolar system. Although reference is commonly made to the 'international system', in reality a new international system, with a new structure for international stability and cooperation, has yet to emerge. The most legitimate, effective and responsive way to build such a system – taking into account not only geopolitical issues, but economic behaviour and social and cultural aspirations – is by democratizing the structures and mechanisms already in place.

Member States

The first priority in this effort must be a fundamental change on the part of the Member States themselves. Despite all the pressures affecting State sovereignty in our time, the concept of sovereignty remains essential for rendering unequal power equal and for making international organization possible; States remain the most important actors of all, and will continue to be the fundamental building blocks of the international system. Yet today only a small proportion of States play their full role on the world stage. Some States, small in size or population, exercise influence far beyond their objective attributes of power. Other States possessing vast power refrain from international involvement commensurate with their strength. Of course, domestic political and constitutional constraints are involved, but the first and greatest step forward in democratization internationally must be increased attention to and engagement with international affairs by all Member States of the United Nations, as an application of the concept of sovereignty.

With this step must come a commitment on the part of all States not only to engage in dialogue and debate but also to discourage isolationism, to oppose unilateralism, to accept decisions reached democratically, to refrain from using force illegitimately, to oppose aggression, to promote and respect the rule of law in international relations and to maintain a general spirit of solidarity, cooperation and community. Unless the majority of Member States have the political will to pay attention to global affairs as they do to national affairs, the democratization of international relations will not succeed.

New actors

Next is the integration of new non-State actors, who are undeniably of increasing influence in world affairs, into existing international structures and mechanisms. There is a great diversity of such actors. They participate in different ways and in different degrees, more effectively within organizations and associations. The vast majority are in the North, and among them are the key actors in the process of globalization: the transnational entities involved in business and finance, which can cooperate closely with the Governments of the countries in which they are based. The degree and nature of the loss of sovereignty brought on by globalization therefore differ between the States of the North and the States of the South. Increasing the participation of the new actors in international institutions must not be allowed to accentuate the gap between North and South. Just as democratization within a State must include an effort to empower citizens to participate in their own political process, so must democratization internationally include an effort to empower all States – developed or developing, North or South, rich or poor – to participate in the international political system, of which they are all a part.

The United Nations is fundamentally and from its inception an Organization of sovereign States. Yet it also has from its inception offered its Member States an indispensable mechanism for cooperation with actors, both governmental and non-governmental, functioning outside the United Nations. The creation in 1945 of an international intergovernmental Organization with provisions for cooperating not only with other such organizations – such as the specialized agencies formally brought into the United Nations system under the aegis of Article 57 of the Charter – but also with regional and non-governmental organizations, was a major achievement. Specifically, Chapter VIII of the Charter is devoted entirely to United Nations cooperation with regional organizations and arrangements in the maintenance of international peace and security. Article 71 of the Charter empowers the Economic and Social Council to make arrangements for consultation with non-governmental organizations active in its area of competence.

Within these provisions and the general framework of the Charter, the United Nations has made great strides in expanding dialogue and practical cooperation with the new actors as their influence on and importance to world affairs has grown. None the less, the discussions on United Nations reform have not dealt adequately with the issue of their integration. It is crucial that in the future they do. Towards this end, the paragraphs below address several of the new actors in turn, outlining the special features which make their integration essential, their present level of involvement in the United Nations and its work, and suggestions to stimulate discussion on the question of their integration into the formal United Nations system. The suggestions touch upon a variety of steps towards deeper integration that could be taken by the United Nations Secretariat, by Member States, either individually or through the intergovernmental machinery of the United Nations, by the actor in question or, most often, by some combination of the aforementioned, acting jointly. Substantively, the steps primarily fall along three main lines, each of which stresses integration as a way to give the new actors a voice in the United Nations: a voice that can be a contribution to problem-solving; a voice on matters before the United Nations, not limited to the situation of each actor; and an avenue of expression to the international community on the prospects, problems and requirements of the sectors that these actors represent.

Regional organizations

The upsurge in activity through regional organizations in the last decade, and especially since the end of the cold war, has challenged the community of States to develop the new regionalism not as a resurgent 'spheres of influence' but as a healthy complement to internationalism. Moreover, at a time of increasing demand but decreasing resources within the United Nations for international action, the potential of regional groups to contribute political, diplomatic, financial, material and military resources has taken on even greater importance. Especially in the area of international development assistance and cooperation, where donor fatigue and indifference have set in, and in peace-enforcement, where the United Nations at present has no capacity, regional groups are for the United Nations increasingly important potential partners whose cooperation could be engaged.

Many regional intergovernmental organizations participate as permanent observers in the sessions and work of the General Assembly. Regional groups have long cooperated with the United Nations in the development field through the United Nations regional economic and social commissions, established in the earliest years of the Organization. Only in the vastly changed circumstances of the post-cold-war years has the United Nations been able to explore new forms of cooperation with regional groups in the maintenance of international peace and security and to delegate responsibility in particular cases to states and organizations of the regions concerned. Under the flexible framework provided by Chapter VIII of the Charter, different forms of United Nations regional cooperation have developed: consultations, diplomatic support, operational support, co-deployment and joint operations. In August 1994 and again in February 1996, I convened at United Nations Headquarters a high-level meeting with regional organizations that have cooperated with the United Nations in peace and security, to examine patterns of and principles for improving cooperation, and to explore the potential for expanded cooperation in the future.

The integration of regional organizations into the United Nations system is a cornerstone of democratization internationally. To build upon this basis, consideration should be given to holding regular meetings at United Nations Headquarters every year or every two years between the Secretariat and regional organizations cooperating with the United Nations in peace and security. The pivotal role of regional organizations in democratizing development should be enhanced by opening channels to the regional level for the views of those at the local level, and by reducing bureaucratic obstacles to the flow or volume of assistance; the United Nations regional economic and social commissions are well placed to contribute to such an effort. Regionalism should be strengthened internationally through United Nations-sponsored agreements on horizontal, inter-regional connections in all areas of endeavour.

Non-governmental organizations

In the last few decades the number of non-governmental organizations (NGOs) has grown at an astonishing rate – the number of international non-governmental organizations alone having risen from roughly 1,300 in 1960 to over 36,000 in 1995 – and their functional scope has expanded considerably. The thousands of NGOs that operate today, from the grassroots to the global level, represent a wide diversity in size, stature, field of activity, methods, means and objectives. However, all are self-governing, private institutions engaged in the pursuit of public purposes outside the formal apparatus of the State. Such organizations are taking on an increasingly important role in world affairs by carrying the voices and needs of the smallest communities to international attention, forging contacts between citizens' groups across the world and offering citizens direct channels of participation in world affairs. To international organizations, non-governmental organizations can bring not only strengthened legitimacy but also field experience and expertise across a vast array of human concerns, as well as a valuable capacity for information-gathering and dissemination. Non-governmental organizations are proving extremely powerful in fighting isolationism and indifference among both Governments and citizens, and in mobilizing public opinion and support, especially financial support and donor assistance.

Some 200 non-governmental organizations were present at the 1945 United Nations Conference on International Organization at San Francisco, where the Charter of the United Nations was agreed and signed. Since that time, the United Nations–NGO partnership has grown into a global network, encompassing some 1,600 non-governmental organizations in consultative status with the Economic and Social Council under Article 71 of the Charter, some 1,500 associated with the United Nations Department of Public Information, and the many other non-governmental organizations affiliated with United Nations offices and agencies in every part of the world. On the legislative/policy-making side, NGO participation in United Nations work is most advanced in the human rights and treaty bodies, with NGO involvement also having been critical to the establishment of those bodies. Less advanced but moving definitively forward is NGO participation in legislation and policy-making in the economic and social field. Recognizing the vital role played by non-governmental organizations at the Earth Summit (Rio de Janeiro, June 1992), the Programme of Action adopted there, Agenda 21,[2] provides for NGO participation in the Commission on Sustainable Development established for its follow-up. Agenda 21 encourages the entire United Nations system and all intergovernmental organizations to review and report on ways of enhancing NGO participation in policy design, decision-making, implementation and evaluation. The momentum generated by Rio for strengthened NGO participation has been carried forward in subsequent conferences and led, among other outcomes, to the adoption by the Economic and Social Council in July 1996 of a new resolution on the consultative relationship between the United Nations and non-governmental organizations.[3] On the operational level, NGO participation is most advanced in humanitarian emergencies, but it is also substantial in the development field, where NGO participation is facilitated by the United Nations Non-Governmental Liaison Service at Geneva and by various NGO committees and advisory bodies established by United Nations departments and agencies.

To deepen further the democratizing potential of the NGO phenomenon, non-governmental organizations and other representatives of civil society (including those addressed specifically below) should be invited to participate in Member State delegations on a regular basis. The Open-ended High-level Working Group on the Strengthening of the United Nations System has suggested that consideration be given to the establishment of a 'civil society forum'. In addition, the Conference of Non-Governmental Organizations in Consultative Status with the Economic and Social Council should be empowered to make more precise and operational recommendations for the consideration of the Council and to help ensure that the non-governmental organizations in such status are representative and of recognized utility.

Each of the actors discussed below is already represented in some way through non-governmental organizations in consultative status with the Economic and Social Council. Therefore, participation via the Economic and Social Council should deepen on all fronts if these actors obtain some formalized or semi-formalized connection with the Council.

Parliamentarians

Parliamentarians, as the directly elected representatives of their constituents, are for international organizations an essential link to international public opinion. Without such a link it has become extremely difficult to build recognition, understanding and support for international efforts, especially in recent years as those efforts have become more complex and the international environment more uncertain. At the same time, by carrying the views and concerns of their constituents to the international arena, parliamentarians offer a direct channel for increasing the legitimacy, responsiveness and effectiveness of international organizations. Situated between citizens of States and the community of States, and by definition committed to dialogue, discussion and agreement, parliamentarians are a direct and motive force for democratization at the international level.

Parliamentarians have participated in the work of the United Nations in a variety of ways. Acting both individually and in concert, they have cooperated with the United Nations in the field across the full range of support for democratization. At the United Nations, they have engaged in informal consultations with the Secretariat, participated in Member State delegations, contributed to preparations for international conferences and fostered international dialogue by occasionally convening their own conferences at the United Nations through the Inter-Parliamentary Union,[4] the world organization of parliamentarians. The Inter-Parliamentary Union has long had consultative status with the Economic and Social Council. Following a request of the General Assembly in its resolution 50/15 of 15 November 1995, I concluded in July 1996 an agreement of cooperation between the United Nations and the Inter-Parliamentary Union which will strengthen that cooperation and give it 'a new and adequate framework'. As Secretary-General, I also continue to meet with parliamentarians and members of state legislatures, upon their request, during my official visits to Member States, as do my Special Envoys and Special Representatives and other representatives of the United Nations system.

To consolidate and take further advantage of the contributions of parliamentarians as a factor of democratization internationally, Member States should consider: encouraging and facilitating the closer involvement of parliamentarians in United Nations efforts to provide international support for democratization within states; establishing a continuing committee or commission on the United Nations within their national parliaments; and urging the Inter-Parliamentary Union to convene every three years at a United Nations location in order to foster international dialogue and debate on the United Nations and issues before the United Nations and its Member States.

Local authorities

While today's major challenges are undeniably global in character, it is at the local level where their impact is felt most directly, which is why local authorities, such as mayors and metropolitan officials, have become notably more active on global issues and, in some cases, collectively organized across countries on matters of common concern. Local participation enhances the legitimacy and effectiveness of global decisions by helping to ensure that those decisions emerge from the realities of local life and are supported by local action. Yet vigorous and effective local governance is essential not only to global problem-solving: by contributing to health and sustainable human settlements, it is also essential to international peace and security in the broadest sense. With the global trend towards urbanization, human settlements increasingly will be urban settlements. Already, the city is where global problems converge and where their interconnections are most apparent; mass migration, overpopulation, natural disasters, air and water pollution, land degradation, the rights of women and children, minority rights, unemployment, poverty and social disaffection are just some of the prime examples. At the same time, however, the city may also be the place where a sound basis for solving these problems can be built, for of all human settlements, cities are best placed to foster dialogue and diversity, to engender community and a spirit of civic engagement while also opening windows to the world. Mayors and metropolitan authorities have therefore become indispensable agents for social integration within and among cities and thus within and among states.

Since the Earth Summit, where local authorities were identified as one of the 'major groups' of society responsible for sustainable development, the involvement of local authorities in United Nations efforts has advanced considerably. Following the Summit, a Local Agenda 21 initiative was launched by the International Council for Local Environmental Initiatives, whose members are cities and towns actively promoting participatory development processes at the local level. Mayors and metropolitan authorities participate in the work of the Commission on Sustainable Development and many exchange information and consult informally with the Commission's secretariat. Mayors and metropolitan authorities have also mobilized in support of the United Nations Framework Convention on Climate Change and contribute to its Conference of Parties. The organizational framework for the United Nations Conference on Human Settlements (Habitat II) allowed for a more formalized involvement of local authorities. In the area of operational activities for development, programmes requested by Member States increasingly involve United Nations cooperation with local authorities. In the peace and security sphere, many local authorities support United Nations efforts through 'sister cities' and other such cooperation and cultural exchange programmes, and many cities have declared themselves nuclear-weapon-free zones. Cities have also been strongly supportive of the United Nations by hosting international gatherings and events and by providing homes to the many United Nations offices around the world.

To strengthen local frameworks for global problem-solving and deepen the involvement of local authorities in the United Nations system, consideration should be given to instructing United Nations resident coordinators to maintain regular dialogue with local authorities, making the interaction an integral part of the work, at the country level, on operational activities for development. The possibility of establishing a joint committee of concerned Secretariat entities and apex organizations of local authorities should be examined; such a committee would serve to raise awareness and promote exchange of experiences among local authorities and could be established along the lines of the Committee for the Promotion and Advancement of Cooperatives, which brings together the United Nations Secretariat, United Nations agencies and international non-governmental organizations to promote and coordinate assistance to cooperatives and is financed by contributions from its members. Member States should also consider a more formalized involvement of local authorities through the establishment of a small subsidiary body of the Commission on Sustainable Development, which would contribute regularly to the work of the Commission and to other relevant United Nations bodies.

Academia

At this time of profound change, academia, including universities, research institutes and public policy centres, has taken on increased importance in world affairs by helping to uncover the dimensions of change and to construct an intellectual platform upon which future efforts may be built. By expanding the flow of ideas, academia has become increasingly powerful in encouraging public participation in national and international dialogue on the future and, more importantly, in shaping that dialogue. Thus, by its very nature, academia also contributes to democratization. At the same time, academia is providing important new evidence on the complementarity among peace, development and democracy, and on the contribution of international organizations to all three.

Many academic groups have engaged in informal consultations with the Secretariat and United Nations departments, agencies and programmes. They have also participated in practical assistance programmes. The United Nations itself has several research centres and institutes, as well as its own United Nations University, which promotes scholarly debate, research and training across the range of issues relevant to the operation and efforts of international organizations. The Academic Council on the United Nations System, established by scholars, teachers and practitioners from around the world active in the work and study of international organizations, fosters dialogue and cooperation between academia and the various components of the United Nations system.

To enable the widest range of the world's peoples to benefit from advances in thought and research, and to give greater recognition to the views and needs of academic institutions and enterprises, consideration should be given to expanding informal consultations with academia across the United Nations system in order to facilitate the contribution of individual scholars, scientists and research institutions to United Nations projects and problem-solving. Integrating the programme of work of the United Nations University with the overall work of the United Nations system would be an important contribution towards that end, as would the inclusion by the periodic conferences of academic disciplines of panels or programmes involving United Nations practitioners. The United Nations University and its subsidiary institutions should be strengthened to forge stronger links between academics and research institutions in the North and the South, with a view to fostering global networks where this might not otherwise be easily accomplished. Member States should consider offering a United Nations centre as the venue for academic gatherings to discuss the problems and prospects of research universities and institutions related to the work of that centre. These could serve both substantive scholarship and the capacity of academia to play a more direct role in world affairs.

Business and industry

Business and industry today have more power over the future of the global economy and the environment than any Government or organization of

Governments. The cooperation of business and industry, whether informal producers, small or medium-sized enterprises or large-scale corporations, is critical to the achievement of development that is both socially and environmentally sustainable. Transnational or multinational corporations in particular – which are today estimated to be 40,000 in number, controlling some 250,000 foreign affiliates worth approximately $2.6 trillion in book value and accounting for some one third of world private-sector productive assets – are playing an extremely important role in economic development. This occurs not only through foreign direct investment in transitional and developing economies but also through the transfer of technology and skills and the stimulation of host-country business enterprise. Moreover, and most importantly, by increasingly integrating the various functions of production across State borders, and as the world's main investors, traders, transferrers of technology and movers of people across borders, transnational corporations are today driving the emergence of an integrated international production system. A development agent and a positive factor for social integration within and among States, the private business sector – especially transnational business – must be recognized as an integral player in international organization and more closely involved in international decision-making.

While business and industry have become increasingly important for shaping the world economy, the United Nations has become increasingly important for shaping the environment in which business and industry operate. United Nations efforts for peace help to maintain a stable environment in which business and industry can flourish. Less well known is the significant role played by the United Nations system in establishing the regulatory framework in which business and industry act internationally. This is done, for example, by the World Trade Organization in trade and intellectual property rights, by the International Monetary Fund in financial transactions, and by the United Nations Environment Programme, the International Labour Organization and many other United Nations programmes and specialized agencies. United Nations entities also set industry guidelines and standards and offer policy analysis and technical assistance to Member States in improving their business and industry-related policies, infrastructure and institutional framework. While United Nations efforts having an important bearing on business are extensive, interaction between the two is at present sporadic, primarily informal and not reflective of the influential role that has been achieved by business and industry in international affairs. The only major exception to this is the International Labour Organization, which brings together in its General Conference Member States represented by delegates from government, employers and workers, each of which are entitled to vote individually on all matters. The need and, in today's more open and increasingly globalized environment, the possibility now exists to transform the role of business and industry within the United Nations into that of an active partnership in pursuit of common objectives. In this regard, the role played by business and industry at the Earth Summit and its continuing participation in the work of the Commission on Sustainable Development are foundations upon which to build. The same can be said of the pioneering efforts under way towards linking international organizations, both governmental and non-governmental, with national and private multinational banks in order to provide the funds and services which small and medium-sized entrepreneurs in transitional and developing countries require for sustainable development activities.

To further the widest possible mutually beneficial involvement of business and industry in the work of the United Nations, consideration should be given to establishing both a roster of United Nations technical and managerial personnel for temporary assignment to business and industry and a roster of business and industry executives and technical personnel for United Nations technical assistance activities. The effort to build the latter roster could be made in conjunction with an initiative to expand the United Nations Volunteers programme to encourage business and industry executives to engage in United Nations work and, *inter alia*, to join in early-stage planning for post-conflict peace-building, with the aim of encouraging foreign investment to facilitate recovery and reconstruction. Member States should also explore the expansion of the tripartite representational structure of the International Labour Organization to other parts of the United Nations system. Also to be considered is the expansion of United Nations efforts to achieve agreement on key issues required for a favourable environment for business, such as uniform commercial codes and intellectual property and accounting standards, and to deal with transnational problems, such as crime and corruption, which inhibit both good governance and good business.

The media

Responsible and independent global communications media can engage Governments and people in global affairs and enable them to be informed, to discuss and debate, and to express positions on the issues of the day. In this way, the global communications revolution and the global wave of democratization are mutually reinforcing: a free press is a vehicle for democratization; democratization promotes the open society in which a free press can flourish. However, in this age of instant information and near total communication, the media has become not only the major venue for dialogue and debate within and among States, but also, definitively, an international actor with a distinct role on the international stage. The media can help keep international politics open, responsive and accountable. Without that essential link to the world public, organizations such as the United Nations would be nothing more than forums for the mutual mutterings of national and international bureaucracies. At the same time, the media itself, especially through the immensely powerful imagery of television and film, has the ability to set the terms of international debate and to shape world public opinion. Through the issues, peoples and places it chooses to highlight – or to ignore – the media today has enormous influence over the international agenda. If this influence is to be constructive and effective, the media must focus not only on the drama of conflict and confrontation in certain areas of the world, but on the global pattern of violence and the broader economic, social, political and humanitarian issues that dominate the international community's long-term agenda.

The United Nations has an obligation to protect the independence and freedom of news organizations and to defend the right of all peoples, as set out in article 19 of the Universal Declaration of Human Rights,[5] to the freedom of opinion and expression, including the freedom 'to seek, receive and impart information and ideas through any media and regardless of frontiers'. The United Nations Educational, Scientific and Cultural Organization (UNESCO), along with various news organizations, has endorsed a Charter for a Free Press, committed to the unfettered flow of news and information both within and across national borders. Through UNESCO, the Department of Public Information of the Secretariat and various other entities, the United Nations offers its Member States support for the development of free, responsible and independent communications media. While striving to promote responsible and independent communications media worldwide, the United Nations also endeavours, without intruding on that independence, to engage the cooperation of the media by making information about the United Nations and its work easily accessible to the media, and through it, to non-governmental organizations and the public at large.

While the media is a powerful force for democratization, efforts to involve them closely with the international system would contravene their highest principles of independence and objectivity. At the same time, however, thought should be given to the many issues which have arisen with the vast new role of the media in global affairs issues which affect not only people, cultures and Governments but the media itself. Among steps to be considered could be: endeavours by the United Nations and its Member States to offer greater transparency and access to world media; strengthening the information capacity of United Nations operations to help focus media interest and attention on international problems at risk of international neglect; and consideration by the General Assembly's Committee on Information of the establishment of a forum where members of the media, if they choose, and without compromising their independence, could report to the international community on the state of the media.

Integrating these new actors into the daily practice of international politics and decision-making will not be a simple task. In some cases, where involvement is relatively limited and where the actor is of a most private nature, the path towards deeper integration may not at this time be clear. But whether or not Member States confront this challenge, these new actors will continue to influence the shape of the new international system as it emerges through the gradual construction of new rules and procedures. Only a concerted effort to take account of these actors will pave the way for the major structural changes now being contemplated.

The benefits of such an approach to reform are seen most clearly in the United Nations practice of convening special international conferences and summits. By organizing such gatherings, the United Nations has created issue-based constituencies and provided conditions under which declarations are being reached that are akin to general referendums on transnational issues. The democratic nature of these conferences contributes to the legitimacy and effectiveness of the programmes of action they are producing. Through the series of global conferences on interlocking economic and social issues, the United Nations has been providing an ongoing democratic process through which a new international consensus on and framework for development can be built. The process has given new direction to the reform and strengthening of the United Nations development machinery, which has advanced considerably, particularly in the past year. This makes manifest the critical relationship between engaging with the new actors on the international scene and reforming the architecture for international relations, the third step in promoting democratization internationally.

The architecture of the United Nations

By promoting democratization within its own architecture, the United Nations, as the world's largest and most inclusive organization of Governments, can make a major contribution to democratization at the international level. Since entering office, I have made democratization a guiding objective of Secretariat reform, as evidenced, for example, in the decentralization of decision-making that has already been enacted.

This reform needs to be advanced by reform in the United Nations intergovernmental machinery, for which democratization can also serve as a guiding objective. There is a clear need to move towards intergovernmental machinery that is less fragmented, better able to affect global forces and more open to civil society. There is also a clear need for an Organization in which all principal organs function in the balance and harmony contemplated by the Charter. This means an Organization which operates more consistently at the political level, with a clear sense of its comparative advantages and priorities, conscious of the linkages among all dimensions of its mission, and equipped with mandates and resources that are effectively matched.

The General Assembly is the embodiment of the universality of the United Nations and the cornerstone of representation and participation within the United Nations system, today bringing together 185 Member States on the basis of sovereign equality and democratic principles, along with several permanent observers. Improvements in the functioning of the Assembly have been a major focus of the Open-ended High-level Working Group on the Strengthening of the United Nations System. I see the Assembly performing on a continuing basis the role that the special international conferences have been playing in recent years, addressing comprehensively, and at the highest political level, the major global issues facing the international community, and fostering national and international commitments. Each session on a particular theme could consolidate and follow through on earlier meetings and set the agenda for work that lies ahead. The Assembly's role should be one of synthesis and overall policy assessment and coordination *vis-à-vis* the membership as well as the United Nations system.

The strengthening of the Economic and Social Council has been a long-standing item on the reform agenda. It received special attention in the Halifax Summit Communiqué of the Group of Seven major industrialized nations in June 1995[6] and has been considered over the past few years by two working groups. The General Assembly has acted, in its resolution 50/227 of 24 May 1996, to reinforce significantly the coordinating role of the Economic and Social Council. Equally important, in the resolution the General Assembly also instructed the Council to undertake further reviews of its functional and regional commissions and its expert groups. The resolution thus set the stage, not only for greater balance in the functioning of the Assembly and the Council, but also for a further streamlining and strengthening of the intergovernmental machinery in the economic and social field. With a view towards the continuing revitalization of the Economic and Social Council, I see three priority requirements: more regular and formalized participation in the work of the Council by the new actors on the global scene; ministerial participation, and increasing involvement of the new actors, in the high-level segment; and a decision to bring the reforms initiated so far in relation to operational activities a step further, so as to enable the Economic and Social Council to exercise an effective role of governance over all the operational funds and programmes of the Organization.

Enhancing the General Assembly and the Economic and Social Council should help to correct the growing imbalance in the functioning, responsibilities and authority of those organs and of the Security Council. At the same time, the new international environment and the marked expansion in the level and scope of Security Council activity call for the reform of its membership, procedure and working methods, towards a more efficient, representative and open body.

The question of Security Council reform is the focus of ongoing debate in the General Assembly through its working group on the matter and other Council-related issues.[7] Member States have welcomed the positive steps taken thus far to improve the flow of information between the Council and the membership at large and to increase the participation of States not members of the Council, especially troop-contributing countries, in Council debates. Progress on the more complex and difficult issue of Security Council membership and voting procedures has been slow. However, the reports of the working group and the remarks made during the Special Commemorative Meeting of the General Assembly, held from 22 to 24 October 1995, reveal an emerging consensus on a number of important points. Most Member States seem to concur that the present size and composition of the Security Council are no longer representative of the general membership of the United Nations or of geopolitical realities. Bearing in mind the need for manageability, most also seem to agree that more effective, equitable and representative participation in the Security Council could be achieved by increasing the overall number of its seats. Once full consensus is reached, the question will ultimately be resolved by the Member States through the processes set out in the Charter, as in 1965 when the membership of the Council was expanded from 11 to 15 by Charter amendment and the minimum number of votes needed for the Council to act was raised from 7 to 9.

The vision and the will required to bring about the changes currently being contemplated concerning the composition, the procedure and the working methods of the Security Council will not be easy to achieve, as balancing capacity to contribute with geopolitical representation will be one of the most difficult obstacles to overcome, but transformation in some form may become essential for the future success of the Council and for the Organization itself. The achievement of those changes would be a major contribution to the realization of a United Nations Organization in which each element plays its full and proper role.

A fundamental part of this effort must be to encourage and facilitate the use of the International Court of Justice. The Charter envisions the Court as an integral component of the peacemaking apparatus of the United Nations as a whole, through its roles in arbitration and the peaceful settlement of disputes. In this regard, the establishment by the Security Council in 1994 of a United Nations Observer Group to monitor, at the request of the parties, the implementation of the Court's judgement in the case concerning the Territorial Dispute (Libyan Arab Jamahiriya/Chad)[8] has created an impressive precedent, which shows much promise for international law and its functioning in an increasingly integrated United Nations system.

All Member States should accept the general jurisdiction of the Court without exception; where domestic constraints prevent this, States should provide a list of the matters they are willing to submit to the Court. The dispute settlement clauses of treaties should permit the exercise of the Court's jurisdiction. The Security Council, under Articles 36 and 37 of the Charter, can recommend that Member States submit disputes to the

International Court of Justice. I have on several occasions urged that the Secretary-General be authorized by the General Assembly, pursuant to Article 96 of the Charter, to turn to the Court for advisory opinions, providing a legal dimension to his diplomatic efforts to resolve disputes. Beyond this, the General Assembly should not hesitate to draw upon that same Article in referring to the Court questions concerning the consistency of resolutions adopted by United Nations bodies with the Charter of the United Nations.

With the International Court of Justice as one of its principal organs, and as the world body of sovereign states, the United Nations provides the forum and the mechanism for the advancement of international law and jurisdiction. This aspect of United Nations endeavours deserves wider recognition and attention from its Member States, not least because international law is another essential aspect of the United Nations architecture which holds enormous potential for democratization at the international level. International law promotes mutual respect among States and peoples, provides a rigorous analytical framework for approaching problems of mutual concern and offers a powerful basis for multilateral action. As such, it is a powerful tool for democratization. At the same time, democratization internationally will strengthen respect for international law. Democratic processes are designed to accommodate diversity. Democratic processes at the international level therefore provide the best way to reconcile the different legal systems of States. With continued democratization internationally, one can contemplate the eventual creation of a common international legal system, not to replace national legal systems, but to serve in certain kinds of cases as a core institution of democratic cooperation within and among states.

The establishment of the International Tribunal for the Law of the Sea and the actions of the Security Council establishing international tribunals on war crimes committed in the former Yugoslavia and in Rwanda are important steps towards the effective rule of law in international affairs. The next step must be the further expansion of international jurisdiction. The General Assembly in 1994 created an *ad hoc* committee to consider the establishment of a permanent international criminal court, based upon a report and draft statute prepared by the International Law Commission.[9] The Assembly has since established a preparatory committee to prepare a draft convention for such a court that could be considered at an international conference of plenipotentiaries.[10] This momentum must not be lost. The establishment of an international criminal court would be a monumental advance, affording, at last, genuine international jurisdictional protection to some of the world's major legal achievements. The benefits would be manifold, enforcing fundamental human rights and through the prospect of enforcing individual criminal responsibility for grave international crimes, deterring their commission.

This area of United Nations activity, promoting democratization internationally, exemplifies the seamless connection between the United Nations' roles in peace-building at the State level and in the maintenance of the international system. As is apparent in the diversity of new actors to be accounted for and in the changes in architecture to be addressed, this task of the United Nations has become increasingly complex in recent years. It amounts to nothing less than managing the construction of a new international system in an increasingly globalized environment, marked by a rapidly expanding array of non-State actors. It amounts to nothing less than peace-building at the international level, in the aftermath of the cold war.

Notes

1   *Editor's Note:* This chapter consists of the key fifth section (reproduced here with the author's permission) of Boutros Boutros-Ghali's *An Agenda for Democratization*, a text published by the United Nations in 1996. The 'Editor's Note' in the original text explains that it 'was presented to the General Assembly by the Secretary-General on 20 December 1996 as a supplement to two previous reports on democratization, and has been circulated as an official document...[as part of the] "Support by the United Nations system of the efforts of Governments to promote and consolidate new or restored democracies"'. (The background to, and the importance of, this text is discussed in Chapter Eight of this volume.)

   An Agenda for Democratization is a publication of some 56 pages, consisting of six sections; but Section V is the most important and takes up nearly half the text. The remaining sections are concerned with relating international democracy to the emerging international consensus in favour of democracy and the role of the United Nations within this.

2   Report of the United Nations Conference on Environment and Development, Rio de Janeiro, 3–14 June 1992, vol. I, Resolutions Adopted by the Conference (United Nations publication, Sales No. E.93.1.8 and corrigendum), resolution I, annex II.

3   Economic and Social Council resolution 1996/31.

4   [General Assembly document] A/51/402, annex.

5   General Assembly resolution 217 A (III).

6   [General Assembly document] A/50/254-S/1995/501, annex I, paragraph 36.

7   Open-ended Working Group on the Question of Equitable Representation on and Increase in the Membership of the Security Council and Other Matters related to the Security Council.

8   International Court of Justice. Reports 1994, page 6.

9   See Official Records of the General Assembly, Forty-ninth Session, Supplement No. 10, (A/49/10), chapter II.B.I.

10 See *ibid.*, Fifty-first Session, Supplement No. 22, Vols I and II. [In fact the statutory charter of a new International Criminal Tribunal was decided at an international meeting in June 1988 – see Chapter Five. Ed.]

8 The United Nations as an agency of global democracy

Daniele Archibugi, Sveva Balduini and Marco Donati

Introduction

In the aftermath of the cold war a considerable number of countries have turned towards democratic political institutions. The so-called 'third wave' of democratization has encompassed all those countries belonging to the former Warsaw Pact, as well as countries like South Africa, Cambodia, Chile, El Salvador, Nicaragua and so on. With due regard to the fact that an increasing number of countries in the world have democratic institutions, it has been argued that democracy is becoming a universally recognized goal for the countries of the world.

However, although the third wave of democratization has allowed an increase in the number of countries ruled according to democratic principles, so far, it has not implied substantial changes in the development of democracy beyond borders. According to the cosmopolitical perspective (see Archibugi and Held 1995; Held 1996; Archibugi, Held and Köhler, 1998), there are at least three separated but interconnected issues that need to be addressed in order to assess the full extent to which democracy can be considered today a successful political model. These are:

1 To what extent can democratic institutions bring about a democratic state, and which exogenous attributes might support a typically endogenous process?
2 To what extent do democratic states apply the principles of democracy in their foreign policy and in their relationship with other states?
3 Taking into account the level of interdependence involved in economic and social globalization, as well as the fact that most political and economic dynamics take place today at a transnational level, is democracy within states and among states sufficient to assure a democratic control of such dynamics? Or should there be not the inclusion of other actors, besides states, in order to have a broader participation in and control over those processes that influence people's everyday life?

First, it is obvious that democratic institutions cannot create democracy by themselves. This is why the only way to achieve democracy stems from an endogenous process which has to be put into place by society. However, the building of a democratic architecture in a particular state, as well as being fostered by democratic dynamics within the relevant society, can benefit from external experiences and from the support (and therefore the legitimacy) that the international community may give to the democracy-building process. This is even more true when democratization takes place in a country recently ravaged by war or internal conflict and where strife, hatred and mistrust can negatively affect the establishment of a democratic society and political regime. In other words, although the development of democracy in a state needs to stem from endogenous forces and dynamics, at a time of increased international interdependence the democratic process cannot rest only on the narrow basis of a state's domestic policy and has to be strengthened by external forces.

Another clear sign of weakness of democracy at the state level is the fact that even those countries commonly considered as being models of democracy seldom implement democratic principles when relating with other countries. Power, rather than democracy, seems to be the dominating principle in interstate relationships, regardless of the political regimes of the states concerned. More generally, it is often unclear what it means to behave democratically beyond borders. While a consolidated body of theoretical literature and historical experience has developed the idea and practice of democracy within states, very little has been done in order to define and apply democracy among states. Considering that the peaceful settlement and resolution of conflicts are among the cornerstones of democracy, it can be argued that conforming international relations to the principles of democracy would considerably strengthen peace and security in the world.

Third, the impact of economic, financial and media globalization has a threefold consequence for democracy. On the one hand, it implies that economic, and consequently political, processes are increasingly abstracted from the policy purview of a single government and that single states are in a difficult position in terms of their control of their economic, social, political, environmental and even cultural development.

On the other hand, the 'porosity' of state boundaries has allowed a broader circulation of information and a higher level of interaction, which – together with the emergence of global problems – has consolidated the role of civil society both at a local level, benefiting also from similar experiences in other countries, and at an international level, creating transnational networks.

By blurring traditional state boundaries, globalization is offering a momentum for an increased interdependence between the domestic and the international level, which in the case of democratization is represented by the role of external guarantor and source of general support that international organizations, especially the United Nations (UN), may play in fostering a democratization process within states – in particular, in those cases where internal tensions and disputes might jeopardize a weak endogenous process of democratization. This is not to say that the United Nations should offer a 'model of democratization or democracy, or to promote democracy in a specific case. Indeed, to do so could be counter-productive. Rather, the United Nations aims to help each state to pursue its own particular path' (Boutros-Ghali 1996: 4).

It emerges clearly that in the era of globalization, and with the ending of the cold war, the issue of democracy has to be understood in a way much more extensive than the traditional narrowly state-based idea of it involves. In order for democracy and for the process of ongoing democratization to develop their full impact on the world's politics and on people's lives it is necessary to consider simultaneously the promotion of democracy within states, among states and at the global level, including other actors besides states, like civil society and international organizations. This is basically the idea underpinning the cosmopolitan democracy model (Archibugi and Held 1995; Held 1995, 1996; Holden 1996; Archibugi, Held and Köhler 1998; Falk 1995; Linklater 1998) which, without dismissing the role that the state plays as the main frame of reference for international politics and economics, also emphasizes the important role that citizens should have in controlling the decision-making processes affecting their lives, both at a national and at a global level. This is to say that democracy within states cannot be truly established if democracy is lacking in interstate relations or if the citizens of the world – represented on the one hand by their democratic governments and on the other hand by civil society – are not fully involved in the democratic management of global problems.

The interdependence among the three 'levels of democracy' has been clearly recognized also by the former Secretary-General of the United Nations, Boutros Boutros-Ghali: '[G]rowing recognition of the practical importance of democracy within states has nevertheless contributed to growing recognition of the practical importance of democracy among states, and generated increased demand for democratization internationally' (1996: 25–6).[1]

Civil society plays a crucial role not only in promoting democracy within a particular country but also at the global level, lobbying on common problems (e.g. environment, health, violations of fundamental human rights, etc.). Supposedly, the more a state is democratic and committed to democracy, the more it will be able to promote and support democratization among states. The more democratic the international community is, the more effective international organizations, and especially the United Nations, can be in enhancing democratic control of global economic and political dynamics as well as being more effectively supportive of endogenous processes of democratization within states.

Summing up, global democracy can be fully achieved only when all of the three levels are affected by the democratization process.

The issue now at stake is this: who can best promote global democracy, tackling simultaneously democracy within states, among states and in the global dimension? It has to be an international actor with the legitimacy and the impartiality that can enable it to engage in states' internal affairs, an actor with the authority to mediate among states and the scope to represent a point of reference for civil society. In other words: it has to be the United Nations.

Things are undoubtedly more complex than this simple statement would make them seem. Nevertheless, as will be illustrated in the following sections, the United Nations has the authority, the means and the opportunity to be a central actor in promoting democratization at all levels. While there are still serious institutional obstacles, to consider reform of the UN to be impossible is politically counterproductive and shows lack of motivation (for a sceptical view on the possibility of UN reform, see Zolo 1997, and his chapter, Chapter Five, in this volume).

To a large extent this is the role envisaged by former Secretary-General Boutros-Ghali for the United Nations in the years ahead. 'From the very first sentence of its preamble, the United Nations Charter suggests, implicitly but strongly, not only the advent of a global, transnational society, but also the need for a collective, democratic project. In other words, the United Nations must act to promote democracy not only within states and among states, but also within the global society in which we will be living' (Boutros-Ghali 1995: 3–4). These same concepts were stressed by Boutros-Ghali on several occasions and, together with the remarks made in *An Agenda for Peace* concerning the crucial importance of democracy in strengthening peace, and the two reports on the 'Support by the United Nations system of the efforts of Governments to promote and consolidate new or restored democracies' in August 1995 and October 1996, they became the backbone of *An Agenda for Democratization*. The latter was the very last contribution of Boutros-Ghali to the UN, since it was published in December 1996 when the new Secretary-General, Kofi Annan, had already been appointed.

An Agenda for Democratization and the cosmopolitan democracy model

When in 1992, at the request of the Security Council, Boutros-Ghali issued *An Agenda for Peace* he underlined the existence of a close link between peace and development and suggested a 'comprehensive approach' to all peace and security problems. Moreover, he underscored the fact that democracy within states enhances the social and political stability necessary for long-lasting peace. Two years later, this time at the request of the General Assembly, the Secretary-General issued a second document, *An*

Agenda for Development, which was strictly correlated with the first and devoted to the complex and 'multidimensional enterprise' of development, and which encompasses a broad set of dimensions of development that go beyond the traditional issue of economic growth. Thus, democracy was included as a crucial asset for development.

In 1996, the trilogy was logically completed with *An Agenda for Democratization*, in which Boutros-Ghali remarked on the inextricable link between peace, development and democratization, and which was intended to provide his own contribution to the debate on the matter and to stimulate a further discussion at the international level.

Enjoyment of stable and long-lasting peace and a certain degree of development are, in the view of the former Secretary-General, preconditions, for any country, for starting a process of democratization or for renewing old democratic institutions. On the other hand, democracy and development within a state system are a warranty of inner peace and of stable and peaceful international relations. Furthermore, though development does not necessarily require a democratic regime, Boutros-Ghali asserts that only democracy can ensure a sustainable development (1996: 53).

These three objectives – peace, development and democratization – are therefore strictly linked and should be pursued by all the states of the international community. Being fully aware of the fact that democracy is still a controversial concept, Boutros-Ghali reminded us that every state must choose its own way to achieve these goals, since there is no one solution valid for all countries and at all times. The former Secretary-General also acknowledged the fact that, while in some situations the joint pursuit of the three goals has proved to be successful (such is the case in El Salvador, Cambodia and Mozambique), in some others this same strategy has turned out to be a failure and has brought about political instability, economic crises and social conflicts. The questions of prioritization and timing must therefore be solved by states individually, because national authorities are in principle the best placed to assess the real political, economic and social conditions of the country. Nevertheless – according to the *Agenda* – the United Nations can play an active role in this process by giving its fundamental support for the achievement of the aforementioned goals.

As far as the specific issue of democratization is concerned, some preliminary remarks are required. The creation of new democracies from authoritarian regimes, or the restoration of old democracies in order to face new challenges, is a long and often tortuous process. The result of this process, which varies according to the different paths followed (for an assessment, see Linz and Stepan 1996; Potter *et al.* 1997), is the establishment of a system of government, generically named 'democracy', which is essentially based on the will of the people. The lack of a unique model of democracy, suitable for all societies and in all times, impels every state to choose its own way of democratizing its institutions. The process must therefore be endogenous and external actors can only support internal forces by providing technical assistance where possible and by contributing to the maintenance of the stability necessary for the democratization process to develop in a favourable context.

Consistently with this view, the former Secretary-General thought that the United Nations could give its positive contribution to the democratization process at three levels: within state systems; among states; and at the global level.

The UN and democracy within states

Within a state system, democratization essentially implies the establishment of 'normative democracy', that is to say a system of government based on ethical and legal rules, respectful of the rights of individuals and minorities, open to political opponents and to a democratic dialogue between all actors. The form, pace and character of democratization must of course be decided by the state itself, the imposition of an external model being contrary to the principle of non-intervention in the internal affairs of a state which is solemnly affirmed by article 2, paragraph 7 of the UN Charter. The United Nations can, nevertheless, offer its assistance and advice to national authorities. In this process of democratization within state systems the United Nations, according to its former Secretary-General, could concentrate on three fields of action: electoral assistance, support in the creation of a local democratic culture, and assistance in building democratic institutions.

Electoral assistance has increasingly become a crucial measure in UN peacekeeping and peace-building missions. Within the UN Department of Political Affairs an Electoral Assistance Division and an Electoral Assistance Information Network have been created with a fundamental contribution by intergovernmental and non-governmental organizations (NGOs) and private associations. Together with traditional methods of intervention, the United Nations has elaborated new approaches not simply limited to the strict monitoring of electoral operations. In some cases (e.g. Cambodia 1993, El Salvador 1994) UN observers have given their support to the organization of fair electoral campaigns by verifying an equal access to media for all political parties and by giving electors the basic instruments for a civic education. In some other cases (e.g. Mozambique 1994), the United Nations has played an active role in the transformation of local revolutionary movements into real political parties (a typology of electoral assistance operations is provided in Koenig-Archibugi 1997; see also UN General Secretariat 1995, 1996).

It is true, nevertheless, that sometimes UN electoral assistance has shown itself to be superficial and ineffective. In those countries where local civil society is weak, and a massive mobilization is neither possible nor allowed, there is no adequate interlocutor and partner for the United Nations' actions. Thus, the simple monitoring of electoral operations may prove useless, if serious violations are committed and no international actor can intervene. This is, somehow, what happened during the general elections in Algeria (June, 1997): UN observers could only certify the regular operation of electoral procedures, but beyond this façade of legality everybody knew that not all political entities were allowed to participate in the competition and that the Parliament was actually deprived of its powers.

The *creation of a democratic culture* in a state with no democratic tradition is a more complex process. UN action aims at promoting respect for fundamental human rights and freedoms; at granting to all subjects an effective participation in the political life of the country; at ensuring free and periodic elections; and at allowing political opponents and minorities to express their views with no conditioning of any kind. When all these principles are systematically violated and state authorities are not aware of the real significance of participation, dialogue and respect for human dignity, the UN system can do very little. Once again, democratization needs an indigenous impetus to be achieved, the role of the United Nations being just one of support and advice (Beetham 1995, 1998).

Assistance in building national democratic institutions is an equally difficult kind of intervention. In this field, according to Boutros-Ghali, the UN must not simply help national governments to create new democratic structures or strengthen the existing ones; it should also act to support the establishment of human rights institutions and adequate legal and juridical systems, the achievement of proper social development, the creation of independent trades unions and the subordination of military forces to the rule of law and respect for human rights. In a word, UN action should pursue, with the essential collaboration of national authorities, the basic aim of good governance of the state.

Electoral assistance, support in the creation of a democratic culture and institution-building all contribute to peace-building missions. Here the UN has the fundamental task of coordinating the activities of all the actors involved in this field, single states as well as groups of states – such as in the case of the Friends of the Secretary-General for Haiti or for Guatemala, which have deployed joint civilian human rights missions – local entities, regional organizations and so on, in order to ensure effective action and to avoid possible duplications.

In Boutros-Ghali's view, valid instruments for peace-building could include, *inter alia*: the organization of periodic international conferences, seminars and workshops to debate world problems and to identify viable solutions; the elaboration of joint activities of UN structures together with local actors, in order to realize common goals; and the definition of specific projects for post-electoral assistance, aimed at verifying the respect for electoral results. All these initiatives, of course, are more likely to be successful in those states lacking proper structures and an institutional organization of their own. But the final result is always dependent upon the degree of collaboration offered by local social and political forces.

The UN *and democracy among states*

Boutros-Ghali argues in favour of the democratization of states also as a means to strengthen international stability and, therefore, peace. He emphasizes that a state with a democratic system of government represents a guarantee of peaceful relations at the international level, while authoritarian regimes are more likely to use intimidation and violence for the solution of all interstate disputes – especially when they need to silence a strong internal opposition – and constitute, therefore, a danger for peace. Democratization within states is, thus, strictly linked to the democratization of relations among all states within the international community. A long-lasting worldwide peace can be achieved, according to the *Agenda*, only through the establishment of stable international democracy; that is to say, a system of relations based on:

- the equal participation of all actors in the life of the community;
- the peaceful resolution of conflicts;
- effective cooperation between all national governments in order to realize common objectives;
- the elimination, or at least the reduction, of the existing gap between developing and developed countries;
- the recognition of the equal rights of all peoples and all individuals;
- a proper division of labour and of burdens among states.

From a practical point of view, democratization at the international level may be achieved – according to Boutros-Ghali – through the creation of an international democratic culture, the reform of the institutional architecture of the United Nations and the involvement of new non-state actors in the activities of the international community. This third aspect, relating rather to the issue of democracy at the global level, will be examined later.

The first area of intervention requires the same kind of actions which are necessary to create democratic culture at the national level and which have already been examined, so do not need further consideration. In fact the crucial issue for the democratization of international relations concerns the reform of the United Nations institutional structure. Since its creation in 1945 the organization has always been the ideal forum for debating international problems and finding proper solutions; its architecture was outlined to reflect the balance of powers existing in the international community in the aftermath of the Second World War. Since then the scenario has radically changed. In order to keep pace with the deep changes which have occurred in the world order, the UN system should therefore be renewed and should achieve, within its own structure, that same democratization that the UN has promoted within states.

There is a widespread consensus on the necessity of a reform of the UN architecture, but different proposals have been submitted for public attention.[2] Boutros-Ghali, in *An Agenda for Democratization*, focuses mainly on the possible strengthening of some existing organs (the General Assembly, the Economic and Social Council, the International Court of Justice) and on the democratization of the Security Council. He does not take into account the possible creation of a new organ directly representing citizens and not governments.

The former Secretary-General begins by reminding us that the General Assembly is the institution where all Member States are represented and which functions on the basis of democratic principles and sovereign equality. This latter argument appears, however, rather weak considering the fact that the criterion 'one state, one vote' does not take into account the different weight of each country in terms of population, territorial extension, resources, income and so on. This same point, that the General Assembly represents governments and not the people, together with the fact that there are still a considerable number of such governments which have not been democratically elected, raises serious questions about the effective democratic legitimacy of the General Assembly. The idea of a People's Assembly (which will be discussed in more depth later in this chapter) has not been taken into consideration by the former Secretary-General.

The reform of the *Security Council* is a somewhat delicate matter, which the former Secretary-General tackles with caution. This issue has long been debated and some steps have already been taken, such as the admittance of non-Council members to the Council's sessions. Nevertheless, there is a strong demand for a major reform, which would modify the present size and composition of the Security Council in order to better represent the new geopolitical reality. Most of the UN Members think that the ideal solution would be to increase the number of Security Council seats, through an amendment to the Charter (as has been done before, in 1965).

Some countries (among which are Germany, Japan and also Italy) ask for a formal recognition of their economic and political power through the attribution of a permanent or semi-permanent seat. Other countries (Brazil, India and Nigeria) lay the same claims on the basis of their geographic and demographic dimensions. *An Agenda for Democratization* supports the idea that the Security Council has to be enlarged in order to reflect the world redistribution of powers.

As far as the modalities of this enlargement are concerned, different solutions can be envisaged: the Council could be constituted of permanent, semi-permanent and elected members; or it could be open to regional organizations; or it could grant a consultative status to non-state entities such as the People's Assembly mentioned earlier. None of these proposals is, however, mentioned by Boutros-Ghali in his *Agenda*. Furthermore, no reference is made in that document to a possible modification of the Council's voting procedure, namely the abolition of the right of veto granted to permanent members – although the power that the five permanent members have to block the Council's resolutions is a legal abuse which has no possible democratic justification and can be considered inconsistent with the principle of equal sovereignty of states affirmed by article 2, paragraph 1 of the UN Charter.

As for the *International Court of Justice*, the *Agenda* underlines its role as arbiter for the peaceful settlement of international disputes and recognizes it as a fundamental instrument for the United Nations' peacekeeping activities. The acceptance of the Court's jurisdiction by all Member States is therefore desirable, in order to achieve an advancement of international law and jurisdiction which could have positive effects also on democratization at the international level. International democracy, in fact, requires the respect of international rules and procedures. The former Secretary-General also envisages, as a possible reform, the empowerment of the Secretary-General with the capacity to ask the Court for advisory opinions in order to give his diplomatic efforts and activities a legal support.

However, these are minor reforms. The crucial concern regarding the role of the International Court should be to make its jurisdiction mandatory. Furthermore, the Court's jurisdiction should also be extended to controversies involving individuals opposed to their governments. If such changes were made to the Court's statute, then this institution really would be applying interstate law and would thereby contribute to the establishment of a new democratic world order. However, any reform implying a modification of the UN Charter needs the approval of all permanent members of the Security Council, and some of these states, the United States above all, are going to be unlikely to support strong supranational institutions, as the case of the permanent International Criminal Court has already shown.

The UN and democracy at the global level

Boutros-Ghali stresses that democratization must not only be achieved within states and among states, but should 'extend to the international arena'. The traditional state borders have been overcome by the phenomena of economic and political interdependence, cooperation among different countries, and an international division of labour and participation in international and supranational organizations. Many problems have acquired a global dimension and therefore need global solutions, as in the case of environmental or sustainable development issues. Governments are no longer able to act individually and need to coordinate their action with other and broader entities; this of course implies a loss of states' traditional sovereignty under the pressure of global forces, reflecting the simple fact that, today, population and territory are not the only variables characterizing sovereignty.

After the end of the cold war and the decline of the bipolar system, states are no longer the only actors in the world community. Even if they remain the 'fundamental building blocks of the international system', they nevertheless have to cope with the emergence of new non-state actors (individuals, civic associations, NGOs) who demand accountability, who claim access to the media and decision-making centres and who insist on representation and participation in national governments and global governance. Democratization at the global level implies the involvement of these actors, at different stages and with different modalities, in existing international structures and mechanisms and particularly in the institutional system of the United Nations.

The new actors that Boutros-Ghali has taken into account in his *Agenda* are: regional organizations, non-governmental organizations, parliamentarians, local authorities, academia, business, industry and the media. In practice, this is an attempt to develop a greater role in the world political community for institutions and actors other than states' governments.

Regional organizations and groups, according to the *Agenda*, could make a fundamental contribution in terms of political, diplomatic, financial, material and military resources, and therefore they are seen by the former Secretary-General as important partners for the UN in support of peacekeeping and development activities. A major involvement of these actors could be obtained through their participation as observers in the General Assembly sessions and through a closer cooperation with UN organs. This would be possible thanks to the flexible provisions of chapter VIII (concerning the UN and regional cooperation) of the Charter, or even through the delegation of some UN tasks at the local level. According to Boutros-Ghali, the involvement of regional organizations in the activities of the United Nations and the establishment of institutional links (for instance by organizing periodic meetings and conferences at UN headquarters with all the delegates of these regional groups) could be crucial for the achievement of true international democratization. However, it is not clear how these organizations, which might not be democratic in their structure or in their scope, would contribute to effective democratization.

NGOs are growing in number and dimension and undoubtedly represent an excellent channel for citizens to participate in the world's affairs. Their legitimacy has therefore been strengthened, and with their activities they have acquired invaluable field experience and a proven capacity to gather information and to mobilize public opinion on sensitive matters, above all in the field of humanitarian emergencies and development.

Such legitimacy has been already partially recognized by the UN and is emphasized by Boutros-Ghali in the *Agenda*. Some NGOs have consultative status with the Economic and Social Council, some others are associated with the UN Department of Public Information. However, it is necessary to strengthen their role in UN structures, for instance by providing for a permanent participation of NGOs and other civil society actors in states' delegations, in order to create a sort of 'civil society forum' (Boutros-Ghali 1996: 36[3]) or by improving NGOs' consultative status with the Economic and Social Council. Furthermore the participation of NGOs at international thematic summits organized by the UN has represented a major opportunity to strengthen the interaction among governments and civil society at the international level (see Segall 1997).

Parliamentarians are seen by Boutros-Ghali as representatives of international public opinion and as a potential link between citizens of states and the community of states. At present they participate in UN members' delegations, they occasionally have informal consultations with the UN Secretariat, and they give their support for the organization of conferences through the Inter-Parliamentary Union (IPU), which has a consultative status with the ECOSOC. According to the *Agenda*, a closer involvement of parliamentarians could require the creation of a United Nations Commission within national parliaments and the establishment of periodic meetings of the IPU, which represents an ideal forum for debate.

There is, however, no mention of the more ambitious project of a People's Assembly (proposed, among others, by Barnaby, 1991, Segall and Lerner, 1992, Archibugi, 1995 and Bienen, Rittberger and Wagner, 1998). The need to encompass the representation of citizens, along with the representation of governments, underscores the need for a substantial reform of the UN system. In its softer version, such reform should provide for the inclusion of representatives of opposition forces and civil society in the existing national delegations to the General Assembly; while in its most radical version it supports the idea of a People's Assembly elected directly by the citizens of the world, on a basis similar to that of the European Parliament. Such a new organ could be established directly by the General Assembly on the basis of article 22 of the UN Charter, which allows the creation of subsidiary institutions for enabling the Assembly to perform its functions. This procedure would avoid the necessity of an approval by the Security Council and would therefore prevent a possible blocking veto.

In the People's Assembly the seats could be distributed according to the population of each state, tempered by other weighting criteria. The representatives would be elected directly by citizens and would therefore be more keen on promoting global policies rather than state-centred ones. To function effectively, the Assembly should be empowered to intervene in states' internal affairs whenever gross violations of human rights or other internationally relevant violations are committed.

Local authorities (mayors or metropolitan officers) are crucial for the solution of global problems – such as unemployment, pollution, overpopulation, poverty, social conflicts, rights of minorities, etc. – which often have a local origin. At present, many local authorities are involved in development projects and in peace and security issues; however, the *Agenda* suggests further initiatives that could be adopted, like the institution of UN resident coordinators establishing a link between the international organization and the local citizens, or the creation of a joint committee of Secretariat entities and representatives of local authorities for a useful exchange of experiences.

Universities, research institutes and public policy centres, in a word 'academia', offer in Boutros-Ghali's view an international platform for discussion and may be a factor in democratization, provided that their role within the UN is strengthened – for instance through the creation of a UN centre for academic meetings.

Business and industry have a huge power in the global economy and are sometimes stronger than single governments. The former Secretary-General supports their major involvement in international decision-making processes, for instance through the extension of the International Labour Organization (ILO) incorporating a tripartite representational structure (governments–employers–workers) as a part of the UN system.

The *Agenda* stresses that the *global communications* revolution has brought about a global wave of democratization, as a free press is both a guarantor of democracy and a factor in further democratization. The UN's information capacity must, therefore, be strengthened in order to focus the attention of the media on particular and delicate international problems. In this perspective, Boutros-Ghali also envisaged the creation of a forum where media could report on their condition to the international community.

To sum up, *An Agenda for Democratization* foresees a wide involvement of various expressions of society, including potentially conflicting forces such as global economic forces and NGOs, but gives few hints on how their involvement could be organized within the UN system. Above all, it provides only generic evidence on the democratization benefits that each could provide. Nevertheless, Boutros-Ghali's exposition represents an important breakthrough in conceiving an international level for world politics which is no longer the monopoly of intergovernmental relations, foreseeing a full involvement of actors constituting a relevant representation of society. Overall, Boutros-Ghali has defined the role of the United Nations in promoting democratization in terms which are very close to, and consistent with, the concept of a cosmopolitan democracy model. The fact that such an important, wide ranging and authoritative document was unfortunately released so late, and when Boutros-Ghali was no longer in his position, constituted the major constraint on its impact.

The United Nations and democratization after Boutros-Ghali

The United Nations that Boutros-Ghali was foreseeing for the twenty-first century, and that he has outlined through his three *Agendas*, was meant to be a strong international actor with considerable autonomy from the traditional fetters that the most powerful states have imposed on the organization. Moreover, the former Secretary-General, even if sometimes underestimating the need to specify which measures the UN should undertake in order to fulfil its new mission, provided a clear and consistent theoretical framework for the future enhancement of global democracy. In doing so, he emphasized the impact that globalization has had on the ability of states to manage global problems and dynamics, thereby declaring the state system as traditionally known to be in a state of serious illness. Such a comprehensive approach to the world's politics and to the future role of the UN could, among other things, only displease those governments – and especially that of the United States – which are still confident in the ability of states to run international politics independently.

The election of the new Secretary-General was very much an outcome of such tensions, and Kofi Annan had to take into account the ambitious and cumbersome inheritance of his predecessor, while acknowledging the fact that the current situation would not have allowed him to carry out a project such as that outlined by Boutros-Ghali. It is not by chance that Boutros-Ghali decided to publish *An Agenda for Democratization* in December 1996, only a few days before Kofi Annan was to take up office. The new Secretary-General's only possible choice was basically to ignore the new document and to tackle the issue of the UN's new tasks on more pragmatic grounds. There was little question that *An Agenda for Peace*, and even *An Agenda for Development*, were fundamental pillars of the UN's strategy. There was also little question that *An Agenda for Democratization* could not receive any attention, as such, by Kofi Annan.

This is not to say that the UN has stopped providing electoral assistance or supporting initiatives required by states willing to move towards democracy, but just that the theoretical framework is much more blurred and that the promotion of democratization is now seen as a by-product of the more general issue of development, or is still linked to the traditional topics of human rights or peacekeeping. Nevertheless, the new Secretary-General committed himself to an overall reform of the United Nations based on the need for streamlining the organization and making it more effective and more responsive to the tasks that the new international environment requires from it. In this sense, the ideological and political project put forward by Annan is far weaker than the one put forward by his predecessor, but as a result is more considerate of states' concerns and might therefore be more appealing to governments.

In July 1997, Annan (1997a) presented to the General Assembly a document entitled *Renewing the United Nations: A Programme for Reform* which sets out clearly some priority areas, among which are:

1   Strengthening the Secretariat by establishing a new leadership and management structure.

2   Assuring financial solvency.
3   Establishing a new management culture, streamlining the organization's system and introducing efficiency measures.
4   Promoting sustained and sustainable development as a central priority of the UN.
5   Improving the organization's ability to deploy peacekeeping and other field operations more rapidly.
6   Strengthening the UN's capacity for post-conflict peace-building missions.
7   Extending human rights activities.
8   Advancing the disarmament agenda.
9   Addressing the need for more fundamental change. This should include a reorganization of the General Assembly's work which, without dispersing its energies, should be focused on major issues with a high priority and aiming at sound results; it is also suggested that there is a need to reform the relationship between the UN and its specialized agencies; and, finally, that the discussion of the role that the UN will need to play in the 21st century should be conducted in a session of the General Assembly specially devoted to it, a *Millennium Assembly*, which could be coupled with a People's Assembly gathering together representatives of civil society.

From this brief overview it appears clear that, while *An Agenda for Peace* and *An Agenda for Development* are widely acknowledged by the reform project set forward by the current Secretary General, the principles of *An Agenda for Democratization* are apparently absent. There is no reference to the United Nations as a promoter of democracy in the world within states, among states and at the global level, and there is no explicit reference to the democratic reform of the United Nations as the main step for enhancing democracy among states.

None the less, the issue of democratization within states is still part of the Secretary-General's concerns, especially with reference to peace-building missions in post-war conditions. It is clearly stressed that, in order to establish 'the foundations of an enduring and just peace...areas of additional activity [for the UN] may include military security, civil law and order, human rights, refugees and displaced persons, elections, local administration...No other institution in the world has the experience, competence, capacity for logistic support, coordinating ability and universality that the United Nations brings to these tasks' (Annan 1997b: 49–50). It appears, therefore, that while Kofi Annan has renounced theorizing the role that the UN should have as a promoter of democracy within states, he is nevertheless maintaining that there is such a function among those that it will have to develop more and more in future years.

There might be no comprehensive design to improve democratization among states; nevertheless, the issue of reforming the Security Council or the Economic and Social Council is still tackled in terms very similar to those used by Boutros-Ghali, with the reference to democratization being the only part missing. Moreover, the project of creating an International Criminal Court – which is supposed to strengthen the role of international law – was realized in July 1998. Even though it might be seen as being too weak to be really effective, it is still a step further in the realization of that legal framework which can enhance global democracy. This may show that it is sometimes easier to induce governments to undertake single steps towards a democratic global order than to commit them to endorsing a general programme promoting such an order.

Conclusions

To sum up, even if the impetus for democratization might have declined under the new Secretary-General, the issue of the UN being a crucial actor for the enhancement of democracy within and among states has nevertheless not disappeared from his agenda. The commitment to democratization is, however, stated in terms of pragmatism rather than of a comprehensive and long-term political project. The crucial question, therefore, concerning the role that the United Nations can play as an agency for democratization is whether a 'low-profile', pragmatic approach to democratization, lacking a consistent theoretical framework, can be effective.

On the one hand, the experience of Boutros-Ghali has shown that too ambitious an approach to the role of the UN in shaping forms of global democracy can hardly find the necessary support from states for it to be implemented. Thus, a pragmatic approach could be more effective in attaining short-term goals and in triggering a process of progressive democratization based on best-practices rather than on a political design. On the other hand, since the enhancement of a culture of democracy is the necessary first step towards democratization at the state level as well as at the international level, it appears likely that the absence of a clear and professed theoretical frame of reference could weaken all possible democratic reforms.

In the end, since the UN is still in essence an intergovernmental organization, in order to fully develop its role as an agency for democratization and overcome governments' reluctance it will need stronger support from global civil society. The apparent paradox is that, in order for the global civil society to strengthen itself, it needs the full support of international organizations such as the United Nations. However, such reciprocity also represents a crucial alliance that will need to develop; at the same time, as a goal it is not that far out of reach, even if perhaps not one to be realized soon.

Notes

1 [See p. 105 in this volume. Ed.]
2 In the first half of the 1990s, in addition to several other contributions, three major studies were published on the reform of the United Nations: Childers with Urquhart (1994); Independent Working Group on the Future of the United Nations (1995); and Commission on Global Governance (1995). See also Stassen (1990), United States Commission (1993), Childs and Cutler (1993), Righter (1995), Russet (1993, 1997, 1998).
3 [See p. 113 in this volume. Ed.]

References

Annan, K. (1997a) *Renewing the United Nations: A Programme for Reform*, New York: United Nations.
——(1997b) *Renewal Amid Transition*, New York: United Nations.
Archibugi, D. (1995) 'From the United Nations to Cosmopolitan Democracy', in Archibugi and Held (eds) (1995).
——(1996) 'Democracy at the United Nations', *Peace Review*, 8, 3: 431–8.
Archibugi, D. and Held, D. (eds) (1995) *Cosmopolitan Democracy. An Agenda for a New World Order*, Cambridge: Polity Press.
Archibugi, D., Held, D. and Köhler, M. (eds) (1998) *Re-imagining Political Community. Studies in Cosmopolitan Democracy*, Cambridge: Polity Press.
Barnaby, F. (ed.) (1991) *Building A More Democratic United Nations*, London: Frank Cass.
Beetham, D. (1995) *Human Rights and Democracy: A Multi-faceted Relationship*, Leeds: University of Leeds.
——(1998) 'Human Rights as a Model for Cosmopolitan Democracy', in Archibugi, Held and Köhler (eds) (1998).
Bienen, D., Rittberger, V. and Wagner, W. (1998) 'Democracy in the United Nations System: Cosmopolitan and Communitarian Principles', in Archibugi, Held and Köhler (eds) (1998).
Boutros-Ghali, B. (1992) *An Agenda for Peace*, New York: United Nations.
——(1994) *An Agenda for Development*, New York: United Nations.
——(1995) 'Democracy: A Newly Recognized Imperative', *Global Governance*, 1: 3–11.
——(1996) *An Agenda for Democratization*, New York: United Nations.
Childers, E. with Urquhart, B. (1994) *Renewing the United Nations*, Uppsala: Dag Hammarskjöld Foundation.
Childs, J. and Cutler, J. (eds) (1993) *Global Visions: Beyond the New World Order*, Boston: South End Press.
Commission on Global Governance (1995) *Our Global Neighbourhood*, Oxford: Oxford University Press.
Falk, R. (1995) *On Humane Governance: Toward a New Global Politics*, University Park, PA: Pennsylvania State University Press; Cambridge: Polity Press.
Held, D. (1995) *Democracy and the Global Order: From the Modern State to Cosmopolitan Governance*, Cambridge: Polity Press.
——(1996) *Models of Democracy*, Cambridge: Polity Press.

——(1997) 'Globalization and Cosmopolitan Democracy', *Peace Review*, vol. 9: 3; 309–15.

Holden, B. (1996) 'Democratic Theory and the Problem of Global Warming', in B. Holden (ed.), *The Ethical Dimensions of Global Change*, Basingstoke: Macmillan; New York: St. Martin's Press.

Independent Working Group on the Future of the United Nations (1995) *The United Nations in its Second Half-Century*, New Haven: Yale University Press.

Koenig-Archibugi, M. (1997) 'International Electoral Assistance', *Peace Review*, 9, 3: 357–64.

Linklater, A. (1998) *The Transformation of Political Community: Ethical Foundations of the Post-Westphalian Era*, Cambridge: Polity Press.

Linz, J. J. and Stepan, A. (1996) *Problems of Democratic Consolidation: Southern Europe, South America and the Post-Communist Europe*, Baltimore: Johns Hopkins University Press.

Potter, D., Goldblatt, D., Kiloh, M. and Lewis, P. (eds) (1997) *Democratization*, Cambridge: Polity Press in association with The Open University.

Righter, R. (1995) *Utopia Lost: The United Nations and World Order*, New York: Twentieth Century Fund Press.

Russet, B. (1993) *Grasping the Democratic Peace*, Princeton: Princeton University Press.

——(1997) 'Ten Balances for Weighing UN Reform Proposals', in B. Russett (ed.), *The Once and Future Security Council*, New York: St. Martin's Press.

——(1998) 'A Neo-Kantian Perspective: Democracy, Interdependence, and International Organizations in Building Security Communities', in E. Adler and M. Barnett (eds), *Security Communities in Comparative and Historical Perspective*, Cambridge: Cambridge University Press.

Segall, J. (1997) 'A First Step for Peaceful Cosmopolitan Democracy', *Peace Review*, 9, 3: 337–44.

Segall, J. and Lerner, H. (eds) (1992) *Camdun-2: The United Nations and a New World Order for Peace and Justice*, London: CAMDUN.

Stassen, H. (1990) *The 1990 Draft Charter Suggested for a Better United Nations Organization*, New York: Glenview Foundation.

Sutterlin, J. (1995) *The United Nations and the Maintenance of International Security: A Challenge to be Met*, London: Praeger.

UN General Secretariat (1995) *Support by the United Nations System of the Efforts of Governments to Promote and Consolidate New or Restored Democracies*, New York: United Nations.

——(1996) *Support by the United Nations System of the Efforts of Governments to Promote and Consolidate New or Restored Democracies*, New York: United Nations.

United States Commission on Improving the Effectiveness of the United Nations (1993) *Defining Purpose: The UN and the Health of Nations*, Washington, DC: US Government Printing Office.

Zolo, D. (1997) *Cosmopolis: Prospects for World Government*, Cambridge: Polity Press.

9 Alternative models for global democracy

Johan Galtung

State/nation-building, democratization and democratic states

Obviously we, humanity, are engaged in a rather ambitious project these days: 'world-building'; and the term used is 'globalization'. We have been through this before, at a lower level of ambition, in processes referred to as state-building and/or nation-building. A distinction should be made between the two. 'State-building' is here conceived of as a process endowing a territory with a certain military, economic and political coherence. 'Nation-building' would be based on the (presumably) sacred nature of (points in) that territory, seen as the motherland/fatherland, and is an effort to endow the people living there with a certain cultural coherence.[1]

Of course the state did not reach into the ultimate niches, nooks and crannies of the steppes, the rain-forests, or whatever, of the country; and of course the nation did not penetrate the deeper crevices of the minds of all the people(s) inhabiting that territory. There has been, and still is, all over the world, resistance, often based on the cultural specificities and identities of non-dominant nations, struggling, violently or non-violently, for economic self-reliance and/or political autonomy in all or parts of the territory. In a world with roughly 200 states, 2,000 nations and only about twenty nation-states, this is to be expected when the nation-state is a model.

State/nation-building generates class, and vice-versa, if we define 'class' in terms of power: in terms of who conditions whom (cultural), who kills whom (military), who exploits whom (economic) and who decides over whom (political).

Take Guatemala as an example: an 'indigenous' majority of Maya descent, to whom the territory is at least as sacred as to the Latino late-comers, with suppressed idioms, killed by the dominant class in cooperation with an outside power, exploited as landless labour, on the receiving end of decisions, to put it mildly. The process has gone on for half a millennium; and the Mayans have resisted all the time.

However, the state has also been endowed with 'sovereignty', meaning that the rulers rule, an obvious homologue to human rights at the individual level. The interstate system is also a highly vertical class system, with a steep gradient between the states that condition, kill, exploit and decide, and those that are on the receiving end. The doctrine of sovereignty does not make the states equal, but has until recently served to preserve an intrastate power monopoly for the domestic ruling class, in that sense making ruling classes equal.

But humankind has also had another project in the last two to three centuries, softening the former: democracy/human rights-building. We are all (well, children are still excluded) endowed with inalienable rights, and one of the rights is to have a share, however small, in the decision-making – to be both sender and receiver. Democracy then establishes a number of rules, according to which the rulers can only rule with the consent of the ruled (in practice that of the 'majority of the ruled'). The human rights tradition goes further, establishing the human body, and the human mind, as private realms over which individuals have sovereignty and are not to be exposed to torture: they have a right to live unmolested with a minimum of basic human needs satisfied and with personal control over their own mental processes.

Fortunately, the democracy/human rights-building project has gone ahead without waiting for the state/nation-building project to be completed.[2] The establishment of the state territory as a single economic market, where factors (resources, labour, capital, technology, management) and products (goods and services) can move freely unencumbered by internal borders, was one such project. These were freedoms to some and repression to others. And of course the 'coherence' was found in the upper classes more than lower down. The introduction of democracy was also a clever effort to solidify coherence by adding consent – protecting the state construction with the argument that 'the majority is always right'. None the less, a great step forward.

Majority-building, then, became a major part of the total process: by changing the composition of the population through conquest (colonialism); by immigration policies (Falklands/Malvinas, Nouvelle Caledonie/Kanaky); by international gerrymandering (Northern Ireland); by killing 'the other side' (Colombia); by buying votes (Southern Italy); by threatening with eternal damnation; by fraudulent numbering and by conditioning people with all the tricks of public relations. And yet: the shift from power by birth to power by number makes non-violent transfer of power possible by rooting power over people in those people themselves. However, there are problems:

1   Democracy *equals* majority rule *equals* 51 per cent dictatorship. The significance for state/nation-building is obvious. But this is where human rights enter as the ultimate guarantee for minorities against majority abuse, like sovereignty in a democratic state-system.

2   Low on choice, low on participation, low on democracy. Choice is a matter of degree, so is participation. If both, or even one, of them is low, so is democracy, making democracy a matter of degree – thereby also unmasking election ritualism.[3]

3   Democracy by debate/vote/majority rule presupposes Western individualism; democracy by dialogue/consensus/common rule would be more compatible with non-Western collective, we-cultures (see Galtung, 1994).

Globalization, democratization and democracy: for whom?

On top of the above three problems comes number four:

4   The sum of state democracies is not necessarily global democracy: the world system is still feudal/hierarchic–anarchic with excess military and political power being held by 'big powers'.[4] If the people concerned with state/nation-building in a number of countries in the Old and the New World, say two centuries or more ago – and with a desire for democracy/human rights – had waited for the first project to be completed (whatever that might mean) before the second project could be embarked upon, then there would not have been many democracies in the world.

Or, rather: the recalcitrant 'minorities' would have been silenced by force rather than by reason, as was done in many places, before the country could be declared safe for democracy. Fortunately the two processes have been on parallel tracks, landing us in a messy reality, but with clearly defined tasks.

But these are not the only two shows in the global village. Since the Second World War they have both been overshadowed by an economic growth project *sans pareil*, not softened, like the state-building project, by civil and political human rights. Economic, social and cultural rights[5] have been, practically speaking, suspended, and the suspension legitimized by the non-ratification of the international covenant by the leading country, the USA. Thus, it passes almost unnoticed that at the global level, under WTO-MAI[6] conditions, only three of the four economic freedoms of the European Union are being practised: the mobility of goods, of services and of capital, but not of labour. Whether goods find customers through world trade more than before is insignificant relative to whether people can find work anywhere, unless we accept very materialistic definitions of globalization.

The moral up till this point is to go ahead with global democratization as the UN/world/humanity[7] has indeed done. There are now around the world numerous intergovernmental organizations (IGOs) where decisions are made by voting, and numerous international people's organizations

(IPOs) – usually referred to as non-governmental organizations (NGOs) – which often have very democratic decision procedures.[8]

More problematic are the transnational corporations,[9] the TNCs, since in these both workers and customers are usually excluded from decision-making. But then it should also be mentioned that, when states vote in the state-system, the citizens are not necessarily consulted either. The feedback to the citizens is mainly through the media, the reporting to the government is slow, and there is little or no feedback to the feedback, except in extreme cases. Low participation means low transparency and low accountability.

Thus there are, as usual, similarities and dissimilarities between the processes at the state and the world levels. A major dissimilarity would be in the definition of 'citizen', if we were to agree that democracy is about participation, including voting, that the participation is limited to the citizens as actors, and that any citizen has rights (such as voting), but also duties (such as paying his dues or taxes). At the state level we have assumed that the citizens are individuals, with ever more categories included. But who are the citizens at the world level?

Obviously there are many potential candidates, and some of them have been mentioned above: states, IGOs, NGOs, TNCs, and above all people. But there are more potential citizens/actors in the world, like the territorial actors incorporated in the states, the local authorities, municipalities. And the 'environment' includes forms of life other than human.

Given their obvious significance for state/nation-building as the major project, until recently, the favoured choice for key world citizens has been states. They even loom so large that many see nothing but states around – a very poor choice given that states tend to be bad world citizens, having character traits reminiscent of their origin in medieval aristocratic castes (Galtung 1994):

- divine self-perception, as wielders of ultimate power (*l'état gendarme*) and ultimate benevolent provider (*l'état providence*)
- a monopoly of violence: 'to he who has a hammer the world looks like a nail'; readiness to fight as self-fulfilling prophecy
- arrogance, as carriers of ultimate power to kill, rule and tax
- expansionism, a general tendency to increase their power
- enemy construction, a general zero-sum orientation possibly deriving from territorial habits: enemies and cheats everywhere
- information monopoly, with secrecy protecting information against internal and external 'enemies of the State', the *Geheimrat* whispering in the ears of the Prince
- closed shops: state officers constituting a *corpus mysticum*, disinclined to listen to lesser humans, as *causa sui*; the chief state officers (CSOs) even being termed 'Excellencies'

- patriarchy, with elements of gerontocracy; typically states are run by older men, usually from the dominant race/nation
- cosmology-driven, enacting – predictably and stereotypically – the deep culture of the (elite layers of the) society[10]
- correspondence: a preference for CSOs whose personalities mirror the deep culture, the cosmology, of the dominant nation
- conventionalism: better to go wrong acting according to conventional wisdom (meaning cosmology) than according to new insights; in the former case the world is wrong, in the latter the actor may be found guilty
- universalism/specificity: action based on intersubjective criteria with much time needed to develop a consensual action basis.

This megalomania-cum-paranoia may become more true for bigger states and their rulers than for smaller states and theirs. They have more to lose. But the logic is built into any state, of any size, and dignified by the term 'sovereignty'.

To base global democracy on states alone is like basing domestic democracy on the nobility alone, which is exactly what was tried for some time. The debate about the organization of the (House of) Lords was permitted to overshadow, for a long time, the much more important debates about the (House of) Lords relative to the (House of) Commons, not to mention whether the common(er)s needed a House at all, or could express themselves directly in referenda or plebiscites. And one special debate was about who was *primus inter pares*, such as those more or less permanently residing with the Sovereign, the King, at the court. This is mentioned here to relativize the debate about that feudal vestige, the veto power of the 'permanent' Security Council members. There are more important discourses.

Capital is basic for the economic growth project, so the next candidate would obviously be the TNCs. But capital logic is not much better than state logic. TNCs are characterized by:

- divine self-perception, partly as creators of wealth and profit, partly as problem-solvers and providers of products and jobs
- money power: 'to he who has money the world looks like a market', equipped with an invisible, obviously divine, hand
- seeking after monopoly, meaning ever-increasing market shares
- arrogance, as carriers of ultimate power to run the market
- expansionism: a general tendency to increase their power
- competitor construction, with market competitors everywhere[11]
- information monopoly, with secrecy protecting information against lesser humans and competitors

- closed circles: executive officers tending to constitute a *corpus mysticum*, disinclined to listen to lesser humans, as *causa sui*, with chief executive officers (CEOs) as dictators
- patriarchy: typically companies are run by men, but not necessarily old and/or of the dominant race/nation
- cosmology-driven, being members of the same society and class.

How did they become that way? To a large extent it was through the reification of the market as something beyond and above individuals, even if to ordinary mortals it looks as if key decisions by key market-players shape the market and its rules. True believers in the market, and they are often on the right wing of the traditional political spectrum, will tend to think that capital is at its best when left to itself, not being held accountable to anybody but the share/stock-holders. And people on the left may also leave capital untouched lest they should dirty their hands. This gives capital considerable action space.

How about the third pillar of modern society: civil society? Whether conceived of as people, or their organizations, in principle we have here the carriers of the democracy/human rights project of protection against the other two pillars. Let us consider an image of people logic:

- human self-perception as fallible, searching for satisfaction of such human needs as survival, well-being, identity and freedom
- object-perception: being perceived as objects of the power of others
- subservience, inclined to obey state and capital
- 'status-quo-ism': at least hold on to what we have and know
- enemy and friend construction, seeing both everywhere
- information monopoly, and sharing, for empowerment
- widening circles, networking for empowerment
- patriarchy, to some extent imitating state and capital
- cosmology-driven, being members of the same society.

People logic, being more open, is more promising – less constrained by one giant institution. But how about local authorities – towns and cities? Let us try an image of motivations, capabilities and possible peace roles:

Motivations

1   Local authorities generally do not possess arms – their possession being state monopoly – and local authorities would be less inclined to see problems as being military and less concerned with 'speaking with one voice'. Many municipalities became nuclear free zones.

2 Municipalities are generally less pathological than states, as they do not serve as depositories of national traumas and myths – such as the idea of being 'chosen' to be above everything else.
3 Towns and cities derive their sustenance from exchange with rural municipalities and with other towns and cities; these exchanges should be preserved and improved. The victims of war, maldevelopment and eco-breakdown are local. The real struggle for peace, including peace with nature, and against structural violence (maldevelopment) also has to be concrete, meaning local.

Capabilities

4 World exchanges are mainly intercity exchanges across borders, and social exchanges are mainly intermunicipal exchanges within borders. Civil society is meaningless without the municipal framework; people meet and interact, within and among municipalities. The phenomenon of town twinning is an excellent and visible example of international civil society.
5 Even many small municipalities are today mirrors of society at large, comprehending both genders, all generations, most classes, often several cultures (religions, languages) and many, if not all, professions. In this they are superior to international people's organizations (NGOs) that tend to be more monochromatic on any one or several of these dimensions.
6 Municipalities have administrations: 'local authorities' are used to handle problems of considerable complexity. That administrative capacity could be enhanced by having a Peace Councillor in charge of municipal peace activities.

Peace roles

7 Before any violence there can be *resolution*: being sites of conferences, seminars and dialogues, municipalities can move diverse nations within and between borders towards more symbiotic relations. Municipal peace and conflict research institutes would be useful.
8 During violence there can be *reconstruction*, using multi-professional teams for assistance and teams cooperating across borders to adopt a municipality in distress; helping displaced persons, political refugees and conscientious objectors.[12]
9 After violence there can be *reconciliation*, bringing conflicting groups together, trying to heal wounds and giving new hope and meaning.
10 Municipalities can act as foci for world politics, helping to bring about a safer world. They can recognize not only other municipalities but

also nations struggling for independence; and they can plan local, non-military defence.

If we should gamble on only one of the candidates for world citizens, then our bet would be local authorities.

Let us then try to organize this characterization of world citizens in a typology for some theorizing (see Table 9.1).

We shall assume that the three terms 'globalization', 'non-territoriality' and 'postmodernity' are close neighbours in a semantic space we do not have to describe in any detail. One simple overarching formula would be 'a borderless world' (with the exception of the lack of mobility for labour); another would be 'fluidity', a third would be 'atomization/fragmentation'. 'Non-territoriality' captures the borderless aspect, 'postmodernity' the fluidity and atomization. The latter is only a part of the story: people disconnect, and old social fabric from the modern and traditional eras disintegrates; but new social tissue is being spun across old borders, for the new global upper class.

But that is also only a partial truth concealing the dissolution of norms and the anomie that is characteristic of the postmodern project with the violence, the corruption, the drug-pushing/consumption, the sect-formation and the nationalism (as the ultimate sect) that follows in its wake.

We are, as humanity always was, at the interface between something old and something new, busily constructing modernity as it is collapsing all around us and yielding to borderless postmodernity with its considerable problems.

But our task here is to identify openings for democracy at this global level. In Table 9.1 there are six types of world citizens: regional state organizations (like the European Union), world ('universal') state organizations like the UNO, states, transnational corporations, local authorities, world people's organizations, and people – most of them still rooted in a territory, others already non-territorial in the sense that how they live is much more important for them than where.

Table 9.1 A typology of world citizens

	Territorial	*Non-territorial*
International community	REGIONAL STATE ORGANIZATIONS	UNO & WORLD STATE ORGANIZATIONS
Pillars of modernity	STATES with State Logic	TN CORPORATIONS with Capital Logic
Pillars of post-modernity	LOCAL AUTHORITIES with Town Logic	WORLD CIVIL SOCIETY with Organization Logic
The sovereign	PEOPLE with People Logic	PEOPLE with People Logic

Daniel Lerner's psychological mobility, in his 1958 classic *The Passing of Traditional Society*, is equally relevant for the present 'passing of modern society'. The latter passing came, probably more quickly than Lerner would have predicted, because of the superiority of video/TV to movies, faxes to telex/cables and e-mail to any other type of mail. But the mechanism is the same: to image oneself, with empathy and ease, somewhere else.

At the core of Table 9.1 are four ways of organizing people: as citizens in a state, as customers of a corporation, as residents in a local community and as members of an organization.

About states, the message is as follows: there is bad news and good news; the bad news is that by and large states are exceptionally bad world citizens, the good news is that they are waning in significance relative to the other five 'citizens'.

About regional state organizations there is also good news and bad news: they may serve to penetrate the sovereignty shell protecting the bad traits of member states, and they may develop those traits themselves, when or if they become super-states. They may start out as organizations, become communities, and end up as unions with federal rather than confederal traits. A super-state has been born, a state, only 'at a higher level'.[13]

About world state organizations, too, there is good news and bad news. The UNO is the major venue for states cooperating on global problems in both senses of that oft-misused term: 'global' in the sense of problems with causal cycles transcending state borders (like pollution) and in the sense of the problems being the same in all states (like improving the livelihood of handicapped people). But the UNO or other state organizations are particularly bad at handling the global problem of accommodating more than one nation within one state (the world average is ten). They reject force as a means of changing borders, but do not offer adequate non-violent alternatives for nations wanting independence.

About corporations, the message is that they are classical in the sense of being pillars of modernity, and yet postmodern in the sense of being non-territorial, fluid and atomizing. Their major concern is survival as corporations; they do not even have the (often) heavy-handed concern of a state for its own citizens. The only language they understand is when people speak money, whereas it is not entirely true that violence is the only language understood by states and those aspiring to state control. No states are total strangers to human rights and democracy, but both are absent from the corporate discourse. They use corruption to lobby the state, rarely listen to the *vox populi* unless forced to do so by a boycott, and do not even listen to their own workers unless forced to do so by a strike. We are dealing with bad world citizens, if we only look at their structurally-given propensities. But this is to disregard the amount of charity lavished on the local, national and world community by benign CEOs (where they are not forced to do so).

About local authorities, the good news is obvious from the above: they are very good world citizens. And the bad news is equally obvious: they are an unused potential, hardly ever mentioned in the literature as serious world-level actors.[14] Why? Probably because they are supposedly one phase behind. Whether their origin was as city-state, as city, town or village, their history has been one of incorporation: the villages into towns, the towns into cities, the cities and the city-states into states. Their role has been to be subservient to the national purpose and the state's will, whether they serve as hosts for state governments, for corporations, or for plain residents. And they tend to take it out on their own hinterland, on the surrounding countryside.

And yet they have the administrative experience in handling all kinds of problems with a minimum of violence, with no more than the city police to draw upon except in special emergencies. They tend to have neither armies to force solutions, nor enough money to buy them. They work through and for people, skilled and unskilled. Their quality of life may vary; if it is low this may be because they have been abused by powers higher up. Being communication centres their cosmopolitanism increasingly covers the whole world.

About people, about civil society: avoid romanticism. Excellent organizations are harboured in such fields as peace and development, the environment and human rights. But there are also rings of drug-dealers, arms-dealers, mafiosi and crime-mongers. Nations are also part of civil society: not all of them are harmless and some of them are very violent. But then it is not always their fault: there are either few or no non-violent alternatives (as pointed out above): they are like prisoners with no court of appeal.

To summarize: we build our world society on about 200 states (with 2,000 nations vying for a state niche of their own) of often very dubious quality, rather than on, say, 2,000,000 local authorities with good inclinations in general, and considerable experience. We leave out highly egoistic corporations, but then we also fail to influence them, and invite them to devote their considerable talents to the purposes of a global democracy. We have probably too romantic a view of civil society, but use the NGOs in policy-forming exercises at the world level, for example, in connection with international conferences and summits organized by the UNO. Regional state organizations have the task of taming states, which is not so easy if the region is lorded over by one hegemonical power (the USA, the former Soviet Union or India). But we are not mindful of the likelihood that the more successful the regional organization, the more likely is the formation of a superstate.

And, above all, we simply leave out people, who are ultimately sovereign, praised in the rhetoric, left out in practice. True, people are mixed, so are their organizations. But we are the best or only people we have, the *demos* in democracy, and that does not change as we move from the local via the state to the world level. If globalization means that decision-making moves to the global level, and democracy is the right to participate in decisions concerning oneself, then only one conclusion is possible: give people the institutionalized right to articulate their concern in such a way that it has a bearing on global decision-making. This means that citizens in country X may make decisions that have a bearing on citizens in country Y. And since that is precisely what globalization is about, decision-making across borders, two-way decision-making must be possible.

Who, then, are the actors in global democracy? Which one of the six world citizens should be the one chosen to articulate the world political will? The only answer we can think of would be all six, every one of them. *Global democracy is interconnected democracy, at the world level.* How to accomplish this institutionally is another matter, and an attempt to deal with that problem will be made in the next section. The concern right here is simply to spell out why it would be a major mistake to gamble on only one actor.

So far the world has gambled on states, i.e. governments. The world is gambling on a loser; there are new actors coming. But Security Council veto power is kept. It is even proposed to add Germany and Japan to the Council, the enemies since the time of the UN's foundation. However, in addition to giving the European Union three vetoes, this discourse is out of touch with reality. Instead, what should be addressed is the inability of states and state organizations to solve issues of statehood as more of the 2,000 nations gain in articulation power.

Then there is another and even more serious problem for states. It is usually taken for granted that what has to be democratized under conditions of globalization is a world state organization, usually the UNO. That should definitely be done. But what if people all over the world turn religious and project their zeal for democratization on the World Council of Churches, asking for a World Parliament of all religions, demanding proportionate representation? In that case an important NGO would become the projection screen for democratic yearnings and zeal. The UN, whose members are states, would recede into oblivion.

There is no unambiguous answer, either to what is going to be democratized, or to who will articulate the political will. Better to leave it open – to all world actors, and all world fora.

The institutionalization of global democracy

Using the United Nations for democratic articulation would require the following:

1   *The abolition of the permanent Security Council members' veto.* Highly recommended for reading here are the accounts of how that veto power was used – to postpone the inevitable (decolonization,

China's entry into the UN, etc.). There are exceptions, but by and large the veto has only served as a brake on history. To the argument that this is the condition for Big Powers being in the UN, a perfectly reasonable answer would be that if having special privileges is the condition for their membership then they do not belong in the key organization of a world heading for global democracy.[15] They would of course be most welcome to come back when they are ready to accept democracy. And the Security Council, like the UN Economic and Social Council (ECOSOC), should be made more representative of all, and not just big, states. In addition to the incompatibility with democracy – i.e. incompatibility with 'one state one vote' – their track record does not justify any privilege. An expanded Security Council would, like the ECOSOC, report to the UN General Assembly (UNGA) which itself would be in a position to pass resolutions in security matters, have special sessions and so on.[16]

2   *The abolition of rich Member States' implicit economic veto.* The membership fees cannot be equal in a very unequal world, but they should not be so unequal that some countries can exercise power by threatening to cripple the institution economically if they withdraw. The right to withdraw belongs to any democratic order,[17] as does the right to join when conditions are fulfilled. But withdrawal of one or a few members should be decoupled from crippling the organization. A membership fee upper limit of 10 per cent of the budget for any one state might be reasonable. And a member not paying dues for a prescribed number of years will of course have its membership suspended.[18]

3   *Greater participation by all Member States.* True, the UN has to balance efficiency with general participation, but in a democratic organization not only decisions but also tasks are shared so as to ensure the participation of all – in the case of the UN this means the participation of governments, delegates and experts from all countries. No doubt technically more competent experts can often be found in one country. However this misses the point: the outcome should be owned by as many Member States as possible by ensuring their participation in all stages of the process. But efficiency and adequacy should also be safeguarded. Not all members have to participate at all levels, but across issues, and over time, they should all be given a chance.

4   *The provision of 'one voice', one vote for the regional state organizations.* It is not unreasonable to give them only one membership if they have as a rule to 'talk with one voice' (the former Soviet Union, the European Union). But some flexibility can be exercised.

5   *Meeting the need for consultation and coordination in the case of the world state organizations.* One important coordinating organ, the Administrative Committee on Coordination, fulfils some of this function for the UN family of organizations. It is a good idea to have a

forum for all IGOs to bear on UN decisions. But this is not what democracy is about. Democracy is not about IGOs influencing IGOs; at that level we need consultation and coordination. Democracy is about 'lower-level' actors, less powerful in terms of coercive and remunerative power (sticks and carrots, military and economic power) having an impact. The ultimate 'lower-level' actor is the individual, all over the world, however humble – perhaps even a pariah – equipped with 'one person, one vote'; democracy is not about additional power for the Brahmin (academics), Kshatriyah (statesmen) or Vaisya (merchants).

6   *Meeting the need for consultation in the case of the transnational corporations.* Given the high correlation in the world between military and economic power, decision-making power within the UN for a body of transnational corporations means additional power to those with 'big bangs and big bucks'. On the other hand it is desirable to give the TNCs the opportunity to articulate their concerns, and to enter into a permanent dialogue about how to work for such major UN goals as peace, development, a clean environment and human rights. This consultative role can be implemented under Article 22 of the UN Charter[19] in the form of a United Nations Corporations Assembly (UNCA), a permanent consultative body.[20] In that dialogue the fine balance between receiving and giving advice and mutual accountability can be drawn. The UN has a right to demand of TNCs a plan for basic needs satisfaction, high employment and a clean environment, to counteract major 'side-effects' of the course of TNC economic cycles. And the TNCs have the right to demand compensation for losses incurred by economic sanctions.

7   *Meeting the need for consultation in the case of International People's Organizations.* The UN has achieved one of the most brilliant strikes for democracy by giving NGOs not only consultative status, but a major role to play in the NGO fora parallel to UN conferences. This is democracy by articulation, not by representation, and could well be imitated by the UN General Assembly and by many parliaments around the world. But there are also NGOs that are more powerful than any state, and in the NGO system the West is over-represented. To give them decision-making power is to double the power of the already powerful. So it would be better to build on the CONGO[21] system that already exists, and give it a higher profile.

8   *Meeting the need for consultation in the case of local authorities.* Practising the principle of subsidiarity, giving the actor at a 'lower level' more weight to compensate for top-down decision-making, should open the doors for local authorities. They are below state governments even if the megalopoleis and metropoleis of the world rank far above many states in significance. As mentioned earlier, they have great potential as peace actors. The Council of Europe has been a

pioneer in the field of cooperation between state and local government; here there is much for the UN to learn. A United Nations Local Authorities Assembly (UNLAA) could relate to the UN in the same way as the UN Corporations Assembly.

9   *Meeting the need for direct decision-making in the world, as in states, in the case of people.* Being the ultimate sovereign, there is no substitute for direct elections to a United Nations People's Assembly (UNPA), which should not be limited to a consultative capacity. In the longer run, world referenda and initiatives will emerge. The UNPA would function like any other parliament, making laws, budgets and appointments. The UNGA would head the executive organ. A parliament would thus be grafted onto the global governance infant that has accumulated experience in two incarnations in this century, the League of Nations and – building on this – the United Nations.

This means adding to the UNGA for governments a Second Assembly, an UNPA, for people; a Third Assembly, an UNCA, for corporations; and a Fourth Assembly, an UNLAA, for local authorities. But only the Second Assembly would have ultimate decision-making power. The Third and the Fourth Assemblies would be there in a consultative capacity, like the Fifth Assembly (CONGO) of NGOs with consultative status. The First Assembly, the UNGA, would only be first in a chronological sense.

This raises questions of conditions for membership of, and interrelationship in decision-making among, these assemblies.

As things stand, applicant states have to be recognized by the current member states to become members of the UN. Admittedly, it is the government of a state that applies, not the people, since governments do not ask their people whether they want to join.[22] The applicant government is then assessed by other governments.

A list of possible criteria for a non-territorial world citizen wanting to be admitted to a UN Assembly might include providing answers to the following questions:[23]

1   Is the organization internationally representative? Does it have members in sufficiently many countries distributed over a sufficient number of continents, preferably also across cultural and political as well as geographical, divides?
2   Is the organization sufficiently democratic? Is the leadership of the organization accountable to its members, and can it be changed through a process of election?
3   Is the organization concerned with basic human needs and rights?[24] Or is the focus on the rather narrow interests of rather special groups?
4   Is the organization capable of reflecting world perspectives, rather than having a perspective which is only regional, or even national? And if so, is this reflected in the power distribution inside the organi-

zation (presidents, executive committees, councils, locations of head-quarters, funding)?

5 Does the organization have a certain permanence? Or is it rather ephemeral, something that easily withers away?

Imagine we now apply such reasonable criteria to states. Point (1) would favour multi-national states, provided the rulers are capable of reflecting that kind of diversity. Point (2) would favour democracies. Point (3) looks for a general human solidarity, as opposed to solidarity with one's own gender, generation, race, class and nation only. Point (4) focuses on world interests, not only on promoting limited state (national) interests. And point (5) favours states with proven permanence, which may also mean proven repression of people and peoples.

Of these five tests, many states would pass only the last one, 'permanence', interpreted as territorial control; with this meaning that neither secession nor revolution are around the corner, and that, if they are, recognition could be withheld. But this criterion is possibly the least meaningful for non-territorial actors, undergoing fission and fusion, coming in and out of existence all the time, operating as they are in an unlimited functional space, not constrained by the finiteness of world territory.

In choosing criteria such as the five mentioned, we would in fact be judging non-territorial actors more severely than we judge states. But then, why not? Why should the criteria remain constant? To demand of an NGO president or secretary-general that he has the members fully 'under control', with no minorities seceding or revolting, would certainly undermine the marvellous flexibility of non-territorial actors.

Would these criteria also apply to the transnational corporations? A TNC is often internationally representative and relatively permanent, but far from democratic. Maybe it should be democratic? And maybe production for basic human needs, and for world perspectives beyond size of assets and turnover, should have priority – including employing as many, rather than as few, people as possible?

Delegates to the UNGA will continue to be selected by governments, but to the UNPA, the UNCA and the UNLAA they should, ideally, be democratically elected.[25] Imagine, then, that we have all assemblies well constituted; how would they relate to each other? To answer that, a comparison with another interstate organization at a higher level of integration, the European Union, may be appropriate.

Using the modern polity as a model, with the usual division of state power into executive, legislature and judiciary, then the UNGA (corresponding to the EU Council of Ministers) is one executive, exercising (soft) governance, and another – albeit in very embryonic form – is the Administrative Committee on Coordination, bringing together the heads of the specialized agencies (corresponding to the European Commission). The legislature, in even less than embryonic form, would be the UNPA, to which both the UNGA and the Specialized Agencies would be accountable. The International Court of Justice would play the role of the judiciary. This is what parliamentary democracy as we know it is about, and something like this is bound to come about, sooner or later. We had better start preparing.

The European Union has two executive heads: the rotating presidency of the Council of Ministers, and the chairperson of the European Commission, corresponding to the territorial and functional tracks. Should this inspire a similar construction at the world level, with one Secretary General for the Member States and one (Deputy) Secretary General for the Specialized Agencies? Or would it be better to continue as today, with one executive head for both, even if the task is superhuman?

The totality would not be that complicated. There would be the UNPA, gradually rising in power relative to the UNGA, taking on more and more functions and decisions; and in addition there would be three consultative organs, for the corporations, the local authorities and the non-governmental organizations (UNCA, UNLAA and CONGO). In return for having consultative status comes accountability: if you are given tasks under a contract, then you also have to make yourself accountable and transparent.

More problematic is how the People's Assembly should be constituted. As mentioned before, some people are more territorially rooted than others, but it seems fair to have the same kind of constituencies or vote catchment areas for all. Practically speaking, everybody is a citizen somewhere, and very many people are even registered somewhere as voters. Voting for a UN representative could be as easily attached to a statewide vote as could a local vote. The general formula might be that each state should have the right to one representative per million inhabitants, the minimum number of representatives being one. An interesting problem would be whether states that are not members should nevertheless have a right to send representatives to the UNPA, making it a true World Assembly.

At present this would give us about 6,000 representatives – somewhat unwieldy but not impossible. The condition for sending an elected delegation would be that the delegation had been truly elected, not selected, by free and secret ballot. Ideally any election should be preceded by a debate on key global issues, and the choice would be between candidates, or between global parties as they emerge (and they will).

The representatives would also be absorbed in committees working between the sessions, which might be during the summer before the UNGA is convened (the third Tuesday in September), using the UNGA agenda and any item they might like to add.[26]

It stands to reason that there will be a limit to what a majority can decide, just as in the case of domestic democracy. Sovereignty shields will blunt the impact of majority decision-making; no doubt they are shields that will gradually be pierced, but never break down completely – like human rights protecting individuals.

Democratization in general

In conclusion, I have only some words about the obvious: the UN is not the only organization to carry the burden of global democratization, but today it is the most important one. The project known as state democratization has been going on for some centuries now. The states have probably been overtaken by such non-states as international people's organizations in their level of democratization. Some NGOs, like some states, have been the products of innovative risk-taking by strong personalities; but even if the role of such personalities should be recognized, their hold on an organization must be time-limited. Local government is probably not much more or less democratic than state government.

Lagging behind are the corporations, organized as private fiefs of strong CEOs, hiring and firing and accountable only to the bottom line. Corporate democracy, and consultative dialogues with consumer organizations, might at first look like tying the hands of the CEOs; but a second glance may reveal new business opportunities. The world cannot in the longer run tolerate major pockets of authoritarian rule in its midst. Where people are affected by decisions they have a right to co-decide.

States beware: as other key actors (NGOs, TNCs, LAs) catch the linkage between globalization and democracy while states fail to do so, and the state system overdoes Westphalian sovereignty (350 years are enough!), these other systems may overtake and pass the state system as carriers of the popular will. Being expressions of an ethos of non-territoriality and fluidity, one of them may one day even overtake and pass the UNGA and relate better to the UNPA than the old state system articulated in the UNGA. If so, then early UN democratization becomes even more significant.

Notes

1 'Country' is used to refer to a, usually contiguous, territory; a 'state' is a particular way of organizing a country, and a 'nation' is a group of people with shared ideas of sacred time and sacred places (whether in addition they speak the same language and hold the same religious beliefs is secondary). Unfortunately, an academic discipline focusing on interstate relations is referred to as 'international relations', although it hardly ever deals with international relations. And the UN, with its Member States, is called the 'United Nations', where 'United States' would have been the more correct term. This is expressed in Boutros-Ghali's chapter by the way he often writes 'international' while the social scientist in him knows very well that it is not international at all.

2 Thus, some chapters in Part I of this book can give the impression that the amount of globalization is insufficient to warrant any special measures. In fact the interconnectedness is overwhelming and it may be much more a matter of

communication than economic interaction. If democracy is the right of co-decision in decisions affecting oneself, the case has already been made.

3 This is the idea underlying the interesting 'Index of Democratization' developed by Tatu Vanhanen (1984). The index is a product of the percentage not voting for the largest party or candidate (the level of competition) and the percentage of the total population which actually voted. Among the top ten in the period 1970–79 were the Scandinavian countries, some other Western European countries, and Australia. The UK was number 11, the USA number 22, Sri Lanka number 23 and India number 24. From there on down there are only Third World and 'socialist' countries, the bottom fifty, down to number 119, having no or very low competition. Obviously democracy becomes increasingly vacuous, with participation below 50 per cent meaning that the majority finds the process insufficiently meaningful. They may register their car, but not their vote; go through anything to get a driver's licence, but not to vote.

Competition is more problematic. In 'choice' we might like to include a number of factors, all of them problematic, like the number of parties/candidates, the political spectrum they cover and the distribution of votes. But the basic point is the idea of a degree of democracy; and a notion of ritualism which includes a poor choice in quantity and quality, and low participation.

4 According to Freedom House (1995–6) 118 of 190 countries (62 per cent) in the world are listed as democracies (the percentages vary from 100 per cent in Western Europe to 34 per cent in Africa). However, the Big Powers still overwhelmingly dominate the arms trade, define more or less residual spheres of interest, and intervene and veto.

5 The International Covenant on Economic, Social and Cultural Rights of 16 December 1966.

6 World Trade Organization, Multilateral Agreement on Investment.

7 Boutros Boutros-Ghali's excellent *An Agenda for Democratization* (1996), a key chapter of which is reprinted in this volume as Chapter Seven, makes the pioneering role of the United Nations in a pragmatic and often very low-key way, very clear.

8 As mentioned by Boutros-Ghali, their numbers have grown from 1,300 in 1960 to 36,000 in 1995.

9 As mentioned by Boutros-Ghali, there are now about 40,000 of these, with 25,000 affiliates, around the world.

10 See Part IV in Galtung (1996) on civilization theory.

11 This corresponds to 'enemy construction' in the case of states.

12 There is an organization doing exactly that, *Gemeinde-gemeinsam, Causes communes* (Municipalities together).

13 We are, of course, thinking of the fifty years of history leading up to the European Union.

14 But see the very positive comments made by Boutros-Ghali in Chapter Seven, pp. 114–15, of this volume.

15 They may then start their own organization and veto each other as much as they want.

16 Concretely this means that Article 12 of the UN Charter will have to be changed, since it is designed to protect the big powers by making it impossible for the UNGA to pass resolutions on matters considered by the Security Council.

17 Like the right not to vote. When that right is used by a sufficient number it constitutes an important, nonviolent, protest, and becomes an important part of the democratic repertoire. The same principle applies to any organization, including states. The USA, the UK and Singapore probably hoped to have that effect when they withdrew from the UN Educational, Scientific, and Cultural

Organization, but they were too few and their arguments too obviously self-centred.

18 Obviously, the United States cannot both struggle to reduce the UN budget and keep the high assessment of 25 per cent and on top of that not even pay. To be able to survive as a member with that record, much informal power is needed.

19 Article 22: 'The General Assembly may establish such subsidiary organs as it deems necessary for the performance of its functions.'

20 Another possibility, hinted at by Boutros-Ghali, is to build on the tripartite structure of the International Labour Organization, which is built on governments, employers' organizations and employees' organizations. At any rate, the ways and means must be found whereby the most dynamic sector of our global reality is brought into the most representative decision-making organization.

21 Conference of Non-Governmental Organizations in Consultative Status with the Economic and Social Council, under Article 71 (Chapter VIII) of the UN Charter. This covers some 1,600 NGOs in addition to the many affiliated with other organs of the UN, including the specialized agencies.

22 In Switzerland the people were asked if they wanted UN membership in March 1986, and the answer was no. And so far (1999) only three governments of the fifteen presumably democratic member states of the European Union (Denmark, France and Ireland) have had a referendum over something so fundamental as the Maastricht Treaty.

23 From Galtung (forthcoming).

24 This would certainly include the third generation of human rights, adding the collective rights to peace, development and a clean environment to the right of self-determination. See the last chapter of Galtung (1994).

25 In practice a transition period of ten to twenty years may be in order, with a governmental pledge to work for a system of election rather than selection, or appointment, of delegates.

26 The proposal by Boutros-Ghali, 'urging the Inter-Parliamentary Union to convene every three years at a United Nations location in order to foster international dialogue and debate on the United Nations and issues before the United Nations and its Member States' would be an excellent beginning.

It is worth remembering that the European Parliament had an initial stage based on state parliamentarians before direct elections were introduced.

References

Boutros-Ghali, B. (1996) *An Agenda for Democratization*, New York: United Nations.

Freedom House (1995–6) *Freedom in the World*, New York: Freedom House.

Galtung, J. (1994) *Human Rights in Another Key*, Cambridge: Polity Press.

——(1996) *Peace by Peaceful Means*, London, New Delhi, Thousand Oaks: Sage.

——(forthcoming) *United Nations, United Peoples*.

Lerner, D. (1958) *The Passing of Traditional Society*, Glencoe, Il.: The Free Press.

Vanhanen, T. (1984) 'Index No. 43', in G. T. Kurian, *The New Book of World Rankings*, New York: Facts on File.

10 Global civil society and the democratic prospect[1]

Richard Falk

Note on terminology

The emphasis of this chapter is upon social forces that respond to the patterns of behaviour associated with the phenomena of economic globalization. As a consequence, it seems preferable on balance to frame such activity by reference to 'global civil society' rather than to 'transnational civil society'. Even so the word 'society' is definitely problematic at this stage of global social and political evolution, due to absence of boundaries and weakness of social bonds transcending nation, race and gender. Such a difficulty exists whether the reference is to 'transnational civil society' or to 'global civil society'. But the transnational referent tends to root the identity of the actors in the subsoil of national consciousness to an extent that neglects the degree to which the orientation is not primarily one of crossing borders, but of inhabiting and constructing a polity appropriate for the global village. Such a nascent global polity is already partly extant, yet remains mostly emergent. (For helpful discussion of these issues of conceptual framing, see Wapner 1996.)

A similar issue arises with respect to the terminology useful in aggregating the actors. It seems convenient to retain the term non-governmental organizations (NGOs) to designate those actors associated with global civil society because it is accurate and widely used, and thus easily recognizable. But it is also somewhat misleading in relation to the fundamental hypothesis of a diminishing ordering capability by the sovereign state and states system. To contrast the actors and action of global civil society with the governments of states, as is done by calling them NGOs, is to confer a derivative status and to imply the persistence of a superordinate Westphalian world of sovereign states as the only effective constituents of contemporary world order. Until recently this hierarchical dualism was justifiable because the pre-eminence of the state was an empirical reality, reinforced by the absence of any other significant international actors capable of autonomous action.

To overcome this difficulty of relying upon this somewhat anachronistic statist rhetoric, James Rosenau has proposed an alternative terminology to that of NGOs by calling such entities 'sovereignty free actors' (Rosenau, 1990). Besides being obscure, such a substitute terminology is still operating in a Westphalian shadowland in which actor identities are exclusively derived from sovereign actors, namely, states. A comparable problem exists if the reference is to 'transnational social forces', although the sense of 'transnational' is more flexible and autonomous than 'sovereignty free'. Another possibility was proposed some years ago by Marc Nerfin (1986), in the form of a framework that recognized the social reality of 'the third system' (the first system being that of states, the second of market forces), from which issued forth civil initiatives of motivated citizens supportive of the global public good. Perhaps the most helpful terminology would be to designate such actors as civil society associations.

There is by now a wide and growing literature on 'global civil society', especially as related to environmental politics on a global level (for a concise overview see Wapner 1996; also Lipschutz 1996). For the purposes of this chapter, 'global civil society' refers to the field of action and thought occupied by individual and collective citizen initiatives of a voluntary, non-profit character both within states and transnationally. These initiatives proceed from a global orientation and are responses, in part at least, to certain globalizing tendencies that are perceived to be partially or totally adverse. At present, most of the global provocation is associated directly or indirectly with market forces and the discipline of regional and global capital. As will be made clear, such a critical stance towards economic globalization does not entail an overall repudiation of these developments, but it does seek to identify and regulate adverse effects and correct social injustices.

To focus inquiry further, I also propose to rely upon a distinction that I have used previously: drawing a basic dividing-line between global market forces identified as 'globalization-from-above' and a set of oppositional responses in the transnational sphere of social activism that is identified as 'globalization-from-below' (Falk, 1993, 1995). This distinction may seem unduly polarizing and hierarchical, apparently constructing a dualistic world of good and evil. My intention is neither hierarchical nor moralistic, and there is no illusion that the social forces emanating from civil society are inherently benevolent, while viewing states, corporations and banks as necessarily malevolent. Far from it. One of the arguments of the chapter is that there are dangerous chauvinistic and extremist societal energies being released by one series of responses to globalization-from-above that are threatening to undermine many of the achievements of the modern secular world, including the gradual progress of an anarchic society of states in the cumulative direction of humane governance. (This normative potential of statism has been most influentially articulated by Hedley Bull, 1977.) To situate the argument, it is important to realize that there are strong positive effects and potentialities arising from the various aspects of globalization-from-above. At the same time, the historic role of globalization-from-below is to challenge and transform the negative features of globalization-from-above, both by providing alternative ideological and political space to that currently occupied by market-oriented and statist outlooks and by offering resistances to the excesses and distortions that can be properly attributed to economic and cultural globalization in its current phase. That is, globalization-from-below is not dogmatically opposed to globalization-from-above, but addresses itself to the avoidance of adverse effects and to providing an overall counterweight to the unhealthy predominance of influence currently exerted by business and finance on the process of decision at the level of the state and beyond.

Deforming historical circumstances

The distinctive challenges posed by globalization-from-above have been accentuated by certain defining historical circumstances. Above all, the ending of the cold war generated an ideological atmosphere in the North supportive of an abandonment of Keynesian and welfare approaches to economic policy, and their replacement by a strong version of neo-liberal reliance on private sector autonomy and an economistic approach to social policy – that is, eroding the social compromises between labour and business by way of achieving fiscal austerity, efficient allocation of resources, privatization, and international competitiveness. There were other pressures to move in these directions, including a pendulum swing in societal attitudes against 'the welfare state' in many states, a generalized distrust of government and public sector approaches to problem-solving, the steadily declining political leverage of organized labour, the waning of industrialism and the waxing of electronics and informatics, an overall disenchantment with ameliorative rhetoric and proposals, and, above all, pressures to neutralize the alleged competitive advantages of countries in the South, especially those in the Asia/Pacific region.

These alleged competitive advantages are associated with the political and economic unevenness of states, and refer especially to cheap skilled labour, minimal regulation and high profit margins that have been supposedly draining jobs and capital away from the North. These differentials have ethically ambiguous consequences, reinforcing neo-liberal rationalizations for harsher economic policy and contributing to chauvinistic backlash politics in the North, while liberating many of the most populous countries in the South from centuries of acute poverty and massive human suffering.

In effect, the material and technological foundation of globalization, based on the possibilities for profitable expansion of business operations and investment opportunities without regard to state boundaries, did not necessarily have to be linked to an ideological abandonment of the social agenda, and downsizing pressures on public goods, including a disturbing decline in support for mechanisms to protect the global commons and the global public good. Neo-liberal approaches and ideological justifications have been latent in market economies ever since the birth of capitalism during the Industrial Revolution, but somewhat surprisingly the nastiest features of early capitalism were moderated to varying degrees in the nineteenth and twentieth centuries in response to the rise of 'the dangerous classes', the labour movement, the ordeal of business cycles culminating in The Great Depression, and the adjustments promoted by different versions of 'social democracy', and what came to be known in the United States as 'liberalism'.

Indeed, the recent change in ideological atmosphere can be rapidly understood by the delegitimation of liberalism in the United States since the 1980s, making even those political perspectives of the most socially sensitive leaders in the Democratic Party unwilling any longer to use or be identified with liberalism. Liberalism fell into such disrepute that it was treated as almost obscene, being referred to as 'the L word'. What has emerged in this first stage of globalization after the end of the cold war is a neo-liberal consensus among political elites in the world, powerfully disseminated by a business-oriented and consumerist global media, a power shift that helps explain the economistic orientation of most governments. (For a more historically grounded view of globalization, see Clark 1997.) In the North, this consensus tends to be justified by reference to the discipline of global capital, or simply by reference to 'competitiveness', the struggle for market shares, the virtues of free trade, and the need to minimize production costs so as to participate successfully in the global economy. Such an ideological setting is often misleadingly merged with globalization to make the one indistinguishable from the other.

The evolving perspective of those social forces associated with globalization-from-below is that it remains possible and essential to promote the social agenda while retaining most of the benefits of globalization-from-above (Hirst and Thompson 1996: 1–17, 170–94). In effect, globalization can be enacted in a variety of governance and fiscal scenarios, including some that are people-oriented and supportive of global public goods and the goals of the social agenda. The ideological infrastructure of globalization is contingent rather than structural, and its reformulation is at the core of the convergent perspectives implied by the emergence of global civil society as the bearer of alternative visions of a more sustainable, compassionate and democratic future world order (Falk 1995). Often this normative convergence is concealed beneath the more particularized banners of human rights, environmental protection, feminism and social justice that have been unfurled within global civil society by issue-oriented social movements that have been transnationally active during the last few decades.

It is also important to acknowledge the limited undertaking of globalization-from-below. It is not able to challenge globalization as such, but only to alter the guiding ideas that are shaping its enactment.

Globalization is too widely accepted and embedded to be reversible in its essential integrative impact. Recent global trends establish the unchallenge-able dominance of markets and their integration. In Jeffrey Sachs's words, ' ... capitalism has now spread to nearly 90% of the world's population, since nearly all parts of the world are now linked through open trade, convertible currencies, flows of foreign investment, and political commit-ments to private ownership as the engine of economic growth' (Sachs 1997: 11). Sachs points out that only twenty years earlier such conditions pertained to only 20 per cent of the world's population, the rest of humanity being subjected either to command socialist economies or to clumsy Third-World efforts to combine capitalism and socialism. Such a shift in so short a time, of course, inevitably produces a fundamental reshaping of the ideas and practices constitutive of world order.

It is this process of economic restructuring according to the logic of markets that establishes the context for globalization-from-below. The strategic question is, how can these forces effectively challenge the uneven adverse effects of globalization-from-above as it is currently evolving? These adverse consequences include insufficient attention to environmental protection and resource conservation, and failures to offset severe vulnera-bilities of certain social segments, countries, and regions that are not currently able to gain sufficient access to the market or to take sufficient advantage of technological innovations. There exists a generalized lack of support for financing the social agenda and global public goods, including the United Nations, especially with respect to its efforts to coordinate and promote moves to overcome world poverty, create jobs and close the gaps that separate rich from poor.

Responding to economic globalization

There have been varied failed responses to economic globalization, conceived of as the capitalist portion of the world economy. Without entering into an assessment of these failures, it is worth noticing that both Soviet-style socialism and Maoism, especially during the period of the Cultural Revolution, were dramatic efforts to reject economic globaliza-tion that ended in disaster. By contrast, despite the difficulties, the subsequent embrace of the market by China under the rubric of 'modern-ization' and even by Russia (and the former members of the Soviet empire) in the form of the capitalist path, has been by comparison spectacularly successful, although the world economic crisis that started in Asia during 1997 has cast a long shadow, at least temporarily. The same is true for many Third World countries that had previously forged a middle path between socialism and capitalism that made the state a major player in their economy, particularly with respect to public utilities and energy. For most of these countries, as well, the change from a defensive hostility towards the world market to a position of almost unconditional receptivity has been generally treated as favourable, or as an adjustment to the new reality.

The learning experience at the level of the state has been one of submission to the discipline of global capital as it pertains to the specific conditions of each country. Once-fashionable ideas of 'delinking' and 'self-reliance' are in a shambles, perhaps most easily appreciated by the inability of North Korea to feed its population while its capitalist sibling in South Korea was scaling the peaks of affluence, at least until it ran aground temporarily in the turmoil of the last two years. In effect, the geopolitical managers of the world economy now use these policies of global market avoidance as a punishment for supposedly deviant states, seeking to legitimize their exclusion under the rubric of 'sanctions', a policy often widely criticized in this period because of its cruel effects on the civilian population of the target society. Even Castro's Cuba, for so long an impressive holdout, is relying on standard capitalist approaches to attract foreign investment and open its economy to market forces. Fukuyama's notorious polemic about the end of history is partially correct, at least for now, if understood as limited in its application to current economic aspects of policy, and not extended to political life (Fukuyama, 1992). But the deeper contention that neo-liberalism is the ultimate idea with respect to political economy seems self-serving and naive at the same time.

Another direction of response to economic globalization has been negative in the form of backlash politics that either looks at some pre-modern traditional framework as viable and virtuous (as is the case with religious extremists of varying identity, or with indigenous peoples) or is ultra-territorialist, seeking to keep capital at home and to exclude foreigners to the extent that this is possible. These responses, aside from those of indigenous peoples, have a rightist flavour because of their emphasis on the sacred religious or nationalist community of the saved that is at war with the evil 'other', being either secularist or outsider. To the extent that such movements have gained control of the state, as in Iran since the Islamic Revolution, or even threatened to do so, as in Algeria since 1992, the results have been dismal – economic deterioration, political repression and widespread civil strife. Specific causes of these backlash phenomena are related to the failures of globalization, and its associated secularist outlook, but the correctives proposed have yet to exhibit a capacity to generate an alternative that is either capable of successful economic performance or able to win genuine democratic consent from relevant political communities.

Related to this predominance of market forces is a series of attempts by civil society to avoid the adverse effects of economic globalization. The most effective of these responses have been issue-oriented, often involving local campaigns against a specific project. One notable attempt to enter the domain of transformative politics more generally was made by the Green parties in Europe during the 1980s. This green movement often exhibited tactical brilliance in its moves to expose the deficiencies of globalizing trends, especially their dangers to the environment. Its political success was less its ability to mobilize large numbers in support of its causes and programmes, than the extent to which its challenge influenced the whole centre of the political spectrum to put the environmental challenge high on its policy agenda. But the green movement's attempt to generalize its identity to provide an alternative leadership for the entire society across the full range of governance, or to transnationalize its activities to promote global reform, met with frustration and internal controversy that fractured green unity, most vividly in Germany, but elsewhere as well. Those that argued for a new radicalism beyond established political parties, within a green framework, were dismissed as utopian dreamers, while those who opted for influence within the existing framework were often scorned as victims of cooptation or derided as opportunists. The green movement, and its political parties, has persisted in the 1990s, but often only as a voice on the margins without either a credible alternative worldview to that provided by globalization or a sufficiently loyal constituency to pose a threat to the mainstream. Contrary to this overall trend, the German Greens are now in uneasy coalition with the governing Social Democrats as of 1998.

Localism has been another type of response directed at the siting of a nuclear power reactor or dam, mobilizing residents of the area facing displacement and loss of traditional livelihood, and sometimes involving others from the society and beyond, who identify with the poor or with nature. These struggles have had some notable successes (Shiva 1987; Rich 1994). But these are reactions to symptomatic disorders associated with globalization, and do little more than influence entrepreneurial forces to be more prudent or to make a more concerted public relations effort.

More relevant have been attempts by elements of global civil society to protect the global commons against the more predatory dimensions of globalization. Here Greenpeace has a distinguished record of activist successes, exhibiting an imaginative and courageous willingness to challenge entrenched military and commercial forces by direct action that has had an impact: helping to discourage and discredit whaling, protesting against the effort of Shell Oil to dispose of the oil rig Brent Spar in the North Sea, supporting a fifty-year moratorium on mineral development in Antarctica and, most memorably, resisting for many years nuclear testing in the Pacific. Rachel Carson's lyrical environmentalism and Jacques Cousteau's extraordinarily intense dedication to saving the oceans suggest the extent to which even single, gifted, individuals can exert powerful countertendencies to the most destructive sides of an insufficiently regulated market. But these efforts, although plugging some of the holes in the dikes, are not based on either a coherent critique or alternative ideology, and thus operate only at the level of the symptom, while neglecting the disorders embedded in the dynamics of globalization.

Some other efforts to awaken responses have arisen from global civil society on the basis of a more generalized assessment. One of the earliest such initiatives was that promoted by the Club of Rome, a transnational association of individuals prominent in business, science and society, that led to the famous study *The Limits to Growth* (Meadows *et al.* 1972). The argument, tied closely to a sophisticated computer program that was measuring trends in population growth, pollution, resource scarcity and food supply, concluded that industrialism as it was being practised was not sustainable, but was tending towards imminent catastrophe. Around the same time a group of distinguished scientists from various countries working with the British journal, *The Ecologist,* issued their own warning call under the title *A Blueprint for Survival* (Goldsmith 1972). These alarms provoked a debate and led to some adjustments, but the resilience of the world capitalist system was such that no fundamental changes occurred, and the warnings issued as signals soon faded into the cultural noise. Neither a sense of alternative nor a movement of protest and opposition took hold, although environmental activism did emerge to weaken the cult of growth.

The World Order Models Project (WOMP) is illustrative of a somewhat more radical effort to challenge the existing order, and find alternatives, through the medium of diagnosis and prescription by a transnational group of independent academicians. The efforts of this group have been confined to the margins of academic reflection on world conditions. Also, until recently, the policy focus and animating preoccupation of WOMP was centred on war, being broadened somewhat later to include environmental danger. Although WOMP did produce overall assessments, its background and participants made it less sensitive to the changing role of the world economy, including the distinctive challenges and contributions of economic globalization (Falk 1995, 1996, 1997a). As such, its emphasis on war and the war-making sovereign state did not come to terms with either the durability of the state or the need to avoid its instrumentalization by global market forces. That is, the principal danger to world order is no longer the absolute security claims of the sovereign state, but rather the inability of the state to protect its own citizenry, especially those who are most vulnerable, in relation to the workings of the world economy, or to mount a sufficient defence of longer-term sustainability in the face of various threats to eco-stability.

A well-financed and prominent initiative to address overall global issues was sponsored by the Commission on Global Governance, culminating in its main report, *Our Global Neighbourhood* (Commission on Global Governance 1995). This initiative, claiming authority and credibility on the basis of the eminence of its membership drawn from the leading ranks of society, and stressing past or present government service at leadership or ministerial levels, seemed too farsighted for existing power structures and too timid to engage the imagination of the more activist and militant actors in civil society. The Commission report failed to arouse any widespread or sustained interest, despite the comprehensiveness and thoughtfulness of its proposals. As an intellectual tool it is also disappointing, failing to clarify the challenge of globalization and the troublesome character of Bretton Woods approaches to world economic policy. As a result, its attempt to anchor an argument for global reform around an argument for 'global governance' seemed more likely to consolidate globalization-from-above than to promote a creative equilibrium relying on the balancing contribution of globalization-from-below. In part, this Commission was unlucky, beginning its work in the aftermath of the Gulf War when attention and hopes were centred on the future of the United Nations, and then issuing its report at a time when the world organization was widely, if somewhat unfairly, discredited as a result of tragic outcomes in Somalia, Bosnia and Rwanda. But this was not the fundamental problem with the Commission. Its most serious deficiency was a failure of nerve when it came to addressing the adverse consequences of globalization, a focus that would have put such a commission on a collision course with adherents of the neo-liberal economistic world picture. Given the claims of 'eminence' and 'independent funding' that characterizes such a commission, it is not to be expected that it would be willing or able to address the structural and ideological deficiencies attributable to the prevailing world-order framework. This means that its unintended impact is to confirm pessimism about finding an alternative world picture to that provided by the neo-liberal prism on globalization.

What is being argued, then, is that the challenges posed by economic globalization have not as yet engendered a sufficient response in two connected respects. First, there is an absence of an ideological posture that is comparably coherent to that being provided by various renditions of neo-liberalism, and that could provide the social forces associated with globalization-from-below with a common theoretical framework, political language and programme. Second, there is lacking a clear expression of a critique of globalization-from-above that cuts deeply enough to address the most basic normative challenges associated with poverty, social marginalization and environmental decay, while accepting the actual and potential emancipatory contributions, as well as the unchallengeable persistence, of state and market. The political goals of globalization-from-below are thus at once both drastic and reformist, seeking to take advantage of global integration and technological innovation, but in a manner that benefits the peoples of the world and protects their long-term interests.

It is central to realize that the world-order outcomes arising from the impact of economic globalization are far from settled, and in no sense predetermined. The forces of globalization-from-above have mainly taken control of globalization, and are pushing it in an economistic direction that considerably instrumentalizes the state on behalf of a set of attitudes and policies: privatization, free trade, fiscal austerity and competitiveness. But there are other options: 'sustainable development', 'global welfare' and 'cybernetic libertarianism'. The eventual shape of globalization will reflect the play of these diverse perspectives and priorities. The perspectives and priorities of globalization-from-above are being challenged in various ways, but mainly in a piecemeal manner. The effort of the final section is to encourage a mobilization of the now disparate forces of globalization-from-below in the direction of greater coherence and political weight. It is my conviction that such mobilization is most likely to occur beneath the banner of democracy, but democracy reformulated in relation to the basic aspirations of peoples everywhere to participate in the processes that are shaping their lives. Democracy can no longer be confined to electoral politics, or even to state/society relations.

The purpose of the next section is mainly to clarify what is meant by 'democracy' in relation to the analysis of globalization.

Towards coherence: the theory and practice of normative democracy

To introduce the idea of 'normative democracy' is to offer a proposal for a unifying ideology capable of mobilizing and unifying the disparate social forces that constitute global civil society, and to galvanize the political energy that is associated with globalization-from-below. The specification of normative democracy is influenced strongly by David Held's work on democratic theory and practice, particularly his formulations of 'cosmopolitan democracy', but it offers a slightly different terminology so as to emphasize the agency role of global civil society with its range of engagements that go from local/grassroots arenas to the most encompassing planetary contexts of decision (Archibugi and Held, 1995; Held 1995). Normative democracy also draws upon Walden Bello's call for 'substantive democracy', set forth as a more progressive movement alternative to the more limited embrace of 'constitutional democracy' (Bello 1997). I prefer normative to substantive democracy because of its highlighting of ethical and legal norms, thereby reconnecting politics with moral purpose and values, which calls attention to the moral emptiness of neo-liberalism, consumerism and most forms of secularism. There is also a practical reason: to weaken the political appeal of resurgent organized religion while at the same time acknowledging the relevance of moral purpose and spiritual concerns to the renewal of progressive politics in a post-Marxist atmosphere.

Contrary to widespread claims in the West, there is no empirical basis for the argument that economic performance is necessarily tied to constitutional democracy and human rights. Several countries in the Asia/Pacific region, most significantly China, have combined an outstanding macro-economic record with harsh authoritarian rule. Globalization-from-above is not an assured vehicle for the achievement of Western-style constitutional democracy, including the protection of individual and group rights. But democracy, as such, is of the essence of a meaningful form of political action on the part of global civil society, especially to the extent that such action, even when revolutionary, refrains from and repudiates violent means. In this regard there is an emergent, as yet implicit, convergence of ends and means on the part of several distinct tendencies in civil society: issue-oriented movements, non-violent democracy movements and governments that minimize their links to geopolitical structures. This convergence presents several intriguing opportunities for coalition-building, and greater ideological coherence in the various outlooks associated with globalization-from-below. Against this background, normative democracy seems like an attractive umbrella for theorizing, not dogmatically, but to exhibit affinities and to build the basis for a renewal of progressive politics.

Normative democracy adopts comprehensive views of fundamental ideas associated with the secular modern state. Security is conceived as extending to environmental protection and to the defence of economic autonomy, for example Mahathir's complaints about George Soros's financial speculations jeopardizing Malaysian development successes (Malaysia 1997). Human rights are conceived as extending to social and economic rights, as well as to such collective rights as the right to development, the right to peace and the right of self-determination. Democracy is conceived as extending beyond constitutional and free, periodic elections to include an array of other assurances that governance is oriented towards human wellbeing and ecological sustainability, and that citizens have broad participatory options, including access to arenas of decision.

The elements of normative democracy can be enumerated, but their content and behavioural applications will require much amplification in varied specific settings. This enumeration reflects the dominant orientations and outlook of the political actors that make up the constructivist category of 'globalization-from-below'. It is thus not an enumeration that is a wish list, but intends to be descriptive and explanatory of an embedded and emergent consensus. The elements of this consensus are as follows:

- *consent of citizenry:* some periodic indication that the permanent population of the relevant community is represented by the institutions of governance, and confers legitimacy through the expression of consent; elections are the established modalities for territorial communities to confer legitimacy on government, but referenda and rights of petition and recall may be more appropriate for other types of political community, especially those of regional or global scope, while direct democracy may be most meaningful for local political activity; the idea is to be flexible and adaptive

- *rule of law:* all modes of governance subject to the discipline of law as a way of imposing effective limits on authority and of assuring some form of checks and balances as between legislative, executive, judicial and administrative processes; also, sensitivity to the normative claims of civil initiatives associated with codes of conduct, conference declarations or societal institutions (for instance, the Permanent People's Tribunal in Rome)
- *human rights:* taking account of differing cultural, economic and political settings and priorities, the establishment of mechanisms for the impartial and effective implementation of human rights deriving from global, regional, state and transnational civil sources of authority; human rights are comprehensively conceived as encompassing economic, social and cultural rights, as well as civil and political rights, with a concern for both individual and collective conceptions of rights, emphasizing tolerance towards difference and respect for fundamental community sentiments
- *participation:* effective and meaningful modes of participation in the political life of the society, centred upon the processes of government, but extending to all forms of social governance, including workplace and home; participation may be direct or indirect, that is, representational, but it enables the expression of views and influence upon the processes of decision on the basis of an ideal of equality of access; creativity is needed to find methods other than elections by which to ensure progress toward full participation
- *accountability:* suitable mechanisms for challenging the exercise of authority by those occupying official positions at the level of the state, but also with respect to the functioning of the market and of international institutions; the establishment of an international criminal court would provide an important mechanism for assuring accountability by those in powerful positions who have been traditionally treated as exempt from the rule of law
- *public goods:* a restored social agenda that corrects the growing imbalance, varying in seriousness from country to country, between private and public goods in relation to the persistence of poverty amid affluence, pertaining to health, education, housing and basic human needs, but also in relation to support for environmental protection, regulation of economic globalization, innovative cultural activity and infrastructural development for governance at the regional and global levels; in these regards, a gradual depoliticization of funding, either by reliance on a use or transaction tax imposed on financial flows or global air travel, or some form of reliable and equitable means to fund public goods of local, national, regional, and global scope
- *transparency:* an openness with respect to knowledge and information that builds trust between institutions of governance and the citizenry at various levels of social interaction; in effect, establishing the right to

know as an aspect of constitutionalism, including a strong bias against public sector secrecy and covert operations, which would criminalize government lies of the sort recently revealed where for years, to protect Air Force spy missions, the CIA lied about alleged 'UFO sightings'; internationally, transparency is particularly important in relation to military expenditures and arms transfers; it also relates to the operation of international institutions and private sector actors

- *non-violence:* underpinning globalization-from-below and the promotion of substantive democracy is a conditional commitment to non-violent politics and conflict resolution; such a commitment does not nullify rights of self-defence as protected in international law, strictly and narrowly construed, nor does it necessarily invalidate limited recourse to violence by oppressed peoples; such an ethos of non-violence clearly imposes on governments an obligation to renounce weaponry of mass destruction and to negotiate phased disarmament arrangements, but also encourages maximum commitments to demilitarizing approaches to peace and security at all levels of social interaction, including peace and security at the level of city and neighbourhood; such commitments suggest the rejection of capital punishment as an option of government, and an overall commitment to peaceful forms of dispute settlement and conflict resolution.

Globalization-from-below and the state: a decisive battle

Without entering into detailed discussion, it seems that different versions of neo-liberal ideology have exerted a defining influence upon the orientation of political elites governing sovereign states. Of course, there are many variations reflecting conditions and personalities in each particular state and region, but the generalization holds without important exception (Sakamoto 1994; Falk 1997b). Even China, despite adherence to the ideology of state socialism, has implemented by state decree, with generally impressive results, a market-oriented approach to economic policy. The state can remain authoritarian in relation to its citizenry without necessarily jeopardizing its economic performance so long as it adheres, more or less, to the discipline of global capital, thereby achieving competitiveness by reference to costs of production, savings and attraction of capital. In these respects, neo-liberalism as a global ideology is purely economistic in character, and does not imply a commitment to democratic governance in even the minimal sense of periodic fair elections. Of course, it can be argued that the anti-democratic orientations prove to be economically stagnant over time due to bureaucratic overload and the authoritarian antipathy to the creative spirit that is so important in sustaining economic expansion.

Globalization-from-below, in addition to a multitude of local struggles, is also a vehicle for the transnational promotion of normative democracy as a counterweight to neo-liberalism. It provides an alternative, or series of convergent alternatives, that has not yet been posited as a coherent body of theory and practice, but remains the inarticulate common ground of an emergent global civil society. Normative democracy, unlike backlash politics that closes off borders and identities, seeks a politics of reconciliation that maintains much of the openness and dynamism associated with globalization-from-above, while countering its pressures to privatize and marketize the production of public goods. In effect, the quest of normative democracy is to establish a social equilibrium that takes full account of the realities of globalization in its various aspects. Such a process cannot succeed on a country-by-country basis, as the rollback of welfare in Scandinavia suggests, but must proceed within regional and global settings. The state remains the dominant instrument of policy and decision affecting the lives of peoples, and the primary link to regional and global institutions. The state has been instrumentalized to a considerable degree by the ideology and influences associated with globalization-from-above, resulting in declining support for public goods in an atmosphere of strong sustained economic growth and in the polarization of results with incredible wealth for the winners and acute suffering for the losers. An immediate goal of those disparate social forces that constitute globalization-from-below is to reinstrumentalize the state to the extent that it redefines its role as mediating between the logic of capital and the priorities of its peoples, including their short-term and longer-term goals, and promotes greater social equality for its citizens.

Evidence of this instrumentalization of the state is present in relation to global conferences on broad policy issues that had been organized under UN auspices, and were making an impact on public consciousness and behavioural standards in the 1990s. These UN conferences increasingly attracted an array of social forces associated with global civil society, and gave rise to a variety of coalitions and oppositions between state, market and militant citizens organized to promote substantive goals (for example, human rights, environmental protection, economic equity and development). These UN conferences became arenas of political participation that were operating outside the confines of state control, and were perceived as threatening by the established order based on a core coalition between market forces and geopolitical leaders. One effect of this realization is to withdraw support for such UN activities, pushing the organization to the sidelines on global policy issues as part of a process of recovering control over the UN agenda and orientation on behalf of globalization-from-above. Such a reaction represents a setback for globalization-from-below, but it also shows that the social forces that are associated with the promotion of normative democracy can be formidable adversaries.

Such a process of reinstrumentalization could also influence the future role and identity of regional and global mechanisms of governance, especially to the extent of increasing the regulatory mandate directed toward market forces and the normative mandate with respect to the protection of the global commons, the promotion of demilitarization, the overall support for public goods and a concern for socially vulnerable sectors of world society.

Conclusion

This essay has argued that the positive prospects for global civil society depend very much on two interrelated developments: achieving consensus on 'normative democracy' as the foundation of coherent theory and practice, and waging a struggle for the appropriate outlook and orientation of institutions of governance with respect to the framing of globalization. The state remains the critical focus of this latter struggle, although it is not even now a matter of intrinsic opposition between the state as instrument of globalization-from-above and social movements as instrument of globalization-from-below. In many specific settings, coalitions between states and social movements are emergent, as is evident in relation to many questions of environment, development and human rights. It may even come to pass that transnational corporations and banks adopt a longer-term view of their own interests and move to alter the policy content of globalization-from-above to soften the contrast with the preferences of globalization-from-below. It is helpful to remember that such an unanticipated convergence of previously opposed social forces led to bargaining that generated the sort of consensus that produced 'social democracy' and 'the welfare state' over the course of the nineteenth and twentieth centuries. There is no evident reason to preclude such convergencies on regional and global levels as a way of resolving some of the tensions being caused by the manner in which globalization is currently being enacted. Indeed, this prospect is encouraged by the difficulties with neo-liberal management of the global economy that followed upon the Asian economic crisis and the inability of IMF medicine to resolve it. Even the champions of neo-liberalism have been forced to retreat from their earlier embrace of unconditional reliance on market mechanisms to meet economic, social and political challenges. As a result, even the mainstream is more open to debate and compromise, including some renewed belief that the political stability needed for economic recovery may depend on renewing the social mandate of government, especially in relation to those most economically disadvantaged. This rethinking of neo-liberalism as the ideological basis for globalization is also being encouraged by the leftward tilt in a series of elections in important European countries.

As we approach a new century, there appears to be a new beginning of history on the horizon, namely, a spreading and deepening of democracy that has revolutionary implications for the future of politics. As the global village becomes more an experienced, daily reality, this transformed democratic spirit will alter our sense of citizenship, participation, accountability and authority. Such a process is likely to engender some type of global polity over the course of the next several decades.

Notes

1   An earlier version of this chapter appeared under the title 'Global Civil Society: Perspectives, Initiatives, and Movements' (Falk 1998).

References

Archibugi, D. and Held, D. (1995) *Cosmopolitan Democracy: An Agenda for a New World Order*, Cambridge: Polity Press.

Bello, W. (1997) Talk at Bangkok Conference on 'Alternative Security Systems in the Asia-Pacific', *Focus Asia*, 27–30 March.

Bull, H. (1977) *The Anarchical Society: A Study of Order in World Politics*, New York: Columbia University Press.

Clark, I. (1997) *Globalization and Fragmentation: International Relations in the Twentieth Century*, Oxford: Oxford University Press.

Commission on Global Governance (1995) *Our Global Neighbourhood*, Oxford: Oxford University Press.

Falk, R. (1993) 'The Making of Global Citizenship', in J. Brecher, J. B. Childs and J. Cutler (eds), *Global Visions: Beyond the New World Order*, Boston, Mass.: South End Press.

——(1995) *On Humane Governance: Toward a New Global Politics*, Cambridge: Polity Press.

——(1996) 'An Inquiry into the Political Economy of World Order', *New Political Economy* 1: 13–26.

——(1997a) 'Resisting "Globalisation-from-above" through "Globalisation-from-below"', *New Political Economy* 2: 17–24.

——(1997b) 'State of Siege: Will Globalization Win Out?', *International Affairs* 73: 123–36.

——(1998) 'Global Civil Society: Perspectives, Initiatives, and Movements', *Oxford Development Studies*, 26: 99–110.

Fukuyama, F. (1992) *The End of History and the Last Man*, New York: Free Press.

Goldsmith, E. (1972) *A Blueprint for Survival*, Boston, Mass.: Houghton Mifflin.

Held, D. (1995) *Democracy and the Global Order: From the Modern State to Cosmopolitan Governance*, Cambridge: Polity Press.

Hirst, P. and Thompson, G. (1996) *Globalization in Question*, Cambridge: Polity Press.

Lipschutz, R. D. (1996) *Global Civil Society and Global Environmental Governance*, Albany: State University of New York Press.

Malaysia (1997): 'Malaysia PM Mulls Action against Speculators', *Turkish Daily News*, 29 July.

Meadows, D. H., Meadows, D. L., Randers, J. and Behrens, W. W. (1972) *The Limits to Growth*, New York: Universe Books.

Nerfin, M. (1986) 'Neither Prince nor Merchant: Citizen – an Introduction to the Third System', *IFDA Dossier 56* (Nov/Dec), 3–29.

Rich, B. (1994) *Mortgaging the Earth: The World Bank Environmental Impoverishment and the Crisis of Development*, London: Earthscan.

Rosenau, J. N. (1990) *Turbulence in World Politics: A Theory of Change and Continuity*, Princeton, NJ: Princeton University Press.

Sachs, J. (1997) 'New Members Please Apply', *Time*, 7 July, 11–12.

Sakamoto, Y. (ed.) (1994) *Global Transformation: Challenges to the State System*, Tokyo: United Nations University Press.

Shiva, V. (1987) 'People's Ecology: The Chipko Movement', in R. B. J. Walker and S. H. Mendlovitz (eds), *Towards a Just World Peace: Perspectives from Social Movements*, London: Butterworth.

Wapner, P. (1996) 'The Social Construction of Global Governance', paper presented at the American Political Science Association Annual Meeting, August 28–31.

11 Globalization, sovereignty and policy-making

Insights from European integration

Jonathan Golub

There is a widespread popular belief that globalization has undermined the traditional system of territorial state authority and perhaps imperilled the very possibility of meaningful governance (Ohmae 1991; Zürn 1995). Others have argued that the novelty and extent of globalization should not be overstated and that individual nations remain very much in control of their own destinies (Hirst and Thompson 1996; Wade 1996; Garrett 1998). Somewhere between these two positions one finds arguments that the effects of globalization are substantial, but that they are largely manageable through an emerging system of global governance. This nascent new world order comprises international institutions devoted to resolving global issues at the level of high politics (Haas *et al.* 1993; Keohane 1998), and an increasingly dense web of transgovernmental relations among the courts, regulators and agencies of disaggregated states engaged in solving similar issues at the level of low politics (Slaughter 1997). The globalization debate thus involves two primary dimensions: discerning the current intensity and future trajectory of transnational exchange, and ascertaining the need for, and performance of, advanced institutional structures which populate the new world order and mediate how these exchanges affect national sovereignty. Assumptions about these two dimensions in turn underpin accounts of various forms of global democracy, including normative claims made about its appropriateness and inevitability, as well as suggestions for how it should be institutionally configured (Held 1995).

To cut through much of the hype which frequently accompanies discussions of globalization, one must begin with a basic question: why do images of spectacular global financial transactions and increasingly porous national borders provoke such alarm? In and of themselves these descriptions portray events that are perhaps novel, certainly evocative, but not necessarily problematic. I suggest that the real source of alarm in many globalization accounts, including some of those offered elsewhere in this volume, derives mostly from the fear that states have lost national sovereignty over some of their most basic policy-making functions. For these observers, the 'punchline' seems to boil down to this: that democratic states are now unable to maintain the high social and environmental standards which continue to attract public support. Regardless of what citizens might prefer, the argument runs, in a world of global investment opportunities and product competition any environmental policy that imposes costs on producers will price domestic products out of world markets, scare off domestic firms and deter foreign direct investment. Similarly, global regulatory competition allegedly unravels the postwar commitment to Keynesian economic management and generous welfare policies by constraining the ability of governments to raise taxes, run deficits or redistribute wealth without incurring substantial trade imbalances, capital flight, lost jobs and stagnant growth.

Because all states face similar economic pressures, many have predicted a global convergence on a neo-liberal model of governance and a regulatory 'race to the bottom'. Such a race entails the death of the social democratic 'left' and the relaxation of costly welfare and environmental policies to lowest-common-denominator levels. Those who take a more sanguine view contend that the development of international and transgovernmental institutions offers the most promising way to avert this race, assert control over transboundary flows, and actually raise global standards. A third group of writers contends that international institutions might be useful for certain issues, but that in general individual nation-states remain perfectly capable of pursuing their own traditional policies. And finally, there are those who advocate some novel form of global democracy to remedy what they see as the twin problems of obsolete nation-states and inherently inadequate state-centred international institutions.

While smaller in geographic scale, analysis of European integration uncovers lessons which are particularly salient to central aspects of the globalization debate. Development of the European Union (EU) is not only propelled by dynamics identical to those underpinning globalization – the simultaneous drive to increase and cope with complex interdependence – but provides almost a laboratory experiment of what changes might occur to national sovereignty, policy choices and effective governance if one could fast-forward the globalization process.

Cross-fertilization between globalization studies and EU scholarship constitutes an expanding and intriguing research agenda, one to which this chapter seeks to make but a modest contribution. The first section presents the case for viewing the EU as something like a laboratory experiment in globalization and then briefly reviews what competing integration theories predict about how this experiment affects national sovereignty and policy outcomes. The following two sections assess the strength of these predictions against empirical evidence from the fields of environmental and social policy. My three basic findings are: that erosion of sovereignty has occurred, but not to a dramatic degree, and not through processes normally highlighted by integration theories; that substantial policy retrenchment has not occurred; but that in more modest ways integration might constrain the policy choices available to Member States. The chapter then goes on to consider the long-term viability of the status quo compared to what many would view as bleak potential alternatives. In the conclusion I relate the discussion of European integration, national sovereignty and regulatory change to the issue of global democracy.

The process of European integration

To study European integration is to study the process whereby individual nation-states work collectively to orchestrate and manage their growing interdependence. There are economic and institutional reasons why this process resembles an advanced form of globalization.

Economically, through the establishment of the 'four freedoms' the EU has come to exhibit remarkably high and ever increasing levels of transnational exchange among its (now fifteen) Member States. Within the integrated economic area of the common market there are few restrictions on the flow of goods, services, capital and labour, and intra-EU trade constitutes over 70 per cent of all EU trade. The elimination of national trade barriers and impediments to the four freedoms can occur in two ways. One is through negative integration, the dismantling of national regulations that impede the workings of the common market. By contrast, positive integration involves reregulation at the supranational level through the adoption of EU legislation that harmonizes disparate national laws. Negative integration has been driven primarily by rulings from the European Court of Justice (ECJ), whereas positive integration requires the adoption of legislation by the Council of Ministers. What makes the EU such an interesting case, of course, is that alongside the four freedoms and prohibitions on national trade barriers under all but the narrowest of circumstances, one also finds explicit treaty commitments to high environmental and social standards. The tension between extreme economic openness and high standards mirrors precisely what for many observers is really at stake in the globalization debate.

Institutionally, promotion and management of integration emanates from a uniquely advanced set of structures, the likes of which are only beginning to emerge at the global level. These EU structures combine high and low politics through a complex blend of supranational, intergovernmental, transgovernmental and unilateral decision-making, most clearly evident when functional components of disaggregated states meet on a daily basis in the Council of Ministers to hammer out the details of legally enforceable common policies that might have originated in the Commission and that still leave scope for a certain amount of national discretion. In accordance with treaty rules, which have themselves changed over time, decisions in the Council are taken by either unanimous or qualified majority voting, depending on the policy area in question.

If open transnational exchange necessarily undermines the ability of sovereign states to maintain ambitious social and environmental policies, as much of the globalization literature suggests, this should be evident where the EU has pursued negative rather than positive harmonization, and where positive harmonization has involved the adoption of low rather than high common standards. The important point here is that, in theory, there are several ways to induce a regulatory race to the bottom, whereas the only guaranteed way to maintain high standards and counteract the downward pressure unleashed by negative integration is by cajoling reluctant Member States into accepting harmonization near the highest common denominator.

Just as European integration represents an experiment in globalization, European integration theory furnishes predictions about how the experiment will turn out. Established integration theories are often criticized for their underspecification of the causal mechanisms leading to one type of policy outcome rather than another, but generally they do provide sufficient guidance to extract testable hypotheses, particularly when one concentrates on their respective claims about how institutions operate. One might initially suspect that the dramatically disparate welfare and environmental traditions found among the respective Member States would defy harmonization, and that the enormous costs of upward adjustment would present an insurmountable political obstacle to positive integration consisting of highest-common-denominator EU policies. Moreover, one might expect that the possibility of harmonization being vetoed in the Council by a single state (under unanimous voting rules) or blocked by a minority coalition (under qualified majority voting rules) would make the prospects for such policies appear particularly bleak. It is on these crucial issues that the predictions of various integration theories differ. According to functionalists, the traditional system of nation-states posed an inherent threat to peace, social stability and general welfare. For Haas, this dangerous configuration would be slowly but inevitably transcended by an ever expanding web of functional, problem-solving, supranational institutions which enjoyed 'jurisdiction over pre-existing national states' (Haas 1964: 16). Driving this gradual erosion of national sovereignty was the inherently expansionist logic of economic spillover and an unabashed faith in technocratic elitism (Haas 1964: 6–11). The end result of this process, the total withering away of nation-states, would yield a more peaceful and prosperous Europe operating under the enlightened, noncontroversial policies fashioned by technical experts.

For present purposes the most important aspect of functionalist theory was its prediction that substantive EU policies would emerge from a process of problem-solving, rather than bargaining (Haas 1964; Majone 1993; de Zwaan 1995). Supranational leadership from the Commission, combined with the distinctive dynamics which evolved in the Council as a result of frequent meetings among like-minded national ministers, was supposed to result in regulatory measures which maximized joint European gains and transcended national self-interest. Similar to constructivist models of international relations and the sociological strand of new institutionalism, the literature on EU integration is full of references to the 'clubby' atmosphere of the Council, and the 'psychological spillover' and 'collective rationality' which supposedly occurs among national officials who meet regularly in the Brussels 'interaction context'. Member State representatives engaged in problem-solving redefine their interests and eschew selfish national goals and concerns about issues of distribution, which paves the way for unexpectedly high regulatory standards, often at or above the highest common denominator of pre-existing national practices, and even under conditions of unanimous voting. Evidence of this process at work was initially adduced from the field of EU health and safety law, and similar claims have been made about the development of environmental policy (Héritier *et al.* 1996; Eichener 1997). If correct, this would suggest a specific mechanism by which integration avoids the race to the bottom: erosion of national sovereignty should occur primarily in those Member States where positive harmonization 'ratchets up' earlier standards or forces other costly adjustments, whereas states which already conformed to stringent regulations could continue their normal practices. Moreover, not only should there be considerable positive integration, but the Council should frequently produce highest-common-denominator outcomes regardless of the applicable voting rules.

Intergovernmentalists saw a much different process, one where states whose economies had been devastated by the Second World War willingly and rationally 'pooled' (not surrendered) a limited amount of their national sovereignty within supranational decision-making bodies in order to lower the transaction costs of economic exchange and provide an enforcement mechanism for overcoming collective action problems. This limited transfer would foster national growth, accelerate national industrial modernization and allow each state to reap the benefits of scale economies. Instead of eroding the traditional nation-state, the European project would rescue its power, the foundation of which was the ability to govern effectively and satisfy the welfare demands of its citizens (Milward 1992). The expansive logic of automatic spillover, the agency of supranational institutions and the apolitical problem-solving method play a minimal role in the intergovernmentalist account (Moravcsik 1993). Rather, Member States remain very much in control of the integration process and pursue selfish aims through hardnosed bargaining. One would expect the specific policies crafted through intergovernmental bargains to differ markedly from those produced through problem-solving. While self-interested states would endorse widespread negative integration as well as positive harmonization associated with completing the common market, deadlock or outcomes near the lowest common denominator would predominate in areas such as social and environmental policy, with issue linkage and side payments serving as the only mechanisms for averting the type of downward spiral feared by globalization alarmists.

Thus, for those worried about globalization, we arrive at two crucial questions: first, how frequently has the EU followed a functionalist path and managed to harmonize social and environmental rules near the highest common denominator, rather than succumbing to deadlock or low standards associated with intergovernmentalism; second, in the absence of such harmonization has the expected race to the bottom materialized, sweeping away the social democratic left in favour of a neo-liberal convergence? One can phrase these questions in terms of national sovereignty. Is it the countries normally prone to low social and environmental standards that have experienced a dramatic erosion of their sovereignty through being dragged upwards towards highest-common-denominator rules, and if so how can one explain this counterintuitive development? Or is it more the case that European integration has undermined the sovereignty of the traditionally progressive Member States by inducing them, against the wishes of their respective electorates, to undertake a race to the bottom?

Environmental policy

Since its inception in 1973, EU environmental policy has expanded steadily and now comprises several hundred Directives and Regulations governing a wide range of activities. Among these laws, perhaps the most important are the many standards related to characteristics of individual products (product standards) and methods of industrial production (process standards). These two vast bodies of rules, themselves evidence of positive rather than negative integration, utilize two distinct forms of harmonization. Mandatory harmonization obliges all Member States to achieve the same level of environmental protection, whereas in cases of optional harmonization states retain complete discretion over their domestic environmental efforts provided that their national provisions do not hinder transnational flows of goods meeting minimal EU standards, such as energy efficiency, noise and exhaust levels.

The distinctions between product and process standards, and between mandatory and optional harmonization, have enormous practical significance. Consider first the case of product standards. Whereas either type of harmonization will achieve a common market for products by guaranteeing free circulation of goods, regardless of whether a high or low minimum environmental standard is set, low standards produce basically the same effect as does non-agreement or negative integration, potentially triggering a race to the bottom as green states struggle to maintain exports and domestic market shares against presumably dirtier and cheaper products. Moreover, high standards which are merely optional can be used to protect home markets in green states but still might trigger a downward regulatory spiral as nationally based firms unwilling or unable to differentiate their production lines compete for export markets within less environmentally concerned states. Of the various harmonization options, only ambitious and mandatory product standards are guaranteed to prevent EU regulatory competition.

Prior to 1987, any form of harmonization required unanimous voting, and product standards for cars, aircraft, appliances, machinery and other items almost always took the form of optional harmonization, and were rarely set near the highest common denominator of environmental protection. Following the 1987 Single European Act, only a qualified majority in the Council was needed to harmonize national standards, but this still allowed ample scope to form blocking minorities composed of Member States fearful of shouldering expensive environmental improvements to their exported products.

Nevertheless, the lack of highest-common-denominator agreements has not triggered the expected downward spiral, and product standards across the EU have actually risen not fallen over the past twenty-five years. This upward trend, also evident in America and referred to by David Vogel as the 'California effect' (in contrast to the downward 'Delaware effect') in part reflects how market integration transmits across national borders the growing consumer demand for green products (Vogel 1996). While consumers everywhere are increasingly willing to pay a premium for cleaner, quieter, energy-efficient products containing a high proportion of recycled material, such inclinations have been particularly apparent in Germany, the Netherlands and the new Member States in Scandinavia. The demand generated by the sheer size of the German market, let alone the combined demand from all these green markets, has catalysed environmental improvements in other Member States, averting a downward drift.

It is essential to recognize, however, that much of the California effect can be attributed not to consumer-pull across open EU markets but rather to the coercive effects of trade barriers erected by the greenest Member States and effectively condoned by the Commission and the ECJ. Not free and open transnational trade, but the lack thereof, has been the key factor behind rising European product standards. It was Germany's unilateral tightening of vehicle emission limits in the 1980s, its formal exclusion of dirtier imports and its tax breaks for cars equipped with catalytic converters that forced other states to make upward adjustments. France and the UK accused Germany of violating treaty provisions on non-tariff trade barriers and on state aids to industry, but the Commission refused to pursue the case. The German measures were then copied by other green states, particularly the Netherlands and Denmark, thereby replacing a race to the bottom with a drag to the top. Similar unilateral trade barriers have been used by various states to exclude products containing cadmium, mercury and pesticides, as well as those lacking energy efficiency labels. In the few cases where rulings have been made, the ECJ has taken a narrow approach to negative integration and allowed these measures to stand. So unlikely was the chance that the Commission and the ECJ would pursue full-blown negative integration that, in 1989, the Council even agreed to mandatory harmonization of small-car emissions in exchange for Germany and the Netherlands foregoing even more ambitious national measures. Somewhat similar, the 1992 Directive on energy efficiency of hot water boilers was also precipitated by the threat of national green trade barriers and introduced elements of mandatory harmonization, albeit with considerable scope for derogations. Regardless of the scenario – optional, mandatory or no harmonization – the end result of the judicially condoned California effect has been that, in many areas, green states have preserved their sovereignty and remain free to enact stringent product standards demanded by their electorates.

Apart from the cases noted above, most product standards, such as those governing noise pollution, have involved optional harmonization, and in the absence of the legal dimension of the California effect the only force counteracting a stagnation or decline in these standards is green consumer strength in each national market. While there certainly has been no race to the bottom, the incremental tightening of domestic environmental policies has sometimes been delayed or blocked for fear of incurring economic competitive disadvantages. To the extent that this has occurred, it is fair to say that the power of transnational EU markets has eroded some of the national sovereignty traditionally held by green member states.

For process standards, for example rules governing the cleanliness of drinking water or the industrial emission of sulphur dioxide air pollution, optional harmonization is not a possibility, there is no California effect, and Council debates turn solely on whether or not to adopt mandatory common standards and how stringent these should be. While pollution is widely considered a negative externality which distorts the functioning of the common market, until the 1992 Maastricht Treaty the harmonization of disparate national environmental process standards required unanimity in the Council. Failure to harmonize, or harmonization at a low level, would leave green states exposed to regulatory competition. These states were still legally free to tighten their own process standards, as this would in no way block trade or harm the competitiveness of foreign producers, but maintaining ambitious water, waste and air laws meant perpetuating high production costs which might raise unemployment and stifle growth. Highest-common-denominator standards would certainly alleviate this downward pressure, but their adoption required cajoling polluting states and those with distinctive approaches to environmental protection, particularly Southern Europe and the UK, into accepting expensive adjustment costs. Following Maastricht, process standards could be adopted through a qualified majority vote, which at least in theory allowed coalitions of green states to force the pace of regulatory improvements.

Sensitivity to competitiveness and concerns about levelling the economic playing field have always been central to Council deliberations, as green states have pushed to export their preferred policy preferences and avoid unilateral clean-up costs. Nevertheless, with a few extremely notable exceptions, the development of EU environmental process standards during the period 1973–93 reflected not functionalist problem-solving but rather the type of lowest-common-denominator bargains one would expect under conditions of unanimous decision-making (Golub 1996a). Besides cases where a national veto prevented any agreement at all, many Directives merely codified pre-existing conditions within the various Member States, contained a plethora of derogations and loopholes, or imposed only cosmetic legislative changes. Examples of such minimal ratcheting include EU standards covering sulphur dioxide and nitrogen dioxide emissions, ambient lead levels, gas and fuel oil content, large industrial plants, detergents, aquatic mercury levels, PCBs, shellfish and freshwater fish, and waste disposal.

This is certainly not to deny that there have been important exceptions, cases of ratcheting that have rightly received attention for the considerable compliance costs and environmental adjustments which they entail. Even allowing for their abysmal implementation records, ratcheting has been most evident in the Southern Member States, where, prior to their accession, environmental policy was patchy at best. Occasionally EU laws have even forced the greener Member States to improve their practices. Ratcheting might be a residual feature of EU environmental policy, but just a few individual provisions, such as those covering nitrate and pesticide levels in water, can have dramatic consequences.

These cases reveal important lessons about how national sovereignty can be voluntarily relinquished through intentional Council bargaining tactics or unexpectedly lost through negotiating failure and *ex post* judicial intervention, either of which averts regulatory competition. Diffuse reciprocity and issue linkage in the Council are mechanisms by which Member States have willingly forfeited sovereignty and allowed environmental ratcheting, although the scope for such concessions has been limited, in part because package deals are almost never struck across policy sectors. Poor bargaining preparation and (especially in Spain's case) the inability to foresee accurately the consequences of highly complex proposals has led some national officials to accept EU standards which proved far more demanding than originally anticipated. The notorious nitrate standard for drinking water, for instance, was only one parameter among many, and it slipped through despite close scrutiny by all Member States.

Some of the most important instances of ratcheting have occurred not at the bargaining stage, which so frequently yields outcomes that Member States understandably view as vaguely worded and undemanding, but later during implementation, when national courts or the ECJ attach concrete interpretations to vague or controversial legislative provisions.

Infringement proceedings under Article 169 of the Treaty, and preliminary references under Article 177, have forced most Member States to make expensive and unexpected adjustments, such as extending the scope of environmental impact assessment, improving certain aspects of drinking and bathing water quality and protecting endangered species of birds. Of course national courts have also used their discretion to withhold references from the ECJ, thereby shielding government autonomy or at least stalling the erosion of national sovereignty (Golub 1996b).

Bearing in mind the general caveat about Southern states, it should be recognized that ratcheting, whether at the bargaining or the implementation stage, is an important exception to the more general phenomenon of EU process standards being set near lowest-common-denominator levels. And despite dramatic institutional changes in 1993, significant ratcheting has remained just as elusive in the post-Maastricht period. Deadlocked unanimous voting cripples the most sensitive proposals, notably the Commission's ambitious carbon energy tax. Majority voting allows green states to impose ratcheting, as was the case with emission standards for medium combustion plants, but this is certainly not the typical outcome of Council deliberations, as shown by the ill-fated proposal on civil liability for waste and the nearly lowest-common-denominator standards adopted under the hazardous waste incineration and the packaging waste Directives. A very important aspect of the latter case was that majority voting allowed a coalition of Member States to impose waste disposal self-sufficiency rules restricting the ability of Germany, Denmark and the Netherlands to pursue ambitious recycling programmes (Golub 1996c).

Besides the continued infrequency of highest-common-denominator outcomes and the absence of functionalist problem-solving, what distinguishes recent developments in this field is the shift towards fewer and less intrusive EU policies and greater respect for national sovereignty, both in line with the subsidiarity principle (Golub 1996d). For example, the Commission has shifted its focus towards the use of softer instruments which allow considerable scope for national discretion, such as general framework directives, ecolabels and ecoaudits. These trends, it would seem, leave ample space for states to satisfy the demands of their electorates and devise ambitious environmental programmes free from supranational interference. Of course enhanced discretion also allows nation-states to satisfy domestic demands for weaker environmental standards and for the prioritization of growth and employment. As the EU retreats from legislative uniformity and the use of intrusive instruments, the prospects for decisive ratcheting fade accordingly, and the conditions conducive to the race to the bottom emerge.

This brief review provides several lessons about how EU integration has affected both the sovereignty of Member States and the prospects for aggressive environmental process standards. First, in cases of ratcheting, to the extent that EU standards approach highest-common-denominator levels, integration directly curtails national autonomy but to the benefit rather than the detriment of the environment. Second, even lowest-common-denominator outcomes erode national sovereignty in a manner which has at least one positive implication for the environment: the fact that EU laws prohibit Member States from backsliding on their previously announced domestic plans.

But given the prevalence of modest EU process standards (the rarity of highest-common-denominator outcomes) and the trends associated with subsidiarity, the most important and perhaps surprising lesson for those engaged in the globalization debate is surely this: fears that tough environmental laws in an integrated European (and global) market will spark capital flight and industrial relocation have certainly been expressed, for example at national level in the *Standort Deutschland* (Germany as a location for industry) debate and by the Confederation of British Industry, and at EU level by the 1995 Molitor Report, but so far there has *not* been anything like a downward convergence in process standards and green Member States have *not* been induced to undertake widespread retrenchment of their environmental policies. Rather, heightened sensitivity to issues of economic competitiveness has found expression in much less dramatic but still constraining ways. One is the measured enthusiasm shown by green Member States towards further tightening of their current laws. Governments everywhere are also striving to design more flexible, efficient policy instruments which will deliver the same or better environmental protection at considerably less cost to industry (Golub 1998a). To this end, widespread use has been made of voluntary agreements, ecotaxes, ecolabels, and ecoaudits. The relative effectiveness and cost of these new instruments is not yet clear, in part because traditional command and control measures, although much maligned, have shown remarkable resilience, and also because states have been reluctant to impose green taxes on key industrial sectors or set them at high levels for fear of undermining national economic competitiveness.

Social policy

Development of EU social policy has followed a very different path from that of EU environmental policy, in that negative rather than positive integration has predominated. And instead of a California effect, ECJ rulings have, at least in certain ways, consistently stripped away national sovereignty over fundamental aspects of welfare provision and labour market structure. The result of negative integration has been that individual Member States now enjoy far less control over the supply and demand – and hence the overall costs – of their welfare programmes. As part of this 'incremental, rights-based, homogenisation of social policy' (Leibfried and Pierson 1995: 65), Member States are no longer allowed to target welfare benefits solely to their own citizens but instead must cease discrimination and extend benefits to all EU nationals living or working in their territory. Welfare has also become portable, in that Member States can no longer compel citizens to consume their benefits or services in the providing country but instead must allow these payments to be exported anywhere in the Union. States therefore face the challenge of sustaining expensive programmes despite the fact that they can no longer count on the stimulus imparted to their economies when recipients spend their benefits at home.

In sharp contrast to the environmental sphere, there has been practically no positive harmonization of EU social policy. In part this stems from the fact that the original Treaty was not directly geared towards constructing social democracy and contained only vague foundations for a federal welfare state (Rhodes 1998). However, it must be recalled that the Treaty contained absolutely no reference to environmental policy, yet this field developed rapidly after 1973. The more fundamental reason for the absence of social policy is that there has never been a political consensus on translating elastic treaty provisions into common programmes. Since the very beginning of the EU, a plausible case could be made for harmonizing nearly all aspects of modern social policy because of their affect on the functioning of the internal market. Wildly disparate rules governing retirement ages, minimum wages, vocational training, pensions, maternity care, disability pay and income support all contribute to the production costs, investment patterns and competitiveness across Member States, certainly to a much greater degree than environmental rules ever could. However, compared with environmental policy, the obstacles to positive integration in social policy are much greater because these distinctive national traditions have evolved over decades or even centuries, and have become deeply embedded facets of the domestic political landscape. Moreover, many of these areas are so interconnected that the specific content of a potential overarching EU social policy has been seen by many as too complex to conceptualize.

Even following the heroic efforts of Jacques Delors, the 1987 extension of qualified majority voting, the 1989 Social Charter, the opt-out of Britain – traditionally the most intransigent opponent of EU social policy – and the replacement of the Conservative government of Margaret Thatcher by a more enthusiastic Labour government, the Council has still managed to adopt only a handful of social policies: the most prominent of these provide for the health and safety of atypical workers, protection for pregnant women and new mothers in the workplace, protection for young workers, standards for posted workers, organization of working time (the 48-hour working week) and consultation rights for workers in multinational firms (Rhodes 1998). Small in number, avoiding many of the most important welfare issues which are not directly related to the workplace, these policies also exhibit little evidence of functionalist problem-solving and are a far cry from highest-common-denominator outcomes. Instead, proposals for ambitious common standards have been consistently watered down in fierce intergovernmental bargaining.

According to most popular accounts, the progressive establishment of the four freedoms, the increasingly privileged position of capital, and the slim prospects for positive harmonization should have undermined the preconditions for social democracy and sparked a race to the bottom as the now 'semi-sovereign' Member States engaged in social dumping and catered to the demands of employers (Moses 1995, Scharpf 1997). But has such a race materialized? Has the size of the state shrunk and social spending collapsed because governments are reluctant to tax mobile capital or crowd out private investment by spending and running deficits? Has EU economic integration impoverished and divided the position of labour, and resulted in declining union densities and falling wages? Has an atrophied welfare net increased income inequality between the richest and poorest segments of society? Table 11.1 presents data on seven member states for several objective measures which help answer these questions.

Despite extensive negative integration and minimal reregulation at the European level, the figures reveal no evidence of a race to the bottom or anything like a convergence across the EU. In fact, as European integration has proceeded, the overall size of government outlays and the level of social expenditure have remained basically constant or even risen sharply, and both of these measures exhibit increasing cross-national variation rather than signs of convergence. And regardless of constraints imposed by the common market, some of these seven states still manage to spend nearly twice as much on social policy as do governments in Greece, Portugal and Ireland. Governments preaching wholesale welfare retrenchment have been long on rhetoric and short on securing cutbacks, with cost containment efforts taking the form of tinkering with established welfare programmes. As part of this 'consolidation' effort, some governments have extended the waiting periods required before entitlement payments begin, delayed or suspended the indexation of benefits to inflation, and restricted welfare eligibility (Kitschelt 1994; Pierson 1995). But even slight retrenchment exacts an enormous political price and these measures might not stick; the new governments of Tony Blair and Gerhard Schröder have pledged to undo the modest efforts of their more conservative predecessors.

Nor did levels of capital taxation fall or converge as integration progressed. Governments supposedly attendant to the economically damaging effects of non-wage costs on employers have either made no adjustments or have taxed capital more heavily in recent years. And dramatic national differences persist in these tax rates.

There is also no clear evidence that European integration has eroded one of the primary preconditions for social democracy, union density. Garrett suggests that density within most Member States has actually grown substantially throughout the history of the EU (Garrett 1996). In

Table 11.1 Welfare state and social policy indicators in the EU

	Government outlays (%GDP)		Effective rate of capital taxation (%)		Social protection expenditure (%GDP)		Union density (%)		Earnings inequality (% change)
	1960–73	1990–95	levels[a]	change[b]	1980	1993	1967–74	1985–90	
Belgium	39.1	56.0	36.7	2.9	26.5	26.3	33	39	−5.9 (1986–93)
Denmark	33.8	61.3	34.8		28.0	32.3	36	59	+1.9 (1980–89)
Germany	37.5	50.0	28.5	2.4	28.0	29.7	21	22	−13.8 (1983–93)
France	38.0	52.7	26.0	3.2	24.0	29.2	10	7	+1.2 (1979–94)
Italy	33.7	54.3	28.1		18.0	24.5	11	16	−4.8 (1979–93)
Netherlands	40.8	58.1	30.5		29.0	32.1	18	15	+2.0 (1986–94)
UK	36.7	44.2	57.5	1.9	20.7	26.8	30	28	+21.1 (1979–95)

Source: Garrett (1996, 1998), OECD (1996, 1997), European Economy (1997).

Notes:
a Average levels during 1985–92
b Change from average 1965–84 levels

recent years this growth has stabilized, and only in a few states has there been a noticeable decline. By contrast, Bruce Western presents evidence of more widespread union losses, but even his analysis suggests, first, that Belgium, Denmark and Italy bucked the trend, and second, that there are no indications of an inevitable European neo-liberal convergence towards the type of dramatically low union density one finds in France (Western 1997). Furthermore, falling union density is not necessarily a reflection of constraints imposed by EU economic integration, as demonstrated most clearly by the British case, where Thatcher's aggressive union-busting policies were certainly the primary factor.

One important ramification of welfare nets and union densities remaining solid is that most EU states have not experienced the wage stagnation or rising income inequality which has plagued the USA. Since the early 1980s, when negative integration got into full swing, Belgium, France, Germany, Italy and the UK have experienced strong real wage growth (OECD 1996: 67). As for inequality, which is supposedly an inevitable by-product of open trade and capital flows, a standard measure is the ratio of the top 10 per cent of incomes to the bottom 10 per cent. A recent OECD study found that 'contrary to what might have been predicted at the end of the 1980s, only a relatively few countries experienced a significant increase in earnings inequality over the first half of the 1990s' (OECD 1996: 91–2). As shown in Table 11.1, inequality remained almost unchanged in France, Denmark and the Netherlands, and it actually fell sharply in Belgium, Italy and especially in Germany. That the UK is an extreme outlier once again reveals more about the effects of Thatcherism than about the impact of integration.

The bottom line here is that Member States are semi-sovereign in the sense that integration has forced them to adapt the delivery of welfare benefits to accommodate portability and inclusiveness, but integration has not eroded the preconditions for social democracy, nor the ability of Member States to pursue distinctive and generous forms of social policy if that is what their citizens so desire.

Are high standards viable?

Even if EU states have so far avoided a race to the bottom, the question remains whether high social and environmental standards are viable options over the long run. I suggest that the answer hinges on which of two competing models eventually prevails. What I would deem a 'punctuated equilibrium' model envisages a belated, but inevitable and potentially dramatic, downward spiral, whereas the 'win-win' model extols the inherent economic benefits and therefore the durability of high standards and generous welfare provisions. I briefly consider each in turn.

Borrowing the term 'punctuated equilibrium' from evolutionary biology, Stephen Krasner has argued that some of the most important political changes do not proceed by smooth, incremental steps but are instead the products of infrequent upheavals (Krasner 1988). This model would suggest that, even if the EU had achieved complete negative integration – entirely unhindered trade, migration and capital flows – without any positive harmonization, there are fundamental reasons why we would not have seen neo-liberal policy convergence on minimalist social and environmental policies despite strong pressure to improve economic competitiveness: high standards, no matter how economically 'dysfunctional', could survive as long as they have solely because they are deeply embedded, because institutions are extremely 'sticky', and because the politics of retrenchment are so perilous (Wade 1996; Pierson 1995; Garrett and Lange 1996). But the dismantling of expensive welfare and environmental policies is only a matter of time because factors which exert mounting pressure on a system can be ignored, contained or suppressed for only so long. Eventually they result in spectacular reforms or collapse.

Those who subscribe to a punctuated equilibrium model might already detect signs of strain. For example, in some cases compliance with environmental standards accounts for up to 20 per cent of a firm's overall production costs and an even higher proportion of investment costs, high enough plausibly to influence the competitiveness of products as well as plant location decisions (Golub 1998b). Studies have also shown that rising green standards adversely affected certain EU industrial sectors and depressed German productivity growth in the 1980s. These effects might intensify as cheaper methods of communication and transport steadily increase the relative contribution of environmental expenditure to overall production costs. Add to this the enhanced threats of capital flight since the late 1980s and one might conclude that green states are fighting a losing battle and will eventually capitulate in dramatic fashion to irresistible market forces or else face dire economic consequences.

Turning to social policy, one could argue that systemic stress is already evident in the EU to the extent that desperate efforts to preserve social democracy merely cause unemployment levels to balloon. And this stress will intensify over time if it is true that the post-war settlement of 'embedded liberalism' was only made possible as a result of closed financial markets and a fortunate period of unusually strong economic growth. It might simply be too soon to judge the full effects of changing conditions. If so, financial integration 'may yet be the death knell of social democracy' because 'it still takes two to tango and, in a world with free capital movements, your partner may choose not to dance' (Garrett 1996: 103; Esping-Andersen 1990: 188). Finally, there is the obvious possibility that expensive social and environmental policies will be the first casualties of Economic and Monetary Union as the single currency and formal rules on small budget deficits force austerity and an inevitable liberal convergence amongst all Member States.

The alternative 'win-win' model paints an entirely different picture, one in which states do not face irresistible pressure to retreat from intervention, where social democracy has a bright future, and where there is nothing inevitable about a regulatory race to the bottom. Classed broadly under the headings 'strategic environmental policy', 'strategic trade' and 'new growth theory', this expanding literature suggests that ambitious environmental and social standards actually improve both industrial competitiveness and a nation's overall economic performance (Romer 1994; Garrett 1998; Golub 1998b; Rhodes and Van Apeldoorn forthcoming). Under this model, one could easily explain the persistence of national diversity and would even predict or at least advocate a race to the top. In other words, the high standards pursued by Germany, the Netherlands and Scandinavian states not only enjoy long-term viability, they are inherently advantageous.

The Commission has issued several reports advocating a win-win approach to environmental policy, arguing that regulation, so adamantly opposed by industry, actually generates a range of financial benefits which accrue to the individual firm. High standards guarantee clean inputs for manufacturing, spur more efficient modes of production, prevent disruptions caused by environmental accidents or the poor health of workers and position firms to capture first mover advantage in the lucrative EU (and global) market for green technology and services. Those who support this position cite examples from the USA, Germany, Japan and Australia where after-the-fact savings have arguably justified the imposition of stringent environmental regulations.

In the realm of social policy, the very existence of modern welfare states illustrates that to some extent all countries recognize the need to seek 'positive-sum outcomes' by tempering unbridled market forces and providing their citizens with at least a modicum of decommodification (Esping-Andersen 1990: 147). In sharp contrast to current globalization fears, Cameron (1978) and Katzenstein (1985) have argued that, in order to reap gains from international trade, states must intervene with welfare programmes and create a large social buffer with which to compensate the domestic losers. The outcome is win-win in the sense that social policy maintains public support for modern capitalism and averts systemic collapse. New growth theory goes even further and suggests that government spending on public goods such as infrastructure, education and research may actually enhance economic performance. Examples are most obvious in Asia but can also be found across Europe (Evans 1997). Many would say that the same logic extends beyond public goods and applies equally to government provision of general welfare programmes and social policies. The argument is that high wages and non-wage investments do not undermine economic competitiveness but, rather, raise the productivity of well trained, motivated, flexible workers. National welfare provisions for income support, housing benefits, health care and unemployment insurance don't just crowd out private investment and scare firms away, they actually secure the type of social stability and attractive investment climate which lures companies and benefits the economy. Germany, for instance, has one of the most generous welfare states in the EU, yet it boasts extremely high productivity and has remained enormously competitive against states where social wages are considerably lower.

Detractors of the win-win model, as well as globalization alarmists, might counter that, by driving up wages and employer costs, welfare destroys low-skilled jobs and raises unemployment levels for those groups most in need. They might also contend that, given the intense regulatory competition unleashed by the common market and the minimal chances of positive harmonization, EU states must accept a move towards lower wages, lower benefit levels and greater wage dispersion or else face high unemployment. But this is not necessarily the case. There is certainly no shortage of publicity when multinational firms decide to shed jobs from plants located where social and environmental standards are high, or to invest where host governments offer lenient conditions. Undeniably there are some firms that behave in a manner consistent with the race to the bottom logic, which fuels speculation about a possible impending regulatory meltdown, but in general studies show that companies don't necessarily invest where wages and tax levels are lowest or where environmental rules are laxest (Garrett 1998; Golub 1998b). In fact, there is evidence that high standards can actually attract firms and inward direct investment, consistent with win-win presumptions. And when considering evidence to the contrary, one must be careful to distinguish industrial relocation and capital flight from situations where firms have simply outgrown their home markets and invest abroad without curtailing their domestic operations. In the case of women, youth and low-skilled workers, all of whom face the highest chances of being priced out of the market, studies reveal that unemployment rates among these groups are not correlated with wage levels, that there is no straightforward trade-off between unemployment and inequality, and that the welfare state is not a 'job killer' (OECD 1996: 94). In short, 'the problems currently facing European labour markets and welfare states have been caused neither by an absence of a European welfare state nor by regime competition and social dumping' (Rhodes 1998: 12).

If the win-win model is correct, how can we account for the supposed crisis facing EU economies and national welfare states? While it is easy to attribute Europe's economic woes to the effects of globalization and integration, technological and domestic factors are probably the real culprits. In every Member State, rapidly advancing technology jeopardizes low-skilled jobs, low birth rates and ageing populations place severe pressure on pension systems and government budgets, and the long-overdue feminization of the workforce disrupts established patterns of labour relations and generates demand for new and expanded social policies (Esping-Andersen 1990; Rhodes 1998). Besides these general factors there are also important domestic political pressures which are clearly country-specific, most obviously the challenges facing Germany following its reunification. In the struggle to cope with all of these domestic challenges, Member States might well embrace the combination of EU economic integration and unilateral commitment to high environmental and social standards as part of the solution, not the problem, particularly when they consider that their growth, unemployment and inflation levels would have all been worse if it weren't for the single market (Cecchini 1988; EU 1996).

Conclusion

In this chapter I have emphasized some of the implications European integration holds for the globalization debate. Alarmists will be surprised by the fact that European integration has greatly intensified transnational exchange without unleashing anything like a race to the bottom or a convergence in either environmental or social policy. They would certainly be pleased by the extent to which green and socially progressive Member States have retained national sovereignty, and ironically they might also be pleased by the fact that in some cases 'dirty' or less progressive Member States have lost control over their own destinies by being forced to make upward adjustments. Those like Keohane, Slaughter and other institutionalists who study the emerging structures which populate the new world order would be correct in attributing these developments at least in part to the advanced institutional design of the EU; not because it generates some sort of functionalist problem-solving dynamic but because it allows solutions to collective action problems when they arise, occasionally facilitates 'ratcheting' through intergovernmental and transgovernmental political bargains, and it allows for the ECJ-driven California effect as well as the judicial reinterpretation of vague and seemingly innocuous Council decisions. But supranational institutions have not been the primary bulwark against a downward regulatory spiral. National standards still remain extremely diverse, even where the EU has undertaken mostly negative rather than positive integration and where there has been no California effect. Integration has brought some changes in how social policies are delivered, and has imposed a modest constraint on the stringency of new national environmental policies, but pressures for reform stem much more from domestic political factors and general technological advance. Whether over the long term Member States can meet their domestic challenges through a combination of European integration and ambitious (possibly unilateral) programmes depends on the inherent economic benefits provided by high standards (the win-win model).

Insights drawn from European integration also help frame discussions about the future of democracy under conditions of increasing globalization. A constructive treatment of this issue requires more than just forceful statements about competing principles of justice, and must be empirically grounded. Even the most adamant reformers admonish that we 'take the sources of disruption of social democracy seriously' (Cohen and Rogers 1997: 5), but this sound advice still contains an untested assumption that serious disruption has actually occurred, or is just around the corner. Advocates of cosmopolitan democracy are particularly prone to presume that global transactions render policies unresponsive to national democratic control (Held 1995; McGrew 1997). With this as their unsubstantiated starting point they then present remedies which often take the form of utopian visions involving a smoothly operating world government, the spontaneous emergence of globally shared identities and interests, implausible institutional structures in which decisions are taken by global referenda and an unproblematic universal legal code enforced by some sort of global coercive police and military service. Dire assessments of the status quo have even tempted otherwise serious scholars towards a bizarre type of Homer Simpson participatory democracy whereby individuals from around the world are selected at random to devise global policies governing phenomena which in some way affect them personally.

Empirical evidence presented in this chapter sharply contradicts the presumptions of cosmopolitan democracy and undermines the impetus for its utopian prescriptions. Despite unprecedented levels of transnational exchange in the European Union there has been nothing like a collapse of national democratic political control, and nothing like an overarching European demos or a shared identity has emerged amongst the EU's 400 million citizens. Even where EU policies are absent or minimal, the record reveals that the actual level of disruption to social democracy caused by integration has been fairly modest, individual national destinies related to social and environmental policies remain largely in the hands of national electorates, and – barring the punctuated equilibrium scenario – this will remain the case.

This in no way denies that increasing levels of political dissatisfaction and alienation among the public reveal serious shortcomings of traditional democratic governance in modern, complex societies. But erroneously attributing these trends to globalization and advocating fanciful new forms of world government merely obscures the actual source of the problems and diverts attention from realistic solutions. To the extent that global flows do pose modest constraints on national policy choice, one can certainly make the case for some form of 'global new deal' which incorporates social and environmental restrictions into the World Trade Organization (Collingsworth *et. al.* 1994; Ruggie 1994), or for an international legal mechanism which extends the reach of the California effect. But, given that challenges to democracy and policy-making originate predominantly at the national level, this is also where reforms should be concentrated, including such things as greater transparency of governmental decision-making and adequate representation for diffuse interests.

References

Cameron, D. (1978) 'The Expansion of the Public Economy', *American Political Science Review* 72, 4: 1243–61.

Cecchini, P. (1988) *The European Challenge: 1992*, Aldershot: Wildwood House.

Cohen, J. and Rogers, J. (1997) 'Can Egalitarianism Survive Internationalization?', MPIfG Working Paper 97/2, Cologne: Max Planck Institute for the Study of Societies.

Collingsworth, T., Good, J. and Harvey, P. (1994) 'Time for a Global New Deal', *Foreign Affairs*, Jan/Feb: 8–13.

de Zwaan, J. (1995) *The Permanent Representatives Committee: Its Role in European Union Decisionmaking*, Amsterdam: Elsevier.

Eichener, V. (1997) 'Effective Problem-solving: Lessons from the Regulation of Occupational Safety and Environmental Protection', *Journal of European Public Policy*, 4, 4: 591–608.

Esping-Andersen, G. (1990) *The Three Worlds of Welfare Capitalism*, Princeton: Princeton University Press.

European Economy (1997) *European Economy*, No. 4, Luxembourg: Office for Official Publications of the European Communities.

European Union (1996) 'The Impact and Effectiveness of the Single Market', COM(96)520, Brussels: Commission of the European Communities.

Evans, P. (1997) 'The Eclipse of the State? Reflections on Stateness in an Era of Globalization', *World Politics* 50: 62–87.

Garrett, G. (1996) 'Capital Mobility, Trade, and the Domestic Politics of Economic Policy', in R. Keohane and H. Milner (eds), *Internationalization and Domestic Politics*, Cambridge: Cambridge University Press.

——(1998) 'Global Markets and National Politics: Collision Course or Virtuous Circle?', *International Organization* 52, 4.

Garrett, G. and Lange, P. (1996) 'Internationalization, Institutions and Political Change', in R. Keohane and H. Milner (eds), *Internationalization and Domestic Politics*, Cambridge: Cambridge University Press.

Golub, J. (1996a) 'Why Did They Sign? Explaining EC Environmental Policy Bargaining', EUI Working Paper RSC No. 96/52, Florence: European University Institute.

——(1996b) 'The Politics of Judicial Discretion: Rethinking the Interaction Between National Courts and the European Court of Justice', *West European Politics* 19, 2: 360–85.

——(1996c) 'State Power and Institutional Influence: Lessons from the Packaging Waste Directive', *Journal of Common Market Studies* 34, 3: 313–39.

——(1996d) 'Sovereignty and Subsidiarity in EU Environmental Policy', *Political Studies* 44, 4: 686–703.

——(ed.) (1998a) *New Instruments for Environmental Policy in the EU*, London: Routledge.

——(1998b) 'Global Competition and EU Environmental Policy: Introduction and Overview', in J. Golub (ed.), *Global Competition and EU Environmental Policy*, London: Routledge.

Haas, E. (1964) *Beyond the Nation State: Functionalism and International Organization*, Stanford: Stanford University Press.

Haas, P., Keohane, R. and Levy, M. (eds) (1993) *Institutions for the Earth: Sources of Effective International Environmental Protection*, Cambridge, Mass.: MIT Press.

Held, D. (1995) *Democracy and the Global Order: From the Modern State to Cosmopolitan Governance*, Cambridge: Polity Press.

Héritier, A., Knill, C. and Mingers, S. (1996) *Ringing the Changes in Europe. Regulatory Competition and the Redefinition of the State. Britain, France and Germany*, Berlin: de Gruyter.

Hirst, P. and Thompson, G. (1996) *Globalization in Question: The International Economy and Possibilities of Governance*, Cambridge: Polity Press.

Katzenstein, P. (1985) *Small States in World Markets*, Ithaca: Cornell University Press.

Keohane, R. (1998) 'International Institutions: Can Interdependence Work?' *Foreign Policy*, 110: 82–94.

Kitschelt, H. (1994) *The Transformation of European Social Democracy*, Cambridge: Cambridge University Press.

Krasner, S. (1988) 'Sovereignty: An Institutional Perspective', *Comparative Political Studies* 21, 1: 66–94.

Leibfried, S. and Pierson, P. (1995) 'Semi-sovereign Welfare States: Social Policy in a Multitiered Europe', in P. Pierson and S. Leibfried (eds), *European Social Policy: Between Fragmentation and Integration*, Washington, DC: Brookings Institution.

McGrew, A. (1997) 'Democracy beyond Borders?: Globalization and the Reconstruction of Democratic Theory and Politics', in A. McGrew (ed.), *The Transformation of Democracy? Globalization and Territorial Democracy*, Cambridge: Polity Press.

Majone, G. (1993) 'Deregulation or Re-regulation? Policymaking in the European Community Since the Single Act', EUI Working Paper SPS no. 93/2, Florence: EUI.

Milward, A. (1992) *The European Rescue of the Nation State*, London: Routledge.

Moravcsik, A. (1993) 'Preferences and Power in the European Community: A Liberal Intergovernmentalist Approach', *Journal of Common Market Studies*, 31: 473–524.

Moses, J. (1995) 'The Social Democratic Predicament in the Emerging European Union: A Capital Dilemma', *Journal of European Public Policy* 2, 3: 407–26.

OECD (1996) *Employment Outlook*, July, Paris: OECD.

—— (1997) *Historical Statistics*, Paris: OECD.

Ohmae, K. (1991) *The Borderless World: Power and Strategy in the Interlinked Economy*, New York: Harper Collins.

Pierson, P. (1995) 'The New Politics of the Welfare State', *World Politics* 48: 143–79.

Rhodes, M. (1998) 'Defending the Social Contract: The EU between Global Constraints and Domestic Imperatives', in D. Hine and H. Kassim (eds), *Beyond the Market: The European Union and National Social Policy*, London: Routledge.

Rhodes, M. and Van Apeldoorn, B. (forthcoming) *Globalization and Welfare States*, Cambridge: Polity Press.

Romer, P. (1994) 'The Origins of Endogenous Growth', *Journal of Economic Perspectives* 8.

Ruggie, J. (1994) 'Trade, Protectionism and the Future of Welfare Capitalism', *Journal of International Affairs* 48, 1: 1–11.

Scharpf, F. (1997) 'Economic Integration, Democracy and the Welfare State', *Journal of European Public Policy* 4, 1: 18–36.

Slaughter, A. (1997) 'The Real New World Order', *Foreign Affairs* 76, 5: 183–97.

Vogel, D. (1996) *Trading Up: Consumer and Environmental Regulation in a Global Economy*, Cambridge, Mass.: Harvard University Press.

Wade, R. (1996) 'Globalization and its Limits: Reports of the Death of the National Economy are Greatly Exaggerated', in S. Berger and R. Dore (eds), *National Diversity and Global Capitalism*, Ithaca: Cornell University Press.

Western, B. (1997) *Between Class and Market: Postwar Unionization in the Capitalist Democracies*, Princeton: Princeton University Press.

Zürn, M. (1995) 'The Challenge of Globalization and Individualization: A View from Europe', in H. Holm and G. Sørenson (eds), *Whose World Order? Uneven Globalization and the End of the Cold War*, Boulder: Westview.

Globalization and democracy – an afterword

Richard Bellamy and R. J. Barry Jones

Three key questions animate the contributions to this volume: does global-ization challenge established patterns of territorially based governance (democratic or otherwise); do global issues and dynamics require effective governance at a supranational or transnational level; and is it either feasible or desirable for global governance to be based upon democratic principles and practices? Totally positive or negative answers are in their different ways unproblematic and uninteresting. 'Strong' or 'hyperglobal-ists' (for example, Ohmae 1995) reply in the affirmative to all three questions. They argue that the nation-state no longer offers liberal democ-racy's best shell. Globalization has undermined the state's capacity not only to forge a common identity and commitment to the public good, but also to provide its citizens with economic or physical security. Either we need and can have a cosmopolitan democracy that goes beyond the nation-state, or (in libertarian versions of this thesis) we can do without states altogether and rely on the beneficent effects of a global market. By contrast, rejectionists offer negative responses that leave us with the status quo. They contend that nothing has changed: trade, social relations, patterns of identity and systems of effective governance still focus on terri-torially based states. Difficulties only emerge among those offering more ambiguous replies. These weaker globalization positions (see Jones 1995a and Hirst and Thompson 1996) accept that some profound changes have taken place within the world system, but believe they have been uneven in both their incidence and their implication: in some areas, such as global finance, changes have been profound; in others, like the military–strategic system, traditional structures remain more-or-less intact. They acknowl-edge that globalization has enfeebled states without necessarily creating appropriate global institutions or communities to replace them.

All the contributors occupy the problematic ground found along the weak–strong continuum. If David Held, John Perraton, Boutros Boutros-Ghali, Johan Galtung, Daniele Archibugi and his co-authors, Michael Saward and Richard Falk hold stronger positions than Danilo Zolo, Tony Coates, Jonathan Golub, Paul Hirst and Graham Thompson, none of them believes globalization so strong as to be irresistible or so weak as to be negligible. They differ over the degree to which global forces threaten state-centred forms of democracy, the ways they might be adapted to cope with this new environment and their evaluation of the benefits and disadvantages of a cosmopolitan political system. But all agree that globalization challenges to a greater or lesser extent established patterns of democratic government.

We also lie within this range, but wish to examine an assumption commonly held by global democrats of all shades: namely, that democracy is a self-evidently basic good all wish to enjoy, and that the central issue is how it might best be realized in global conditions. We believe the resulting focus on which form democracy should take and where it might best be located begs the further questions of whether democracy is important and, if so, why, for what purpose, when and among whom? There are a variety of forces making for the possible transformation of democracy beyond the nation-state. These call for different sorts of solution, not all of them democratic in kind, and involve different groups of people.

Globalization has altered the modes as well as the levels of government activity, and traditional democratic ideals and styles may not always be appropriate to these circumstances. To see why, we shall begin by looking at the supply and demand factors involved in the shift from state government to global governance. We then investigate the important questions of why democracy is important, for what, where, among whom and when. Finally, we use these frameworks to address the proposals of the various contributors. We shall conclude that global democracy may be a much patchier and more improvised system than certain enthusiasts imagine, but all the more plausible and desirable for that.

From state government to global governance

There are 'supply' and 'demand' aspects to the issue of global democracy, which commentators too often conflate. On the 'supply-side' of the equation lie arguments about how far advancing globalization has undermined the effectiveness, and ultimately the legitimacy, of established state-level government. Proponents of global democracy, like David Held, Boutros Boutros-Ghali, Richard Falk and Johan Galtung, maintain that globally integrated finance, increasingly internationalized business organizations, the growth of 'international' trade and, more generally, of intersocietal interdependence have narrowed the competence of states in some areas; effectively eliminated it in others. The faltering capacities of state-level government lead ineluctably to an ever greater need for new structures and institutions of governance at supranational and transnational levels to supply the regulatory goods states can no longer provide. On the 'demand-side' of the governance equation are those 'new' problems resulting from globalization, most notably environmental issues such as global warming, that call for novel forms of genuinely global governance. These new structures necessarily involve more than relocating traditional state forms of democracy at a supra-state level. They address problems of a different kind to those traditionally tackled by states and that only arise in a global context. Even so, as Zolo notes, a global problem may not need a global authority to address it. New forms of global cooperation between existing state agencies may be sufficient.

Distinguishing the 'supply' and 'demand' aspects of the global democracy debate is important. Though some contemporary global developments, like those created by financial integration, upset this traditional picture by impacting simultaneously on both sides of governance, the distinction remains analytically illuminating. New 'demands' may involve supplying either the same goods in different ways or different goods. Both the supply of traditional democratic goods in global conditions and meeting the demand of emerging global problems may require a rethink of not only the forms democracy must take but also the ideals it instantiates. Conventional notions of representation, sovereignty, authority and citizenship may not be plausible within global structures. Indeed, democracy *per se* may be an inappropriate response to many global problems.

This rethinking of democracy belongs to the broader change from government to governance noted by a number of commentators.[1] Though they define governance in diverse and often maddeningly imprecise ways (see Rhodes 1996: 653–9 for a useful overview), all focus on a common phenomenon: namely, the expansion of regulatory and decision-making mechanisms beyond the various branches of the state and away from formal and hierarchically ordered structures of authority. These mechanisms include intergovernmental institutions possessing their own bureaucracies and decision-making processes and differing degrees of autonomy, scope and power, from the European Union (EU) through the United Nations (UN) to the North Atlantic Treaty Organization (NATO); non- or quasi-governmental sector-specific agencies, such as Housing Trusts, the Child Support Agency and the Bank for International Settlements; professional bodies, like the British Medical Association (BMA) or the Federation of International Football Associations (FIFA); self-validating legal bodies, such as the European Court of Human Rights; semi-autonomous inspectorates, such as the European Ombudsman; the managerial structures adopted by private organizations, from businesses to clubs and associations; and last, but far from least, the discipline of social norms and, most important of all, the market. The making, implementation and monitoring of policy increasingly involves a mix of different kinds of state and non-state, public and private actors, with the former ranging from government ministers to city administrators, and the latter from corporations and unions, through charities and associations, to pressure groups, think tanks, learned bodies and prominent individuals. Moreover they operate at a number of levels, from the international to the local, and employ rules and procedures of varying degrees of formality.

Four dimensions of governance emerge from this analysis: the public and the private, formal and informal. Public governance serves an identifiable population across a range of issues of general concern; private governance is generated by and for a specific group of actors and is concerned with a restricted range of issues particular to them. Formal governance – based upon laws, constitutions or treaties – can also be differentiated, analytically at least, from informal modes – based upon common understandings, mutual accommodations, tacit agreements, and so on. As we have seen, the first two categories contain a wide spectrum of different types of actor or agency, the last two a variety of types of regulation and decision-procedure. A matrix of four types of governance arises from the public–private and formal–informal distinctions (see Figure A1).

All four may to a lesser or greater degree be democratic. Thus, formal public governance can involve democratically elected politicians or enlightened bureaucrats; private formal governance may take the form of market exchanges or the elected committee or executive of a firm or association. Totally informal variants also exist. For example, social reputation can place an individual in a public leadership role and the democratic will often manifest itself more effectively in terms of diffuse public opinion than at the hustings. Nor are these mutually exclusive modes of governance. Most formal mechanisms involve informal elements and vice versa. Indeed, all democracies manifest aspects of these four types of governance, with the recent privatization of large elements of the former public sector greatly increasing the crossover between them.

This schema suggests four corresponding patterns of future governance for a world of growing globalization (or mere internationalization). The first is the status quo of uneven interstate regulation, in which representatives of democratic societies rub shoulders with those of manifestly

	Public	Private
Formal		
Informal		

Figure A1   Types of governance

undemocratic regimes in primarily intergovernmental fora of highly variable effectiveness. The second possibility is the development of the state-based status quo, with the enhancement of the regulatory capabilities of the range of intergovernmental regimes (see Krasner 1983; and Rittberger 1993 for overviews of regime theory) and the extension of the democratic credentials of the states represented in them. The third possibility is the progressive replacement of state-based governance and interstate regulation of the global system by a new global civil society, and a new pattern of 'global democracy' (in addition to contributions to this volume, see Held 1995 for a further discussion of this concept) with new institutions of democratic global governance. The fourth is that of the growing role of private governance, with its characteristically limited perspective, long-term fragility and often undemocratic character. Associations of market-based actors are the main candidates for such private governance.

As noted, these scenarios do not exclude one other. Jonathan Golub notes how the EU, probably the most developed instance of transnational – and hence of proto-global – governance today, manifests features of all four. Thus, the intergovernmental conferences employed to make and revise the European Treaties belong to the status quo; however, acceptance of liberal-democratic principles is now a condition of membership and the Council of Ministers has clearly formalized intergovernmentalism to a large degree. At the same time, the EU has its own bureaucracy, political institutions and judiciary; can make laws, call elections, raise revenue and even engage in certain international negotiations. Consequently, there is a plethora of non-state actors, from individual citizens to regions and European-wide interest groups, that directly or indirectly participate in the EU political system. Finally, the common market remains the prime rationale for European Union and the principal motor of integration and the development of a European civil society. Though some pro-Europeans believe the ultimate trajectory of the EU is towards a unified polity, economy and society, the current picture is much more complex and likely to remain so for the foreseeable future. At present there is a proliferation not only of levels and types of governance but also of the actors involved, with regions, cities, sub-national, national and transnational interest groups and non-governmental organizations all playing a part in the decision-making and regulatory process (Schmitter 1996). This phenomenon of 'multi-level governance' has appeared transitory and unstable to some, but suggests to others that the most likely form of global governance will be some complicated mix of all four of the modes identified above (Marks, Hooghe and Blank 1996). The crux lies in identifying the appropriate mix. This task involves asking what the relative merits of different types of public and private, formal and informal governance are for different sorts of problem, how democratic they need be, and who is to employ them (Bellamy and Warleigh 1998; Schmitter 1998).

Why democracy, which kind, to decide what, among whom, where and when?

The question, 'Why is democracy beneficial?' is rarely addressed explicitly.[2] More commonly, commentators focus on its normative foundations and its empirical manifestations in order to discover what democracy is, taking its virtues for granted. However, we believe that asking why we value democracy provides a clearer picture than either purely prescriptive or merely descriptive approaches to the definition of democracy can offer, of which sort of democracy should be employed, for what purpose, among whom, where and when.

Democracy allows the ruled to control the exercise of power by their rulers, on the one hand, and provide rulers with information about the ideals and interests of the ruled, on the other. These two functions yield four related benefits. First, they protect and help define individual rights and liberties by checking arbitrary and self-interested rule and encouraging (as we shall see below) the formulation of general laws that reflect the common good.[3] Second, democratic mechanisms foster a degree of social equality. Because democratic majorities inevitably contain the underprivileged, the rich find it harder to ignore the poor and are forced to offer at least some redistribution of resources. For example, Amartya Sen has observed how 'democracy spreads the penalty of famines from the destitute to those in authority. There is no surer way of making government responsive to the suffering of famine victims' (Sen 1990: 19). Third, democracy helps identify and inculcate support for the collective good. Democracy encourages the reciprocity needed to construct the general will. Democratic equality obliges participants (at least to some degree) either to strike mutually beneficial bargains or to argue in ways that are open to scrutiny and show equal concern and respect for the opinions of their interlocutors. These processes weed out purely self-interested arguments by turning private individuals into citizens of the commonwealth. This transformation supports the supply of public goods, such as defence, and the tackling of public bads, such as pollution. More controversially, civic participation can also foster solidarity and trust. Such bonds are necessary if minorities are to accept majority decisions and, more importantly, majorities are to modify their demands to take account of minority concerns (Elster 1986; Bellamy and Hollis 1998). Finally, democracy promotes domestic and international peace. People exchange words rather than bullets, with jaw jaw replacing war war (Doyle 1983).

Attempts to define democracy in terms of a set of rules of the game (e.g. Bobbio 1987), no matter how minimal, overlook the fact that democracies are distinguished by the continual contestation of their rules. Qualifications for citizenship (as in struggles over the franchise); the nature of the political system (as in debates over the powers of the executive); the composition of the legislature (the balance between local and central government and so on); the practices of democratic decision-making (whether they should be consensual or adverserial, direct or indirect, for example), their location (for instance, in firms, as industrial democrats argue, or only for politicians) and scope (as when people dispute whether practically and normatively even democratic states should interfere with the market or 'private' life) have been and remain the subject of heated public controversy. What lies behind this redrawing of the rules is not the establishment of some 'ideal' or 'true' democracy so much as the desire to secure the benefits of democratic rule in ever changing circumstances for an increasingly diverse population (Tully forthcoming).

Which model of democracy one should adopt, therefore, rests on what set of procedures and principles will produce the responsive rule and civic education required to deliver the democratic goods. To a large extent, this depends on the complexion of the *demos* and the type of issue being tackled. The more heterogeneous the population the more complex the mechanisms for distributing power are likely to be, with culturally plural societies tending to favour consociationalism over majoritarianism (Lijphart 1977), for example. Likewise, decision-making processes and levels of power vary in their efficiency and effectiveness according to the problem, service or good under consideration. Thus, executives are typically freer from political controls in matters requiring dispatch, decisiveness and discretion, such as war, than when deciding long-term social and economic policy, where greater consultation with and dialogue between the interests and ideals of those concerned seems appropriate.

As we saw in the last section, public and private, formal and informal procedures, are further variables. Balancing these also depends largely on context and in particular on what is to be decided. Certain issues may even be better resolved from a democratic point of view, albeit broadly conceived, by methods that are normally judged nondemocratic. For instance, the privatization of various hitherto publicly managed services, such as trains and telephones, was often defended on the grounds that consumer pressure made them more responsive to popular demands than any plausible form of citizen pressure could.[4] Neo-liberals contended that, epistemologically and practically, economic management by political agencies was necessarily inefficient and oppressive. No state agency could either process all the information coming from consumers and producers, or mimic the innovation of new demands and products that result from a free market (Hayek 1960). Though liberal democrats now accept many of these points, that still leaves plenty of room for debate over the degree to which markets need democratic regulation to prevent their freedom and efficiency being undermined by individually economically advantageous but collectively disastrous behaviour, such as cartels or insider dealing. Differences also persist over which goods can be legitimately delivered in market terms without destroying their intrinsic qualities. That money cannot buy love as opposed to sex is appreciated by most. How far similar considerations apply to health, art, education or sport, say, is less clear-cut. Paradoxically, democracy may itself have to answer such questions about its limits, with different *demoi* operating different procedures and coming up with different answers (see Walzer 1983 for an argument along these lines).

Though general rules of thumb are possible, therefore, one cannot resolve which democracy is best or what issues it should be employed to resolve *a priori*. Though the continuous process of democratic self-definition constitutes one of democracy's central paradoxes, it is only the start of the conundrum. To ask which democracy we should adopt and for what purpose assumes the democratic process is up and running. However, answers to the questions when (in the sense of in what circumstances) can democracy be established or invoked, who is the *demos* and where can the people, once defined, exercise their democratic entitlements, are themselves preconditions for democracy. Consequently their resolutions necessarily lie beyond any democratic process.

Democratic rule only takes root when rival sources of economic, social and coercive power have been subordinated. This has only ever occurred through non-democratic and usually violent means, such as defeat in war, revolution or a *coup d'état*. The people (as opposed to the electorate) and the territorial location of democracy also have non-democratic origins in historical and geographical contingency. The people may be self-determining but cannot determine for themselves who they are. There is no democratic rationale for deciding who to consult, for democracy assumes that there is a political community to ask. Both these related problems arise with secession, for example. For Scotland to secede from the UK, must there be a mere majority favouring it in the future Scottish territory, or must it be a super-majority and perhaps involve the whole UK? The all-affected principle appealed to by many theorists offers little help here. English and Scots might feel equally affected by such a decision, but still debate whether they vote as a single constituency with a simple majority sufficing or as two constituencies involving a concurrent majority. Indeed, many Scots would deny the right of the English to be involved in the decision at all. And that still leaves wide open issues such as whether either or both would still be members of the EU, NATO, or the UN. Likewise the timing of any referendum may have a crucial bearing on the outcome. Once again, however, which *demos* can speak and when are not matters they can decide democratically for themselves.

These complications are related to the more general quandary of democratic agenda-setting. For democracy not only assumes a *demos* but also choices for debate that originate only indirectly from the democratic process itself. As practised, democracy in its usual liberal, representative form, standardly consists of a periodic choice between parties. Electoral success requires their platforms respond indirectly to voter opinion, but parties also have the capacity to collude in sidelining certain topics. A direct democracy that involved everyone listing the preferred policy options on each and every conceivable issue is a practical impossibility, even with the new technology of communications and information gathering, and might defy the adoption of any conceivable collective decision rule. We rely on others to reduce the agenda to manageable proportions. What we vote on, therefore, is decided by the political class. Broadly conceived, this includes people such as activists and journalists as well as politicians, but not the *demos* as a whole. Faith in democracy usually goes hand-in-hand with faith in the elites.

For democracy to be possible, therefore, alternative sources of power must be overcome, the political community be established, and a reliable and accepted political class exist. People may then debate the rules and scope of democracy, and democracy can periodically renew itself. In other words, asking which democracy, and for what purpose, assumes we already know when, for whom and where. In the language employed earlier, the supply-side of the democracy equation turns to a high degree on factors outside the democratic process, though some lie within it. Within those parameters, democracy can adapt itself to meet new demands, and even evaluate its own appropriateness to do so.

Is global democracy desirable or possible?

With these clarifications in mind, we can now address the responses of the contributors to the questions of whether global democracy is desirable or possible. A central claim of David Held's chapter is that the impact of globalization on political community means a resounding 'yes' on both counts. However, this account assumes the supply and demand aspects of the equation are changing in tandem: that the impact of globalization in creating new demands that states cannot solve has also conveniently reconfigured political communities into *demoi* that match the new cosmopolitan institutions. As Saward's discussion of the 'all-affected principle' suggests, however, both 'supply' and 'demand' are problematical and may not dovetail. On the supply side, it is unclear that the preconditions for the establishment of cosmopolitan democracy have been met. Alternative sources of power, both private and public, exist to challenge the capacity of such a regime to control significant aspects of social and economic life. If we again take the EU as an example, then, as Golub shows in his chapter, intergovernmentalism prevails in key areas of decision-making (Moravcsik 1991 and 1993) and the European economies remain vulnerable to the private power of world financial markets and multinational companies. On the demand-side, globalization often has highly differentiated effects. Instead of creating new communities of common fate it may accentuate differences, especially when linked to cultural diversity (Hirst and Thompson, 1996: chs 3, 4 and 5). As Golub notes, even within the EU there have been fierce disputes over environmental controls, such as the setting of fish quotas or emission standards. Typically Member States have tried to either free-ride on, or defect from, collective agreements whenever they have perceived it to be in their national interest to do so. Moreover, popular identities have not changed anything like as much as globalists would lead us to expect, or as is implied by such terms as 'global society' (Shaw 1994). When asked in a recent poll how they describe themselves – by nationality only, nationality and European, European and nationality, or European only – respondents were divided 45, 40, 6 and 5 per cent respectively (Eurobarometer Report No. 48, March 1998). Thus, notwith-standing increased European trade and labour mobility, there is little evidence of an emerging European *demos* or a shared political culture.

If such problems bedevil a relatively well established transnational polit-ical system, the prospects of turning the United Nations into a more effective institution for public global government, as proposed by Boutros Boutros-Ghali, Johan Galtung and Archibugi *et al.* (and see also Held 1995) look dim. The United Nations is, at heart, a 'club of states' (Jones 1995b) and its effectiveness remains, for the present, a function of the effectiveness of its members, or at least its leading members. As presently constituted, democratic global government via the United Nations would remain indirect rather than direct: a function of the representation of democratic states rather than of populations directly – and then only if all Member States were democratic by conventional standards. Galtung and Archibugi *et al.* seek to remedy these failings by curtailing the veto power of the Security Council and broadening its membership, and grafting a 'People's Assembly' onto the existing UN structure. However, if people's allegiances remain state-based, such reforms will lack legitimacy and if instituted might not alter decision-making as much as their proponents might suppose.

In any case, international instititutions that are rooted in a state-based system do not seem particularly favourable even to mild measures of democratization. By and large they have few, if any, democratic features and their rationale is to preserve the economic and military standing of the dominant powers – witness the structure and operation of the recently established World Trade Organization (WTO). Without the preconditions of an absence of alternative sources of power, a sense of community and a suitable founding moment, global democracy is unlikely even when it appears both desirable and logically necessary.

As Zolo points out, globalization has tended to exacerbate differences in economic and military power between rich and poor countries. Opening up markets to global competition can allow stronger economies to exploit their advantages to an even greater degree. The main industrial countries dominate any cosmopolitan body, and exploit the resulting concentration of power to further promote their interests. Zolo argues that the current practice of the UN supports this thesis, with the increasingly proactive role of the UN in global security issues amounting to little more than economic and cultural imperialism. A 'strong' transnational political order is in any case normatively and practically flawed, since no central body can do justice to the plurality of values and functional complexity of modern societies. Instead, he advocates 'weak' decentralized international institutions with local roots.

Zolo grounds his argument in moral and epistemological relativism. However, Coates shows this need not be the case. In fact a concern with human rights might well underpin his proposal for a weaker, more equitable political system far better. Drawing on the pre-Enlightenment natural law tradition, notably Vitoria (Pagden and Lawrence 1991), Coates argues that cosmopolitan morality need not produce arguments for world government: quite the opposite (indeed, this is arguably the case for the Kantian, Enlightenment version too – see Pogge 1994). Respect for rights suggests we should seek institutional arrangements that empower people to negotiate with others of opposed views and avoid being dominated by them. For all the reasons Zolo gives, these conditions are more likely to occur in weak decentralized political systems than in strong centralized and hierarchically ordered ones. That suggests we should look for an emerging global democracy through the development of informal, private forms of governance rather than formal institutions of public government (Dryzek forthcoming). However, a weak form of global governance may not be any more realistic than the stronger version Zolo attacks. Arguably it poses an even greater challenge to the existing order and hence is less likely to come about.

Despite its manifest failings, moves to supplement the present interstate system of global governance appear not only more likely but also in many respects more attractive than schemes to subvert or supplant it. In the absence of global institutions, any weakening of established state-level public government could create a serious regulatory hole that might all too readily be filled, in the short and medium term at least, by undemocratic structures of private governance. As Hirst and Thompson observe, the 'end of the state' could permit the spread of private, and often relatively informal, forms of governance into a growing number of areas of public interest: a privatization of governance in a quasi-medieval manner. Such private governance of the new global system might serve certain interests effectively for a time but would suffer from some fundamental shortcomings: the partiality of the interests represented; the limited availability of legitimacy and enforcement capabilities; and a chronic tendency towards retrospective (and often minimalist) responses to new problems and pressures.

The regulation of the financial sector, both domestically and internationally, has demonstrated the shortcomings of private governance with impressive frequency (Kindleberger 1996). Private governance in this area has been both resistant to public intervention and minimalist in its approach to its own affairs, until one or other major financial catastrophe threatens both the stability of the sector and the collapse of public confidence. At this stage, the intervention of public authorities is suddenly welcome, both as a provider of fall-back resources and, through the introduction of new rules and regulations, as a restorer of public confidence.

The financial sector provides merely the most marked example of the shortcomings of private governance in general, and on matters of public concern in particular. Such private governance, moreover, is far from democratic in any conventional sense of that word. The interests being served are those of the private interests operative within the domain of the particular institutions of private governance: any service to the public interest being incidental and articulated indirectly. The immediate consequence of any weakening of effective public governance at state or global levels is, however, likely to be the opening of the field to the spread of private governance, until such time as the inherent weaknesses of such arrangements become manifest in the face of breakdown and general disquiet.

A shift from interstate to global democratic government may not be possible, therefore, while global governance without government looks likely to be both undemocratic and undesirable. Instead, the most practical and attractive response to globalization may be a mixed solution. For the time being, states alone have the legitimacy to determine when democratic government is possible, either within or between them. Global democratic government is not an option. However, within this statist context, new political actors are developing that challenge established notions of who participates, how, where and what is decided, and push towards new forms of democratic governance both inside and across states. The EU provides probably the best example of how a basically intergovernmental framework can provide the environment for new kinds of transnational democratic governance while resisting moves towards the setting up of a transnational government (Bellamy and Castiglione, 1998). In sum, the possibility of global democracy lies in new forms of governance modifying and complementing, but not replacing, old forms of government.

Conclusion

Even if the strong globalization thesis proves valid, the world might still find itself betwixt and between for the foreseeable future; with traditional state and intergovernmental government reduced in effectiveness, but with the continued absence of the preconditions for a new and effective form of global democracy. Such a situation would raise serious questions about the stability and acceptability of the developing global order. If the strong globalization thesis is not wholly sound, then a mixed picture, with uneven implications, emerges. Effective traditional government might be undermined in some respects, but not in others; global government might be possible in some areas, but prove difficult and costly to establish and sustain in others. Such a mixed situation continues to raise serious questions about the emerging global condition and invites a more critical review of the possibilities, and limitations, of traditional forms and levels of public government. Moreover, the degree to which government must or can always be democratic, and what form that democracy should take, remain open questions. None the less, new types of global governance can emerge in an *ad hoc* fashion, fostering the evolution of, and collaboration between, established liberal democracies rooted in nation-states. Thus, the seeds of global democracy lie in governance *with* governments. The resulting system may prove messier than certain theorists of global democracy would like, but it is much more likely to satisfy the preconditions for the establishment of democracy and deliver the desired benefits than grander schemes for a cosmopolitan political order.

Notes

1 For discussions of this shift from an international and a domestic perspective respectively, see Rosenau (1992) and Rhodes (1996).
2 Three exceptions on which we have drawn are Schmitter and Karl (1991); Holden (1993); and especially Offe (1998).
3 The constitutional protection of rights and democracy can of course conflict when democratic majorities themselves turn tyrannous, but in general democracy is the form of government least prone to this danger. See Bellamy and Castiglione (1997) for a view of democracy as inherently constitutional.
4 Such thinking lay behind UK Conservative Prime Minister John Major's Citizens' Charter programme, for example. For an assessment, see Bellamy and Greenaway (1995).

References

Bellamy, R. and Castiglione, D. (1997) 'Constitutionalism and Democracy: Political Theory and the American Constitution', *British Journal of Political Science*, 27: 595–618.
——(1998) 'Between Cosmopolis and Community: Three Models of Rights and Democracy within the European Union', in D. Archibugi, D. Held and M. Köhler (eds), *Re-imagining Political Community*, Cambridge: Polity.
Bellamy, R. and Greenaway, J. (1995) 'The New Right Conception of Citizenship and the Citizens Charter', *Government and Opposition*, 30: 471–90.
Bellamy R, and Hollis, M. (1998) 'Consensus, Neutrality and Compromise', in R. Bellamy and M. Hollis (eds), *Pluralism and Liberal Neutrality*, London: Frank Cass.
Bellamy, R. and Warleigh, A. (1998) 'From an Ethics of Integration to an Ethics of Participation – Citizenship and the Future of European Union', *Millennium* 27: 447–70.
Bobbio, N. (1987) *The Future of Democracy: A Defence of the Rules of the Game*, trans. R. Griffen, ed. R. Bellamy, Cambridge: Polity.
Doyle, M. W. (1983) 'Kant, Liberal Legacies and Foreign Affairs', *Philosophy and Public Affairs*, 12: 205–35, 325–53.

Dryzek, J. S. (1999) 'Transnational Democracy', *Journal of Political Philosophy* 7: 30–51.

Elster, J. (1986) 'The Market and the Forum: Three Varieties of Political Theory', in J. Elster and A. Hylland (eds), *Foundations of Social Choice Theory*, Cambridge: Cambridge University Press.

Hayek, F. A. (1960) *The Constitution of Liberty*, London: Routledge.

Held, D. (1995) *Democracy and the Global Order*, Cambridge: Polity Press.

Hirst, P. and Thompson, G. (1996) *Globalization in Question*, Cambridge: Polity Press.

Holden, B. (1993) *Understanding Liberal Democracy*, 2nd edn, London: Harvester Wheatsheaf.

Jones, R. J. Barry (1995a) *Globalization and Interdependence in the International Political Economy: Rhetoric and Reality*, London: Pinter.

——(1995b) 'The United Nations and the International Political System', in D. Bourantonis and J. Wiener (eds), *The United Nations in the New World Order: The World Organization at Fifty*, Basingstoke: Macmillan.

Kindleberger, C. P. (1996) *Manias, Panics and Crashes*, 3rd edn, New York: John Wiley and Sons.

Krasner, S. D. (1983) *International Regimes*, Ithaca: Cornell University Press.

Lijphart, A. (1977) *Democracy in Plural Societies. A Comparative Exploration*, New Haven and London: Yale University Press.

Marks, G., Hooghe L. and Blank, K. (1996) 'European Integration from the 1980s: State-centric v. Multi-level Governance', *Journal of Common Market Studies* 34: 341–78.

Moravcsik, A. (1991) 'Negotiating the Single European Act: National Interests and Conventional Statecraft in the European Union', *International Organization* 45: 19–56.

——(1993) 'Preferences and Power in the European Community: A Liberal Inter-governmentalist Approach', *Journal of Common Market Studies* 31: 473–524.

Offe, C. (1998) ' "Homogeneity" and Constitutional Democracy: Coping with Identity Conflicts through Group Rights', *Journal of Political Philosophy* 6: 113–41.

Ohmae, K. (1995) *The End of the Nation State: The Rise of Regional Economies*, New York: Harper Collins.

Pagden, A. and Lawrence, J. (eds) (1991) *Francisco de Vitoria: Political Writings*, Cambridge: Cambridge University Press.

Pogge, T. W. (1994) 'Cosmopolitanism and Sovereignty', in C. Brown (ed.) *Political Restructuring in Europe: Ethical Perspectives*, London and New York: Routledge.

Rhodes, R. A. W. (1996) 'The New Governance: Governing without Government', *Political Studies* 44: 652–67.

Rittberger, V. (1993) *Regime Theory and International Relations*, Oxford: Oxford University Press.

Rosenau, J. N. (1992) 'Governance, Order and Change in World Politics', in J. N. Rosenau and E.-O. Czempiel (eds), *Governance without Government: Order and Change in World Politics*, Cambridge: Cambridge University Press.

Schmitter, P. C. (1996) 'Imagining the Future of the Euro-Polity with the Help of New Concepts', in G. Marks, F. W. Scharpf, P. Schmitter and W. Streek, *Governance in the European Union*, London: Sage.

——(1998) 'Is it Really Possible to Democratize the Euro-Polity?', in A. Follesdal and P. Koslowski (eds), *Democracy and the European Union*, Berlin: Springer.

Schmitter, P. C. and Karl, T. (1991) 'What Democracy Is...and Is Not', *Journal of Democracy* 2: 75–88.

Sen, A. (1990) 'How Democracy can Free the World of Famine', *The Independent*, 2 August.

Shaw, M. (1994) *Global Society and International Relations: Sociological Concepts and Political Perspectives*, Cambridge: Polity Press.

Tully, J. (forthcoming) 'The Agonic Freedom of Citizens', *Economy and Society*

Walzer, M. (1983) *Spheres of Justice: A Defence of Pluralism and Equality*, Oxford: Martin Robertson.

Index

academia 115–16, 137
Academic Council on the United
    Nations System 116
accountability 173; complex 41–2
Administrative Committee on
    Coordination 154
affectedness 33–5, 37–8, 210
Agenda for Democratization, An 8–9,
    105–24, 138, 139; academia
    115–16, 137; architecture of the UN
    120–4; business and industry
    116–18, 137; and the cosmopolitan
    democracy model 128–30; local
    authorities 114–15, 136–7; media
    118–20, 137; member states 108–9;
    new actors 109–10, 135; NGOs
    111–13, 135–6; parliamentarians
    113–14, 136; regional organizations
    110–11, 135; UN and democracy
    among states 132–4; UN and
    democracy at the global level 134–7;
    UN and democracy within states
    130–2
Agenda for Development, An 128–9,
    138, 139
Agenda for Peace, An 128, 138, 139
agenda-setting 209–10
Agenda 21 112, 115
Algeria 131, 167
all-affected principle 33–5, 37–8, 210
Annan, Kofi 128, 138–9
Archibugi, D., 1, 75
arranged marriage 93
Asian financial crisis 54–5, 67, 166
assets, MNCs' 51–2, 64
assistance in building democratic
    institutions 130–2
autonomy: individual 24–5, 33; of the
    state 25–6, 26–7

backlash movements 167
Baily, M. 64
balance of payments constraints 53
Beetham, D. 25, 131
Bellamy, R. 213
Bello, W. 171
Ben-David, D. 62
Blank, K. 206
Bobbio, N. 17, 73, 73–4, 207
Bosnia 78, 123, 170
boundary problems 23–4, 27, 28, 34–7
Boutros-Ghali, B. 127, 128–9, 137–8;
    see also Agenda for Democratization
Boyle, J. 92
Bretton Woods era 50, 65
Budge, I. 43
Bull, H. 27, 79, 81, 163
business and industry 116–18, 137

California effect 185–6
Cameron, D. 195
capabilities 149
capital flows 51, 63, 65–6; Asian crisis
    54–5, 67
capital taxation 191, 192
capitalism 166–7
Capotorti, F. 25
Carson, R. 168
Cassese, A. 73
Castiglione, D. 213
Charter for a Free Press 119
Chile 55
China 23, 166, 171, 174
choice 145
cities 114–15
citizenship, global 10, 29–30, 146–53
civil rights 82
civil society 127, 148, 150–3; *see also*
    global civil society

civil society forum 113
Clark, I. 165
class 143–4; political class 209–10
Club of Rome 169
Cohen, J. 198
collective good 207
commercial banks 55
Commission on Global Governance 169–70
Commission on Sustainable Development 115, 118
Committee for the Promotion and Advancement of Cooperatives 115
communitarian perspective 4
communities of choice 45
communities of fate 34, 37–8, 39, 44–5
competitiveness 48; and national policies 55–8
complex accountability 41–2
confederation 35–6
Conference on Non-Governmental Organizations in Consultative Status with the Economic and Social Council 113
conferences, international 29, 40, 120, 175
consent 27–8, 172
constructive rationalism 93–4
consultation 154–6
cooperation, governmental 35
coordination 154–5
cosmopolitanism 3–4; *Agenda for Democratization* and cosmopolitan democracy model 128–30; peace, law and 6–7, 73–86; and realism 7–8, 87–101
Council of Europe 155–6
Council of Ministers 181
Cousteau, J. 168
Crawford, J. 24
'creolization' 76
cross-border issues 23–4, 27, 28, 34–7
cross-border referendums 42–3
Cuba 167
cultural globalization 75–6
cultural imperialism 7, 90–8
culture: changing forms of regional and global order 22–3; UN and support in creating democratic culture 130–2, 132; *see also* media

Dahl, R.A. 17
Dahrendorf, R. 75

decentralization, territorial 83–4
defence 25–6
deliberative forums 40–1, 43
demand: domestic 56; and supply 210–11
democracy 1, 4–5; among states 126, 132–4; as a double-sided process 30; globalization and 26–7, 197–8; globalization, democratization and 145–53; liberal 17–18, 27; normative 11, 130, 171–4, 174–5; responses to cross-border issues 35–7; rethinking in the context of globalization 27–30; state/nation-building, democratization and 143–5; three levels 125–8; value of 12, 207–10; within states 125–6, 130–2; *see also* global democracy
democratic culture 130–2, 132
democratic mechanisms 38–45; for cosmopolitan democracy 39–44; and political communities 44–5
democratization: in general 159; globalization, democracy and 145–53; state/nation-building, democracy and 143–5; third wave 125; *see also Agenda for Democratization*
Denmark 56
derivatives, financial 55
development: democracy and 106, 128–9; global 76–7
discretion 188
Dobson, A. 41
domestic analogy 75
domestic saving 51
Doyle, M.W. 207

earnings inequality 192, 193
Earth Summit, Brazil 1992 23, 112, 114–15, 118
economic development 76–7
economic globalization 20–2; and global civil society 10–11, 163–4, 164–5, 166–71; *see also* global market forces
Economic and Monetary Union 194
Economic and Social Council (ECOSOC) 110, 112, 113, 121, 139–40, 154
economic veto 154
Eichengreen, B. 67
Ekins, P. 89

electoral assistance 130–2
end-point analysis 60–1
English language 22
environmental policy 179–80, 184–9;
    viability of high standards 193–7
environmental problems 23–4
Esping-Andersen, G. 195
Europe 27, 29
European Convention for the
    Protection of Human Rights and
    Fundamental Freedoms 24–5
European Court of Justice (ECJ) 181,
    188
European Monetary System (EMS) 54
European Union (EU) 11–12, 29, 49,
    157–8, 179–201, 213; difference
    accentuated 210–11; environmental
    policy 184–9; governance 206;
    integration process 181–4; social
    policy 189–93; viability of high
    social and environmental standards
    193–7
Evans, P. 195
Evans, T. 25
evolution of international law 80
Exchange Rate Mechanism (ERM)
    crisis 1992–93 53, 67
exchange rates 53–4, 66–7

Falk, R. 73, 75, 163, 165, 169
Featherstone, M. 76
Fernández-Armesto, F. 26
financial derivatives 55
financial flows 20, 51, 54–5, 63, 65–6,
    67
financial liberalization 54–5
financial sector 212–13; *see also*
    international finance
fiscal competition for international
    capital 64–5
foreign direct investment (FDI) 51,
    63–4, 195–6
formal governance 205–6
'four freedoms' 181
Framework Document 35
France 56, 66
franchise 37–8
Franck, T.M. 1
free trade 62
Fukuyama, F. 167
functional communities 33–8
functional representation 41
functionalism 182–4

fundamentalism 28

Galtung, J. 145, 146
Garrett, G. 191
General Assembly, UN 120–1, 121–2,
    133, 139, 154, 157
general system theory 74–5
Germany 28, 56, 153, 168, 185, 196
Gersbach, H. 64
Giddens, A. 19
Gilpin, R. 77
global citizenship 10, 29–30, 146–53
global civil society 10–11, 162–78, 206;
    deforming historical circumstances
    164–6; domestic analogy 75–6;
    normative democracy 171–4;
    political community and 29–30;
    responding to economic
    globalization 166–71; and the state
    174–6
global commons 23, 168
global community 3
global democracy 1–4; alternative
    models 9–10, 143–61; democratic
    mechanisms 39–45; desirability and
    possibility of 210–13;
    institutionalization of 153–9
'global development' 76–7
global governance 12–13, 169–70,
    203–6, 213–14
global institutions 29
global market forces 47–9; and global
    civil society 10–11, 163–4, 164–5,
    166–71
globalization 2–3, 4–5, 12–13, 106–7;
    changing forms of global order
    19–26; concentration of political
    and legal power 78–9; cultural 75–6;
    and democracy 26–7, 197–8;
    democratization, democracy and
    145–53; end-point conception 60–1;
    evidence for 5–6, 32–3, 49–55,
    60–72; and 'global development'
    76–7; historical forms 19; hyper-
    globalization and sceptical school
    19, 21, 60–1, 202–3; and levels of
    democracy 126–7; rethinking
    democracy in the context of 27–30;
    weak–strong continuum 202–3; *see
    also* economic globalization
Goldblatt, D. 22
Goldsmith, E. 169
Golub, J. 187, 188, 189, 194

governance: global 12–13, 169–70,
    203–6, 213–14; international
    finance and trade 55–6; and the
    market 47–9; private 205–6,
    212–13; without government 83
government 27–8; governance without
    83; levels of 36–7; from state
    government to global governance
    203–6, 213–14
governmental cooperation 35
governmental democratic mechanisms
    38–45
Green movement 167–8
Greenpeace 168
Greider, W. 61
Grotian natural law 79–81, 94
growth, cult of 169
Guatemala 143–4
Gulf War 88–9

Haas, E. 182
Habermas, J. 73, 74
Hadenius, A. 1
Haiti 78
Halifax Summit Communiqué 121
harmonization of policies 181–98
Hayek, F.A. 21, 80, 90, 92, 93–4, 208
Heater, D. 3
Held, D. 1, 25, 32, 61, 73, 179, 211;
    civil society 75, 171; cosmopolitan
    model 36, 171; cross-border issues
    33–4; cross-border referendum
    42–3; decision-making levels 28, 36;
    democracy as a 'double-sided
    process' 30; globalization 19
Heylen, F. 65
Hirst, P. 19, 50, 52, 54, 165, 210
Holden, B. 2
Holy Alliance 79, 85
Hooghe, L. 206
human rights 24–5, 92, 144; normative
    democracy 171–2, 173
humanitarian intervention *see*
    interventionism
Huntington, S.P. 75–6
Hurrell, A. 79
hyper-globalization 19, 21, 60–1, 70–1,
    202–3

ideology 164–5
imperialism, cultural 7, 90–8
income inequality 192, 193
Indian society 95

individualism 145
Indonesia 54
industrial policy 64–5
industry and business 116–18, 137
inflation 56
informal government 205–6
institutionalization of global democracy
    153–9
institutions: democratic 130–2; global
    and regional 29
instrumentalization of the state 175–6
integration, European *see* European
    Union
interest rates 65–6
intergovernmental organizations (IGOs)
    107, 145–6, 150–3, 154–5
intergovernmental regimes 206
intergovernmentalism 183–4
international conferences and summits
    29, 40, 120, 175
International Council for Local
    Environmental Initiatives 115
International Court of Justice 122–3,
    134, 158
International Criminal Tribunals 7,
    78–9, 81–2, 123, 140
international finance 52–5, 55–6, 65–8
International Labour Organization
    (ILO) 117, 118, 137
international law 24–5, 78–82, 123; *see
    also* legal globalism
International Law Commission 123
International Monetary Fund (IMF) 54,
    117
international political associations 108
international regimes 79–81
international relations 108, 109;
    democratic 126, 132–4
international trade 20, 50–1, 61–3, 68
International Tribunal for the Law of
    the Sea 123
International War Tribunals 7, 78, 123
Inter-Parliamentary Union (IPU)
    113–14, 136
interstate regulation 205–6
interventionism 78, 91, 96–8; weak
    82–4
investment, foreign 51, 63–4, 195–6
Iran 167
Iraq 88
Italy 57

Japan 28, 55–6, 57, 153

Jones, R.J.B. 211

Kantian universalism 73–4, 79
Katzenstein, P. 195
Keegan, J. 89
Kelsen, H. 73, 74
Keohane, R. 23, 81, 197
Keynes, J.M. 50, 69
Kindleberger, C.P. 212
Kissinger, H. 88
Köhler, M. 1
Korea, North 167
Korea, South 54, 167
Krasner, S. 81, 193–4
Krugman, P. 61

labour 48–9
Latouche, S. 76
law: international 24–5, 78–82, 123;
    rule of 173; *see also* legal globalism
Lawrence, J. 95
Lawson, N. 53
left, political 49
legal globalism 6–7, 73–86; alternative
    philosophy of international law
    79–81; concentration of political
    and legal power 78–9; cultural
    globalization 75–6; general system
    theory 74–5; globalization and
    'global development' 76–7; new
    international criminal tribunals
    81–2; weak international
    interventionism and weak pacifism
    82–4
legal power: concentration of 78–9
legitimacy 27–8
Leibfried, S. 189
levels of governance 36–7
liberal democracy 17–18, 27
liberalism 165
liberalization, financial 54–5
Lijphart, A., 208
local authorities: *An Agenda for
    Democratization* 114–15, 136–7;
    global citizenship 148–53, 155–6
localism 168
Long Term Capital Management fund
    55
Louvre Accord 1987 54, 66

Maastricht Treaty 1992 186
McGrew, A.G. 24

macro-economic policy 47–8, 56, 65–8
Mahathir bin Mohamad 172
Majone, G. 42
Major, J. 53
majority rule 144
Malaysia 172
mandatory harmonization 184–9
Mann, M. 19
markets 208–9; governance and 47–9;
    international finance 52–5, 65–8;
    and public policy 52–5, 68–9; *see
    also* global market forces
Marks, G. 206
May, J.D. 34
mayors 114–15
Meadows, D.H. 169
media 22–3, 107; *Agenda for
    Democratization* 118–20, 137
metropolitan authorities 114–15
military intervention *see*
    interventionism
Mill, James 18
Milward, A. 183
minimum international order 82–3
MNCs *see* multinational/transnational
    companies
mobility 48–9
moral universalism 7–8, 79, 91–6
Moravcsik, A. 183, 210
motivations 148–9
Multilateral Agreement on Investment
    65
multinational/transnational companies
    (MNCs/TNCs) 20–1, 51–2, 63–5,
    69, 117; world citizenship 146,
    147–8, 150–3, 155, 157, 159
Murdoch empire 22

nation-building 143–5
national policies 5–6, 21–2, 47–72;
    competitiveness and 55–8;
    effectiveness 68–70; governance and
    the market 47–9; international
    finance 52–5, 65–8; international
    trade 50–1, 61–3; MNCs 51–2,
    63–5; political parties and
    globalization 49; security and
    defence 25–6
national political communities 18, 26
natural law 79–81, 87–8, 93–6
negative integration 181–4, 189–93
neo-liberalism 164–5, 174, 176
Neoscholastics 94–5

Nerfin, M. 163
Netherlands 56–7
new growth theory 195
New Right 49
new social movements 29
nitrate standard 187
nobility 147
non-governmental democratic
    mechanisms 38–45
non-governmental organizations
    (NGOs) 108, 145–6, 152, 155, 159;
    An Agenda for Democratization
    111–13, 135–6
non-state actors 109–20, 135–7
non-territorial world citizens 150–3,
    155–6, 156–7
non-violence 174
normative concept of law 79–80, 93
normative democracy 11, 130, 171–4,
    174–5

OECD 193
Ohmae, K. 19, 75–6
OPEC 53
Open-ended High-level Working Group
    on the Strengthening of the United
    Nations System 113, 121
openness of national economies 50–1
optional harmonization 184–6

Pagden, A. 95
Paine, T. 18
Pappell, D. 62
parliamentarians 113–14, 136
participation 105–6, 145; normative
    democracy 173; UN and greater
    participation by member states 154
peace 7, 73–86, 96–8, 207; *An Agenda
    for Peace* 128–9; roles and local
    authorities 149–50; weak pacifism
    82–4
peace-building 131–2
Peace of Westphalia 6, 73
peacemaking institutions, weak 83
people 145–6, 150–3, 156
people logic 148, 150–3
People's Assembly, UN 10, 133, 136,
    156, 157–9, 211
permanent democratic mechanisms
    38–45
Perraton, J. 20
Pierson, P. 189
Plaza Accord 1985 53–4, 66

Pogge, T.W. 212
political class 209–10
political communities 4–5, 17–31, 94,
    209, 210; changing forms of
    regional and global order 19–26;
    democracy and globalization 26–7;
    global democratic mechanisms and
    44–5; presuppositions of liberal
    democracy 17–18; rethinking
    democracy in the context of
    globalization 27–30
political parties 49
political power 22, 26; concentration of
    78–9
pollution 23
positive integration 181–9
power 126; democracy and 207–8;
    global democracy and 211–12; legal
    78–9; political 22, 26, 78–9
private governance 205–6, 212–13
private/informal democratic
    mechanisms 38–45
process standards 184, 186–9
product standards 184–6
public expenditure: EU 191, 192;
    globalization and national policies
    56–8, 70
public/formal democratic mechanisms
    38–45
public goods 173
public governance 205–6
'punctuated equilibrium' model 193–4
punishment 81–2

ratcheting 187–8
rationalism 79–80, 90–6
realism 7–8, 79–81, 87–101
reciprocal representation 41
referendums, cross-border 42–3
regional institutions 29
regional order 19–26
regional organizations 110–11, 135
regional state organizations 150–3, 154
regulation: environmental policy
    184–9, 195; interstate regulation
    205–6; of MNCs/TNCs 52; re-
    regulation and financial derivatives
    55; UN role 117
Reich, R. 49, 70
rejectionists 19, 21, 60–1, 202–3
*Renewing the United Nations: A
    Programme for Reform* 138–9
representative democracy 17–18, 27

research and development (R & D) 64
resource consumption 23
Rhodes, M. 190, 196
Rhodes, R.A.W. 204
right, political 49
rights 33, 38, 82, 207, 212; human
    rights 24–5, 92, 144, 171–2, 173
Rogers, J. 198
Rosenau, J.N. 83, 162–3
rules 207–8
Russia 166
Rwanda 78, 123, 170

Sachs, J. 62, 166
sales, MNCs' 51–2, 64
sanctions 167
Sandel, M. 18
saving, domestic 51
sceptical school 19, 21, 60–1, 202–3
Schmitter, P. 41, 206
secession 209
Secretary-General of the UN 134
security, national 25–6
Security Council 121–2, 133–4,
    139–40, 211; abolition of veto 134,
    153–4
Segall, J. 136
self-interest 48
Sen, A. 207
Sepúlveda, J.G. de 94
Shaw, M. 211
Singapore 56
Single European Act 1987 185
Slaughter, A. 179, 197
Sobel, A. 67
social democracy 176
social equality 207
social expenditure 191, 192
social policy: EU 179–80, 189–97;
    national policies 47–8, 56–8, 70;
    viability of high standards 193–7
socialism 166–7
Somalia 78, 170
Soros, G. 172
sovereignty 24–6, 26–7, 39, 108–9,
    143–4, 147; European integration
    and 11–12, 179–201
spontaneous order 75, 90–1
state-building 143–5
states: democracy among 126, 132–4;
    democracy within 125–6, 130–2;
    global civil society and 174–6; from
    state government to global

governance 203–6, 213–14; as
    world citizens 146–7, 150–3, 154,
    157; *see also* sovereignty
strategic environmental policy 195
strategic trade 195
substantive democracy 171
Suganami, H. 75
supply and demand 210–11
Sweden 56

technology 64, 68
telecommunications 22
temporary democratic mechanisms
    38–45
territorial decentralization 83–4
Territorial Dispute (Libyan Arab
    Jamahiriya/Chad) 122
territoriality 33–8; territorial world
    citizens 150–3, 154–5
Thailand 54
third wave of democratization 125
Thompson, G. 19, 50, 52, 165, 210
Time-Warner 22
TNCs *see* multinational/transnational
    companies
tourism 22
trade, international 20, 50–1, 61–3, 68
trade barriers 185–6
transnational companies (TNCs) *see*
    multinational/transnational
    companies
transparency 173–4
tribalism 28
Tully, J. 208
Turner, B.S. 76

unemployment 196
union density 191–3
United Kingdom (UK) 49, 53, 54, 57–8
United Nations (UN) 7, 28, 89, 105,
    106, 211; as an agency of global
    democracy 9, 125–42; amendment
    of the Charter 133, 134; conferences
    and summits 29, 40, 120, 175; and
    democracy among states 132–4; and
    democracy at the global level 134–7;
    and democracy within states 130–2;
    and democratization after Boutros-
    Ghali 137–40; democratization of
    UN architecture 120–4, 132–4;
    ECOSOC 110, 112, 113, 121,
    139–40, 154; global citizenship 10,
    150–3; human rights covenants 25;

institutionalization of global
democracy 153–9; international
justice 73, 78; member states 108–9;
and non-state actors 109–20 *passim*,
135–7; Security Council 121–2,
133–4, 139–40, 153–4, 211; *see also*
Agenda for Democratization
United Nations Commission 136
United Nations Conference on Human
Settlements 115
United Nations Conference on
International Organization 112
United Nations Corporations Assembly
(UNCA) 155
United Nations Educational, Scientific
and Cultural Organization
(UNESCO) 119
United Nations Environment
Programme 117
United Nations Framework Convention
on Climate Change 115
United Nations General Assembly
(UNGA) 120–1, 121–2, 133, 139,
154, 157
United Nations Local Authorities
Assembly (UNLAA) 156
United Nations Non-Governmental
Liaison Service 112
United Nations Observer Group 122
United Nations People's Assembly
(UNPA) 10, 133, 136, 156, 157–9,
211
United Nations University 116
United Nations Volunteers programme
118
United States (USA) 49, 55–6, 66–7, 78,
165; competitiveness and national
policy 56, 57

Universal Declaration of Human Rights
1948 74, 119
universalism 7–8, 73–4, 79–80, 90–6

veto: economic 154; Security Council
134, 153–4
Vitoria, F. de 95–6
Vogel, D. 185
volatility 53–5

wages 62, 193, 195–6
Wagner, P. 162
Waltz, K.N. 96
Walzer, M. 38, 209
war 84, 96–8, 169; *see also*
interventionism
Warner, A. 62
waste disposal 188
weak international institutions 82–4,
212
Webb, M. 65–6
welfare state 56–8, 63, 70, 176; *see also*
social policy
Western, B. 193
Westphalia, Peace of 6, 73
Whelan, F. 37, 42
Wight, M. 79
Williamson, J. 62
'win-win' model 193, 194–7
world citizens 10, 29–30, 146–53
world government 73, 87
World Order Models Project (WOMP)
169
world state organizations 145–6,
150–3, 154–5
World Trade Organization (WTO) 63,
117, 198, 211

Zolo, D. 87, 90, 98, 128